GAWKER SLAYER

THE PROFESSIONAL AND PERSONAL ADVENTURES OF FAMED ATTORNEY

CHARLES HARDER

CONTENTS

1

THE GIRL ON THE BATHROOM FLOOR

The footage was grainy, but what it showed was clear enough: a young woman, obviously extremely drunk, with a man on top of her, having sex with her, on the filthy floor of the men's restroom in a sports bar in Indiana.

The video was posted on Deadspin.com, a "sports" blog owned by Gawker Media. A few days later, Deadspin's editor, A.J. Daulerio, got an email from a woman begging him to take it down. "I know the people in it and it is extreemly [sic] hurtful," she wrote. "please, this is completely unfair."

Daulerio wasn't moved. "The best advice I can give you right now: do not make a big deal out of this," he wrote, warning that if she did go public, it would simply mean that more people would see the video. He added that due to the footage's poor quality, she was unidentifiable.

But to people who knew her, the college student was very much identifiable. In multiple emails with Daulerio and a lawyer for Gawker, she kept begging for the video's removal. Daulerio dug in his heels, telling her, "It's not getting taken down. I've said that. And it's not a very serious matter. It is a dumb mistake you (or whomever) made while drunk in college. Happens to the best of us." He offered some condescendingly smug advice: "I'm sure it's embarrassing but these things do pass, keep your head up." Gawker's attorney Gaby Darbyshire (who was also the company's chief operating officer) told the woman the video would remain on the site and was "completely newsworthy."

Daulerio then got an anguished call from the girl's father, who had watched the video of his daughter make its way around the internet. "He had this basic breakdown on the phone," Daulerio later revealed. Daulerio and Darbyshire did eventually take the video down—after it had been lifted and posted to multiple porn sites.

Years later, Daulerio admitted he wasn't sure if the woman in the video wasn't so drunk that she was past the ability to give consent. Meaning that when he posted the video, he wasn't sure whether she was being raped.

* * *

On-air NFL reporter Erin Andrews was stalked. Her stalker checked into the same Nashville, Tennessee, hotel and asked for the room next door to the ESPN personality. He hacked the peephole of her door and filmed her naked in her hotel room. The video ended up on the internet.

When she learned from a friend that a nude video of her had been posted online and was being widely shared, Andrews was hysterical. She called her parents. "I was just screaming that I was naked all over the internet, and I didn't know what it was," she would later reveal. When she had to watch the footage—accompanied by FBI agents and her father—Andrews was so traumatized, she ran into another room and vomited.

Many media outlets reported on the sick and illegal invasion of privacy Andrews had suffered.

Gawker, however, took a different approach. It directed its readers straight to the video itself: Daulerio "broke the story" for Deadspin by posting a link to an obscure website that featured the stalker's video of Andrews. Deadspin helped the little-seen video quickly reach a wide audience, and Deadspin's own page views reportedly tripled as a result of the Andrews post. According to experts, the video has been seen an estimated 17 million times.

* * *

THESE ARE JUST two examples of the vile handiwork of Gawker Media and its senior editor, Daulerio. Gawker also obtained topless photos of Duchess Kate Middleton, the mother of the future king of England, while she sunbathed on a balcony in France. Accompanying posts on Gawker sites screamed headlines like "These Topless Photos of Kate Middleton Put Us at Two for Three on Royal Nudie Pic Scandals [NSFW]" and "Duke and Duchess Enjoy Their Southeast Asia Tour, Even Though We've All Seen Kate's Boobs." The "NSFW" tag stood for "Not Safe for Work," code for racy or pornographic content you wouldn't want your boss seeing on your office computer.

Gawker's founder, Nick Denton, was so pleased with traffic from the Kate Middleton photos that he gave Gawker staff a 20 percent bonus, boasting in an email that Gawker had "scored with royal breasts." It was another coup for Daulerio, who was revered at the company, which showered him with annual bonuses for the massive traffic he drove to the Gawker Media empire. He was promoted for his work time and again, from editor-in-chief of Deadspin to editor-in-chief of the flagship site Gawker.com, and given a huge raise.

Daulerio was running Gawker.com in 2012. A few weeks after he posted Kate Middleton's breasts to the site, he posted a 1-minute, 41-second video of Hulk Hogan (real name Terry Bollea) in a bedroom, showing full-frontal nudity and sexual intercourse—without any censoring: no pixilation, no blurring, no blocking. Daulerio even provided English subtitles so viewers could understand every word of the pre-sex, during-sex and post-sex dialogue on the video. His head-line: "Even for a Minute, Watching Hulk Hogan Have Sex in a Canopy Bed is Not Safe For Work But Watch it Anyway."

Bollea's partner in the video was Heather Clem, the wife of his closest friend, radio shock jock Bubba the Love Sponge Clem (this was his legal name—which he changed from Todd Clem a few years earlier). The wrestler's marriage was falling apart, and both Clems had implored him, for over a year, to be intimate with Heather. In a moment of weakness, Bollea agreed—unaware his friends were secretly recording the tryst.

Five years later, Bollea (and the rest of the world) found out about the existence of the recording, Gawker posted the 1:41 video, and Bollea sued. Gawker claimed the video was protected by the First Amendment. But was a surreptitious sex video (not the story, but the video itself) newsworthy? And was Gawker even a "news" outlet deserving of protection?

Before the Hulk Hogan lawsuit, Gawker did not consider itself a journalistic enterprise. Its leaders were almost offended by the idea. "We don't seek to do good," Denton told *The Washington Post* in an interview. "We may *inadvertently* do good. We may *inadvertently* [emphasis added] commit journalism," he said, as if it were a crime. "That is not the institutional intention."

When *Playboy* asked Denton if he placed a lower value on privacy than most people, Gawker's CEO and founder replied, "I don't think people give a f---, actually."

It wasn't until Denton and Gawker were sued by Bollea that they suddenly became "journalists" seeking to wrap themselves in the First Amendment. Ironic, though: Nick Denton was a dual citizen of Hungary and the United Kingdom, two places without anything remotely similar to the First Amendment to the *United States* Constitution. He brought their brand of ruthless tabloid media to the U.S., to expose people for profit and then try to take advantage of the U.S. laws that protect actual journalists.

The moment Denton got into trouble, he cried "First Amendment" as if his blood was red, white and blue. The only Americans involved in his stories are those he exposed and exploited—like Erin Andrews, Terry Bollea (Hulk Hogan), the girl on the bathroom floor, and so many countless others whose privacy and reputations Gawker had invaded and assassinated over the years.

During our case for Hulk Hogan against Gawker, I told the attorneys and staff at my firm that the case was not just about Hulk Hogan, it was about *all* of Gawker's victims. And the verdict that the heroic Florida jury eventually delivered may have taken them *all* into account.

In the second year of our four-year legal saga against Gawker, I announced to my entire law firm, loud enough for all to hear: "Everyone, listen up. This case is not about Hulk Hogan. **It's about the girl on the bathroom floor.** This case is about privacy in America. If we don't win, the right to privacy will be lost for everyone."

2

INTRODUCTION, PART I:
THE GAWKER SLAYER

W hat do Hulk Hogan, Halle Berry, Julia Child and Donald Trump have in common?

Me.

Despite many famous cases—and clients—I'm not a celebrity myself, nor do I aspire to be one. I'm an attorney. For 25 years, I've represented some very famous people and also many people you've never heard of. I'm also the editor and co-author of the legal treatise *Entertainment Law & Litigation*. I own and run a small law firm in Los Angeles. There's really nothing flashy about my lifestyle. I've lived in the same starter home for nearly two decades, though I could buy a bigger one if I wanted. I still drive the family SUV that I bought more than 16 years ago, though I can afford to trade up. The parties I attend are potlucks with friends. And truth be told, the only thing I dislike more than wearing a suit is putting on a necktie.

People in certain circles who know my name—powerful people who run or represent media companies—will sometimes get a letter from me and are not happy when they do. It means they've been caught doing something wrong and need to make up for it. Why?

Two words: Hulk Hogan.

I was lead counsel for the former professional wrestler, 12-time world champion, and Hall of Famer. His real name is Terry Bollea, and he sued the website Gawker after its editors posted 101 seconds of surreptitiously recorded video of him, including 10 seconds of consensual sexual relations with a partner in a private bedroom. *Bollea v. Gawker* captured the public's attention. It had the ingredients of a modern-day soap opera: sex, lies, videotape, an American pop-culture icon, and a powerful company that made money from publishing invasive, mean-spirited, destructive gossip disguised as "news."

Gawker's leaders were ruthless, even sadistic. They humiliated people. They seemed to get joy out of ruining lives. We didn't just win the Hulk Hogan case; we won *big*. The jury's $140 million verdict in March 2016 put Gawker where it belonged: out of business.

The case put me on the national map, so to speak. It led to even more high-profile cases against irresponsible media, like when first lady Melania Trump hired me to sue the *Daily Mail* for a false story that she had once worked in an illegal trade. I've also prevailed for her husband, President Donald Trump, against porn star Stormy Daniels in her failed defamation suit, and against former Trump campaign staffer Alva Johnson, who falsely claimed the president had forcibly kissed her. He didn't, and I located a cellphone video that proved it.

Does this make me a hater of the media, as some reporters have claimed? Am I the "Gawker Slayer" who wants to rip apart the First Amendment and its guarantees of free speech and freedom of the press? Absolutely not. Nothing could be further from the truth.

One misguided journalist even said I'm viewed as "the media's Darth Vader." Not in my view. If anything, I'm the media's Luke Skywalker. I want responsible media and journalism, and for the First Amendment and its guarantees of free speech and free press to thrive and prosper. But for that to occur, the Dark Side of media and journalism must be neutralized, or eliminated. That's my job.

Gawker, thankfully, is gone—reduced to an ugly footnote on the story of American media. The case gave me a unique vantage point where law, media and society converge. That view has me very concerned. Gawker was a malignant lesion on a media establishment that, as a whole, is suffering from a silent, creeping cancer.

The disease takes many forms: Irresponsible journalism. Hidden editorial agendas. Advocacy disguised as factual news. Sensational and invasive content that hurts people. Propaganda—for the left, the right or other. Fake news.

This cancer has already killed "the truth" as many of us know it. Pulitzer Prize-winning newspapers, cable news shows that attract millions of eyeballs each night, popular websites, national magazines —all are suffering from massive failures of responsibility at every level. This hurts people like you: readers who turn to the news for facts, truth and help making sense of the crazy and complicated world we live in. This cancer also hurts the media itself. People have developed a mistrust for reporters, editors and news outlets, and often don't believe what they read or hear. Journalism exists to help people make sense of a confusing world. But if people can't trust what they read, they become more confused and stressed, rather than better educated and calmed, and journalism fails in its mission. The cancer also hurts the subjects of the stories: people who are lied about and whose lives are impacted greatly, sometimes forever. Many of them call on me to be their champion.

I want this cancer to be eliminated so that the patient—the American people, the American Way, American journalism and American politics—can be healthy and thrive. I have some ideas about how to do it. I would love nothing more than to *put myself out of business* when it comes to media cases. If journalists acted responsibly, my defamation and privacy cases would all disappear. I'm fine with that. I'd love it, in fact. I'd be happy to go work on something else—don't worry about me. But until then, worry about the accuracy of the news being delivered to your doorstep, TV, computer, tablet, or phone.

My father drilled two lessons into my head:

> 1. *Never give up, and*
> 2. *Find a way.*

It's time to kill the cancer in the America media and restore responsibility, accountability, accuracy, ethics and privacy to our daily news, for the benefit of everyone: the American people who rely upon the information they receive from the news, those covered in the news, and everyone who writes, edits, publishes and profits from the news itself.

People have great power to change what they don't like. The way the news is being gathered and disseminated should upset you. It certainly upsets me. In the spirit of my father's mantras, I will not give up working to fix it, and will continue to think creatively, and act boldly, to find ways to do that. I hope you will do the same. I want you to help me to put *me* out of business.

This book will outline ways we can do that. It also will share my ideas about how to make the whole world better—and hopefully entertain you with tales of my trench warfare with evil corporations, many of them in the media industry. Along the way, I will fill in the blanks created by flattering, sometimes critical, but always reductive media descriptions of me, like "Gawker Slayer" and "the media's Darth Vader." They don't tell the full story of who I am, how I became me, or what I stand for. That's why I wrote this book.

In sharing my adventures and hard-fought wisdom with you, and revealing how taking on big companies on behalf of individuals became my life's work, I invite you to join me in the battle.

3

THE WORLD'S BIGGEST CYBERBULLY

The Hulk Hogan sex video went live on Gawker on Oct. 4, 2012.

In Gawker's newsroom, the "big board"—a large screen displaying the company's best-performing posts in real time—tracked the number of readers watching footage of Terry Bollea (known to fans as his alter ego, Hulk Hogan) in a private bedroom doing very private things.

The video had been filmed five years earlier, when Bollea was in a dark place. His 23-year marriage to his wife, Linda, was essentially over. After a four-season run, their VH1 reality show, *Hogan Knows Best*, had been canceled. Linda and their children, Brooke and Nick, had just left the family's longtime home in Tampa, Florida, for California, and Linda could not have been clearer: Their marriage was over.

Bollea, by then retired from wrestling, was depressed and alone. He considered suicide. His closest friend was a local radio shock jock, Bubba the Love Sponge, who had an open marriage with his wife, Heather. Both had pressured Bollea to have sex with Heather for more than a year. Bollea always declined and snapped at Bubba to stop asking.

But in 2007, Bubba was worried about Bollea and insisted he come over. The three talked over wine, the Clems doing what they could to cheer up Bollea. In a moment of both weakness and a feeling of connection to the couple, Bollea gave in. He had a fling with Heather in her bedroom. Over the next few weeks, they were intimate on two more occasions. He had no idea that each time, a hidden camera was recording them.

* * *

By 2012, five years had passed and Bollea had gotten his life back on track. He and Linda had completed a long, bitter divorce battle in 2009, and he remarried in 2010. In March 2012, the first story of a Hulk Hogan sex tape was posted at TMZ, and then a month later TheDirty.com posted grainy still images, but no video and no identifiable nudity. Bollea and his lawyer, David Houston, were frantically trying to track down the tape and those responsible. In September 2012, a DVD containing 31 minutes of footage of Bollea and Heather Clem (who had since divorced Bubba) being intimate in her bedroom landed on the desk of A.J. Daulerio, then the editor-in-chief of Gawker.com.

Whoever wanted to humiliate or ruin Bollea with the footage (a practice known as revenge porn) sent it to Daulerio—well known as a master of exploiting people. In late 2011, Daulerio was promoted from head of the "sports"-themed Gawker-owned site Deadspin.com, to being the head of its flagship site, Gawker.com. In just a short time, he took Gawker.com from 700,000 visitors a month to well over 2 million. He didn't do this with enlightening stories, balanced coverage or impactful investigations.

Daulerio was fixated on sex tapes and photos of people's private parts. He once handed over an envelope containing $12,000—in cash —to a source in return for below-the-belt selfies that New York Jets quarterback Brett Favre allegedly had sent to a female sports reporter. Daulerio wrote the post himself and gave it the headline "'Brett Favre Once Sent Me Cock Shots': Not a Love Story."

Sports heroes, celebrities, average Joes, women, men—everyone was fair game to Gawker Media. Sex sells. The company's business model was clickbait, and its success or failure depended on eyeballs, the ensuing advertising dollars, and increased popularity of the growing Gawker Media empire, which also included sites devoted to technology, video games, cars, sports and, ironically, feminism.

But their motivation went beyond eyeballs and money. As I would soon learn, Gawker was a twisted place. The very idea of changing the world or doing good inspired revulsion at its downtown Manhattan offices, where leaders cultivated an image of jaded outsiders with nothing to lose, tearing down people's reputations and lives, one "asshat" and "douchebag" (two of the site's favorite insults) at a time.

Go back to that interview Gawker Media's founder and CEO, Nick Denton, did with *The Washington Post* in 2011, when he boasted, "We don't seek to do good.... We may inadvertently do good. We may inadvertently commit journalism. That is not the institutional intention." That was Gawker.

Gawker editors portrayed themselves as antihero crusaders who were channeling the rage of the creative underclass to take down the wealthy and powerful. But in reality, Gawker was a place where resentful, underpaid young bloggers working in sweatshop-like conditions (hundreds of its writers were interns who received little or no pay at all, nor school credit for that matter) could channel their own personal rage, target anyone (and everyone), and spread it to many thousands, or even millions, simply by pushing a button.

Gawker's depravity wasn't just directed outward at the people it covered. It was baked into the company's culture.

Former Gawker editor Emily Gould revealed that after she quit the company, Denton himself wrote vicious stories about *her* for the site. "He posted about my 'bed-hopping' in the guise of making some kind of point about literary culture. I was, while this was happening, unemployed, not protected by any kind of institutional power," she wrote in an essay for TheCut.com in February 2020.

At one point Gould clicked on Gawker and saw an image of

herself "drunkenly fellating a plastic tube." It had been taken while she worked at Gawker, after she and other staffers who had attended a party together were "goofing off" on a Soho street. "Nick had somehow found the video, sent it to an employee with instructions to post it, and then the staffer did, probably because Nick was his boss," Gould wrote. (Denton denied to The Cut that he had directed the staffer to post the video.) "In 2008, I didn't know how to contextualize what I was experiencing. Now, we have a term for this: 'revenge porn.'"

* * *

WHEN GAWKER.COM LAUNCHED IN 2003, it mainly focused on skewering NYC's media and cultural elite. But under Denton's—and, later, Daulerio's—leadership, it grew into an all-purpose purveyor of smut, snark and shame. In a 2010 internal memo to staff, Denton explained the company's mission this way: "The staples of old yellow journalism are the staples of the new yellow journalism: sex; crime; and even better, sex crime."

Sometimes it was simply gross, like the time the site documented, *with photos*, a used condom hanging on the handrail of a New York City subway car. Gawker at its "best" was juvenile and crass. Gawker at its worst was cruel, vindictive, invasive and vicious. And no one was safe.

They outed gay people in the most insensitive ways. They had a regular feature where they mercilessly taunted subjects of local wedding announcements, mocking the bride and grooms' last names, alma maters and parents' careers. Gawker once devoted an entire post to attacking a *preschooler*—seriously—because his blogger dad had written a story about the little boy's taste in gourmet cheese that offended the sensibilities of Gawker writer Josh Stein. ("When is it okay to hate a 4-year-old?" Stein's post began.)

Simply put, Gawker was the world's biggest cyberbully.

* * *

WHEN THE HULK HOGAN video arrived in the mail from a so-called "anonymous" sender (though Daulerio spoke by phone with New York talent agent Tony Burton of the Don Buchwald agency, who arranged the DVD shipment), there was no moral struggle or legal ambiguity for Daulerio and his team. They didn't question whether Bollea knew he was being recorded, or how the video's release might affect him and his family, or *why* the person shipping it was trying to destroy Bollea's life—and likely engaging in revenge porn.

Daulerio and company simply sat at their editing machine and spliced a 1-minute, 41-second "highlight reel" (Daulerio's words to Tony Burton) from the original 31 minutes. Daulerio wrote the accompanying commentary: salacious, graphic descriptions of oral sex and intercourse, along with a demeaning recap of mundane pillow talk that was never meant to leave that Tampa bedroom. Daulerio told readers the full 31-minute sex tape was "a goddamn masterpiece."

On Oct. 5, 2012, the day after it went up, Bollea's personal attorney, David Houston, sent a letter to Gawker demanding that the video come down. "Any attempt to hide behind the veil of the 'newsworthiness privilege' will fail," he wrote. The next day, with the video still up, he personally emailed Denton, imploring him to do the right thing and remove the video. "I'm sure you understand as a human being," he wrote, telling Denton that if the video was taken off the site, Bollea would consider the matter closed. Yes, you heard that right: Gawker would still be alive today if it had simply removed the video—no payment, no apology, nothing more required.

But the video remained. A few days later, Cameron Stracher, a lawyer for Gawker and Denton, sent a letter saying the posting of the video was legal (though it wasn't) and would remain on Gawker.com for all the world to watch. Imagine if Stracher had simply told his client: Take the video down; you've gotten what you wanted—you exposed Bollea, attracted lots of eyeballs and revenues, promoted the Gawker brand; let's avoid a legal fight. But such advice or instruction does not appear to have been communicated. And if it was, Denton ignored it.

I got involved the week Stracher sent his letter refusing to remove the video. "We should sue Gawker for $100 million," I told Houston, "and do a press conference on the courthouse steps." We filed the lawsuit days later and did just that.

At the time, I had been practicing law for about 16 years. I had filed more than 30 lawsuits for major celebrities as of then, but this was my first press conference. Why was this case different?

We needed to send a strong message. Articles were pouring out saying—falsely—that Bollea was involved in the release of the video and was doing so for publicity or money, or both. It was essential for people to know the truth: Bollea was being severely victimized and had no role in the video's creation, release or promotion. He wanted the video off the internet and destroyed. We also wanted to send the strongest possible message to Gawker to take the video down immediately, because Houston's two emails to Gawker and Denton hadn't worked. I wanted to pull out a sledgehammer and hit Gawker as hard as I could. Our demand to Gawker, Denton and Daulerio was $100 million—a very high number, no doubt, but one that we believed was both justified and achievable.

Press conference on Oct. 15, 2012, at the U.S. Courthouse in Tampa,
Florida, to announce the filing of the $100 million lawsuit against
Gawker. Terry Bollea (aka Hulk Hogan) and his personal attorney,
David Houston, are standing behind me.

That day on the courthouse steps marked the start of a four-year journey that exposed Gawker for the cyberbully it was and ultimately achieved full retribution: landing Gawker Media in bankruptcy court and seeing its assets sold to the highest bidder.

Our lawsuit included claims against Gawker of invasion of privacy, name and image infringement, and infliction of emotional distress. Six months into the case, the Florida state court judge ordered the video removed from Gawker.com, and the company complied.

We then sent more than 60 takedown demands to porn sites, blogs and others who had lifted the video, attaching the court order, and they all complied. Months later, the Florida Court of Appeal reversed that order, but Gawker kept the video down pending the outcome at trial. (We received a permanent injunction against the video at trial.) During the six months the video was up, it was viewed well over 7 million times, 2.5 million at Gawker.com and the remainder at the various porn sites.

The trial began in St. Petersburg, Florida, on March 7, 2016. This book was published on the fifth anniversary of the trial. One of the most infamous moments came during Daulerio's videotaped deposition, which we played for the jury. The exchange is still cringeworthy:

Q: "Can you imagine a situation where a celebrity sex tape would not be newsworthy?"

Daulerio: "If they were a child."

Q: "Under what age?"

Daulerio: "Four."

When Gawker presented its defense, Daulerio took the stand and tried to explain that he was only "joking" when he gave that testimony—but no one was laughing in the video. He also gave the same answer ("Was she under 4?") to a different question regarding the newsworthiness of a possible Miley Cyrus sex video.

Either he really believed that child pornography was acceptable news content, or he was treating his deposition, and also Gawker's First Amendment defense, and ultimately the entire lawsuit, as a joke. The jury was not impressed.

Gawker's trial presentation was miscalculated. It attempted to portray Daulerio as a "bold and brilliant" journalist; Denton as a publisher of important, non-tabloid news; and the Bollea footage as necessary to telling the story of the sex tape's existence. But both in his deposition and on the stand, Daulerio admitted the opposite. He testified that each of the 10 reasons Gawker's counsel gave for the supposed newsworthiness of posting an uncensored, secretly recorded sex video were not true. He admitted that "Bollea's penis" was not newsworthy, as one example. He also testified that all of those 10 reasons were *not even considered* by Daulerio at the time he posted the video.

An important moment at the two-week trial was when Gawker.com's managing editor, Emma Carmichael, testified. She acknowledged that, as the site's managing editor (its No. 2 editorial position), she and Gawker had made no effort to find out whether Bollea knew he was being recorded, or whether the tape could have constituted "revenge porn," which is illegal and criminal. She was calm and stone-faced as I asked, "You were aware that Mr. Bollea was likely to feel distressed, hurt, upset, and embarrassed, and yet Gawker.com posted the sex video of him anyway, correct?"

"Yes," Carmichael responded.

"Do you believe it was a good thing that Gawker.com posted a video of my client fully naked and having sex?" I asked.

"Yes, I'm comfortable with the story that we published," she said.

"And if you had it to do over again, you would do the same thing?" I asked.

"If history were to repeat itself, yes, I would republish the story," Carmichael replied.

Her callous detachment was mind-bending. The jury later cited her testimony (as well as Denton's and Daulerio's) as a reason for its unprecedented verdict.

* * *

WHEN IT CAME time for the verdict to be read, my heart was in my throat.

It was March 18, 2016. For three and a half years, I had felt like we were swimming upstream. Gawker always had more attorneys working the case than we did; they buried us in paper, citing the many, many U.S. Supreme Court and appellate court decisions siding with the First Amendment in other circumstances. Two early decisions in the case (in Gawker's favor) showed us that simply by litigating against a "news" organization, we were automatically the clear underdogs.

The room was dead silent as the court clerk read the entire 10-page verdict form, word for word. There were 14 questions. We needed 13 yesses, and one very important "no" (to question No. 2). The clerk read the form: Yes. No. Yes. Yes. Yes. Yes.... By that point, I started to break down. The jury had answered every question exactly as we had asked them to.

Bollea was sobbing loudly. I was sobbing too, but quietly. Tears streamed down my face and soaked my collar. I couldn't stop. The clerk continued: Question No. 7: Yes. Yes. Yes. Yes.... After all the ups and downs, hard work, and so much time away from my wife and children, this was the payoff: justice being served, and privacy in America being enforced. These were tears of joy. Our heroic jurors were ruling for privacy over exploitation, in a big way.

We filed out of the courtroom and went into a private room in the courthouse. That's when Bollea asked us, "What was the verdict?" He hadn't heard that the jury had just awarded him $110 million. (They would award another $30 million the following week at a separate hearing on punitive damages.) We told him, and he was floored.

I was too. The jury gave us more money than we'd asked for, but the joy wasn't just about the money. The permanent injunction preventing the video from ever being posted again: That was a tremendous victory as well. I knew there would be an appeal; this verdict was hardly the end. There were battles still to fight. But for the moment, we were going to savor our euphoria over the trial victory, and then get to work to do everything in our power to make it stick. There was so much on the line: a man's reputation and mental health; a large monetary verdict; and to me, the grand prize—ensuring every American the right to privacy.

Our jury of four women and two men resoundingly determined that what happened to Terry Bollea, aka Hulk Hogan, was a massive violation and should never happen to another human being. Gawker could not wrap itself in the First Amendment and destroy people's lives. Just the opposite: It had to be punished for its intentional harmful conduct.

*Terry Bollea, my associate Seema Tilak, David Houston and me in a
photo taken late in the trial.*

I SHOULD MENTION HERE that the work of others at my firm, particularly Dilan Esper and former associates Sarah Luppen, Matthew
Blackett and Seema Tilak, as well as the exceptional talents of our co-
counsel in Tampa, Kenneth Turkel and Shane Vogt, and other attorneys and staff at their firm, as well as David Houston, Esq., and trial
consultant Michael Boucher, all made our successful result possible.

Once a judgment is issued, the plaintiff (now called a "judgment
creditor") can collect on the debtor's assets: its bank accounts, property, and so on. The only way to stop collections is to post a bond of
the amount of the judgment, plus interest for two years to account for
the appellate process. But Gawker did not have enough hard assets to
obtain a bond for the $140 million jury verdict. So in post-trial
proceedings, after filing and losing two motions challenging the
verdict, Gawker then did something very clever: It offered 100 percent
of its stock in lieu of a bond to stop Bollea from collecting on Gawker's assets (which would have destroyed it), to allow Gawker to remain

in business and appeal the judgment. If Gawker lost on appeal, Bollea would own all of its shares. If Gawker won on appeal, it would be free of the judgment.

We had little choice but to agree to the proposal because, if we hadn't, the court of appeal likely would have stayed enforcement of the judgment and might have required no bond, stock pledge or any other collateral—a terrible scenario for us. But something unexpected happened: When we accepted Gawker's proposal in court, its lawyers asked for a break, and then went into the empty jury room to talk. My guess is they were talking by phone to Nick Denton, who was in New York. After 30 minutes, Gawker's team returned to the courtroom and told the judge they were withdrawing their offer. The judge said "OK" and signed the $140 million judgment against Gawker.

A few days after the strange proposal and then prompt withdrawal of the proposal, Gawker filed for Chapter 11 bankruptcy: protection from creditors during a reorganization. If they wanted to stay in business, and believed in their case on appeal, they should have gone through with their stock pledge proposal. I think Gawker got cold feet. They were afraid they would lose on appeal, and all of the company's stock would end up in the hands of Bollea. They had grown to hate him so much over the three and a half years of litigation, they seemingly would rather kill the company themselves than take a chance that Bollea would end up with it.

Gawker also decided not to go through with a reorganization plan, and instead opted to sell its assets in a bankruptcy auction. A second suicidal act. So two months after Gawker Media filed for bankruptcy, its assets—websites, URL addresses, office lease, furniture, equipment and so on—sold to the highest bidder: The Spanish-language network Univision paid $135 million.

Univision reportedly absorbed 99 percent of Gawker's staff; the other 1 percent went elsewhere, by their choice. Univision maintained seven of Gawker Media's eight sites: Gawker.com being the exception. That site was sold a few years later to a fellow named Bryan Goldberg who started to relaunch it, and then had some employee issues and abruptly stopped. But the other seven sites continued on, with their staff, with little or no interruption from the trial—though I noticed that the sites seemed to become noticeably more responsible in their reporting after the Bollea verdict.

Nick Denton left the company he had founded and filed for personal bankruptcy. A.J. Daulerio, who was ordered to pay $115.1 million for his part in the case, had his checking account frozen and at one point offered up a rice cooker and a single golf club in lieu of the money he owed. (We ignored his publicity stunt.) While Gawker had vowed to vigorously pursue an appeal of the jury's verdict while its bankruptcy case was pending, it instead ended up settling with Bollea in October 2016 for $31 million.

I don't mind that people call me the Gawker Slayer. But the truth is, no one *slayed* Gawker. The company made decisions that led to its eventual demise. Gawker, Denton and Daulerio made the decision to post the Bollea video in the first place—even TMZ and TheDirty.com were smart enough not to do that. Gawker made the choice to ignore David Houston's two emails, the second of which said if the video were removed, the matter would be closed. Gawker made the decision not to settle the case: It had numerous opportunities but did not offer a single dime of settlement for the first two years of litigation. Bollea would have accepted a reasonable offer. Gawker also chose its trial strategy: miscalculations, in my view. Gawker also chose to file for bankruptcy rather than pledge its stock, appeal the judgment, and remain in business pending the conclusion of appeals to the Florida Court of Appeal, Florida Supreme Court and U.S. Supreme Court. Gawker also chose not to pursue a reorganization and instead sold its assets in a bankruptcy auction. It could have settled with Bollea instead and remained in business.

Yes, we brought Gawker to trial. The jury's verdict and the judge's affirmation of it pushed Gawker to the edge. But Gawker made the Thelma and Louise decision to go over the cliff.

4

INTRODUCTION, PART II:
CONQUERING EVIL

"The only thing necessary for the triumph of evil is for good men to do nothing." —Edmund Burke

I've tried to make this book entertaining and thought-provoking. My goal is a good read. I don't read a lot of books. The ones I do read are entertaining, thought-provoking, or both. I can't get through a book if it isn't, and I wouldn't put a book out for people to read if I, as a reader, wouldn't want to read it myself, or find it enjoyable and meaningful.

Many famous people have spent their adult lifetimes on a mission to see good triumph over evil: Jesus Christ, Mahatma Gandhi, Martin Luther King Jr., Mother Teresa, Princess Diana and countless others. I certainly don't place myself in their category, though I am inspired by them. But the mission of my life, and my law firm, is, has been, and will continue to be, to act as a force for good and to conquer evil.

Examples of conquering evil are provided throughout this book. Many of them relate to media law—one of my specialties of practice. There is no better example in my personal career of conquering evil than the case of *Terry Bollea (aka Hulk Hogan) v. Gawker Media.* Gawker was, in my view, an almost purely evil organization. It existed to exploit people, cause them harm, and profit from that exploitation and harm—and many within its ranks obtained some sort of sick pleasure from its harmful acts. That type of behavior is known as *sadism*—deriving pleasure from inflicting pain, suffering or humiliation on others.

When evil exists, like it did with Gawker, it is incumbent on everyone who witnesses it to do their part to eradicate the evil. But in the case of Gawker, no one was doing that. For decades, Gawker committed sadism, unhindered and unabated. I was hired to do something about it, and I did.

Several chapters in this book pertain to experiences in my life, not just in my law practice. I've included those chapters in the hopes that others will learn from the lessons that I have learned myself. My parents, Paul and Catherine Harder, were instrumental to me during my formative years and beyond, and I acknowledge their love and skilled parenting in shaping who I am today. The combination of nature and nurture they provided set me on a path to always stand up for what is good, and always take action against evil.

5

THE MYSTERY BACKER WHO LEVELED THE PLAYING FIELD

The first time I ever heard from the representative of the billionaire who would end up funding the entire Hulk Hogan case against Gawker, it was an unusual email from an unknown sender. I almost hit delete.

A man—I'll call him Mr. A—said he represented somebody wealthy who disliked Gawker and wanted to bring maximum pressure to bear on the company. I thought it might be a phishing scam. I scanned the email again; it didn't read like it was coming from an internet café in Nigeria. I wrote back and set up a phone call.

The reception was terrible on that first call with Mr. A. He was using some kind of internet-based phone service. Still skeptical, I thought, "He represents a guy with tons of money and he doesn't even have decent phone service?" But as we talked, it became clear he was both legit and highly intelligent. By the end of the call, he told me I was hired.

It was a strange arrangement—communicating through an intermediary, not knowing who was paying the bills. Before signing on, my partners and I thoroughly researched the codes of ethics that apply to attorneys. Having a financial backer, whether known or unknown, is not a violation of any laws or ethical codes.

In the U.S., people are allowed to financially assist others with lawsuits. If someone wants to file a civil suit, a rich uncle can pay the bills. A *pro bono* case is essentially funded by the law firm that handles it. There are companies that provide "litigation finance" and get a percentage of the recovery. Public interest law firms take contributions from people—who may remain anonymous—and use those contributions to fund the lawsuits of their choice.

Bollea and his personal attorney, David Houston, understood that the mystery backer would fund the case but (by law) the backer had no decision-making authority. Decisions would rest with Bollea alone.

* * *

AFTER THE JURY's verdict and the "outing" of Bollea's financial backing, our mystery benefactor was attacked by the press. The fact of the matter was that Terry Bollea could not have self-financed his own case. Gawker was a $250 million company that carried two insurance policies and borrowed millions more to finance the case. Gawker openly revealed that it spent more than $10 million for the world's best media defense lawyers to try everything in their power to defeat Bollea's case. Bollea, on his own, was no match for Gawker's resources —not even close. And who wants to spend all their retirement savings on a lawsuit that could lose?

I knew that Gawker had acted illegally when it posted a surreptitiously recorded sex tape of my client. I believed we had a strong case. But I could not have taken the case on contingency, where payment comes in the form of a percentage of the recovery. A case like this could have taken eight years to be resolved, including trial and appeals. I could not have afforded to keep the lights on, the rent paid, and the attorneys and staff employed at my firm, on the *possibility* of a payment after many years of litigation. No attorney is that foolish, and even if I were, I would have gone bankrupt in the process and been required to pull out of the case.

The amount of work and expense involved in a complex four-year case like *Bollea v. Gawker* is tremendous: numerous motions, oppositions, replies, hearings, written discovery requests and responses, numerous live depositions of witnesses spread around the country, three mediations, trial preparation, and trial. Our mystery backer did nothing more than allow Bollea to level the playing field against Gawker. He spent about $7 million to finance Bollea's case through trial—about $3 million less than what Gawker spent. But without the $7 million of help, Bollea stood no chance against Gawker and its ability to easily spend $10 million on a single lawsuit.

I dealt exclusively with the intermediary, Mr. A, for the duration of the case. He would occasionally fly to meet me, usually in Los Angeles, but when the case went to trial in St. Petersburg, Florida, he flew in for it. During one day of jury selection, Mr. A took a seat in the audience section of the courtroom, a few rows behind Gawker's trial team. Most people in the audience were reporters typing away on their laptops. Defendants Nick Denton and A.J. Daulerio entered the room and sat down right next to him. (Mr. A remained anonymous, but his heart nearly stopped.) After the next break, he moved toward the back of the room.

It wasn't until after we won, and a Florida jury awarded Bollea $140 million, that I (along with the rest of the world) learned the identity of our mystery benefactor.

* * *

PETER THIEL IS one of Silicon Valley's most successful tech entrepreneurs. He co-founded PayPal and the data analytics juggernaut Palantir, and was Facebook's first outside investor. Gawker Media was on his radar for purely personal reasons. A 2007 post on the company's Valleywag tech blog outed the billionaire venture capitalist in a post with the headline: "Peter Thiel is Totally Gay, People."

Was he personally targeted and hurt by Gawker? Yes. Did he want to put them out of business? Yes. But Thiel didn't reach into his pockets merely to get even.

"It's less about revenge and more about specific deterrence," he told *The New York Times* in May 2016, after *Forbes* revealed him to be the man who financed the Hulk Hogan case. "I can defend myself. Most of the people they attack are not people in my category. They usually attack less prominent, far less wealthy people that simply can't defend themselves."

Thiel, a German-born former chess prodigy, would read Gawker's stories and see that they were getting bigger and meaner, and meaner and bigger. They weren't just "punching up" at the privileged and powerful few. They were "punching down" at regular folks who were defenseless. They went beyond outing someone's sexuality; they were destroying lives. So Thiel decided to find people with legitimate cases against Gawker and help them afford to seek justice and stand a fighting chance. He wanted everyone to stand on an even playing field against Gawker.

"I saw Gawker pioneer a unique and incredibly damaging way of getting attention by bullying people even when there was no connection with the public interest," he has said, calling Gawker's articles "very painful and paralyzing for people who were targeted."

He's right. Take the case of one mid-level employee at ESPN. After a co-worker filed a lawsuit falsely accusing the employee of certain behavior toward her, and also of having an affair with another colleague (another false allegation), the Gawker sports blog Deadspin ran detailed accounts of the allegations, making no effort to ascertain whether they were true.

My firm investigated—and determined they weren't. But by then, the man's life was wrecked. His wife divorced him because of Deadspin's story amplifying the false allegations, and moved thousands of miles away with their children. He moved to the same state, just to stay in his children's lives. To be able to obtain a new job, without the Gawker stain raising questions about his character, he had to legally change his name. Any Google search of his birth name showed the Deadspin story as the first search result.

* * *

THE DECK IS STACKED against any person who has been hurt by a media company, whether it's a salacious blog, a sensational tabloid or a mainstream news outlet. There are so many disadvantages for the average Joe.

Imagine for a moment that you wake up tomorrow to find your name and image attached to a horrific story that is either highly unflattering, totally untrue, a massive privacy invasion like what happened to Bollea, or some combination of these. Perhaps your worst enemy, or your neighbor, or your ex, has a vendetta against you and has told a reporter something about you—real or made up—and it's now widely available for public consumption in the great echo chamber of the internet. It's being forwarded to everyone you know: your family, your friends, your colleagues, your employer, your business associates.

What do you do? Here's what you can expect: Most requests for a correction, removal, retraction and/or an apology are refused. "We stand by our reporting" or "Our reporting is protected by the First Amendment" are the typical responses.

If you decide to call a lawyer, here's what you're up against:

1. **The cost:** Lawyers with experience in media litigation typically charge between $500 and $1,000 per hour. Sending a letter, which gets ignored by the media company, typically costs a few thousand, while a lawsuit can cost a few hundred thousand—or more than a million.
2. **The law:** Under the "actual malice" standard set by *The New York Times Co. v. Sullivan* case in 1964, which applies if you are a "public figure" (and the definition of "public figure" has been getting broader every year—Nick Denton even testified that anyone with a Facebook page is a public figure, though that is not true), the statements disseminated about you by the media can be false, and there's nothing you can do about it, as long as the person

who wrote it did not have "reckless disregard" in doing so. The U.S. Supreme Court put it this way: Actual malice means the defamatory statement was made "with knowledge that it was false or with reckless disregard of whether it was false or not."

3. **Anti-SLAPP laws:** Enacted in a majority of the states in the country, they mean that you, as a plaintiff, could be ordered to pay the legal bill of the media company that ruined your life. The legal bill could be as high as $200,000 or more, and the fact that the company's insurance carrier paid for it does not even matter. You have to prove, with evidence, that you are "more likely to prevail" in the case, and if you can't, you lose and have to pay up—big time. Even if you win the motion, the media company can take an immediate appeal, and your case is stalled in anti-SLAPP proceedings for one to two years. If you lose the appeal, your case is over and you have to pay for the anti-SLAPP motion *and* the appeal. Now you could be ordered to pay $300,000-plus.

4. **Insurance:** U.S.-based media companies tend to be fully insured. This means they literally have a blank check to pay for legal counsel and associated costs. It also means the media company is not particularly concerned about a judgment, because the insurance company will pay for it, up to policy limits, which are usually very high. As a result, the media company has little or no fear of litigation, and can fight in court for years and years and years, and it will not affect them at all.

5. **The wealth of a private company:** If the insurance money isn't enough, multimillion-dollar media companies (and often multi*billion*-dollar media companies) have vast resources to keep fighting.

6. **Defense counsel:** Media outlets have highly experienced and skilled defense counsel, who have memorized every case in America that favors a media company. They have a

template for every possible motion, discovery request, deposition outline, motion to exclude evidence, trial brief and litigation playbook, and they will spend as much time as needed to fully litigate the case, and indeed overwhelm the plaintiff from inception through trial and the exhaustion of all appeals.

7. **Outside help:** On appeal, there are numerous pro-First Amendment organizations that file "amicus" briefs to lend support to the media defendants, groups like the ACLU, Public Citizen, Reporters Committee for Freedom of the Press, Association of American Publishers, First Amendment and Media Law Scholars, and PEN American Center, Inc. Plaintiffs have no such help.

8. **Judges:** Since 1964, the case law has evolved to where the media companies usually win. This means that judges become increasingly reluctant to side with the plaintiff, and feel the "safe thing" is to side with the media company, to avoid a possible reversal on appeal. It also takes one more case off their overcrowded docket. Dismissal is an easy choice for any overworked judge.

9. **Publicity:** A lawsuit regarding the worst thing that can be said about you is likely to generate *more* news stories about exactly that. Some call it the "Streisand Effect" after a lawsuit by Barbra Streisand against a person who photographed her home from the air, along with all other homes along the California coast, and put it on an obscure government website that no one paid attention to. The lawsuit got the whole world focused on exactly the thing Streisand wanted to remain private: an aerial photo of her home. News companies don't sweat the publicity of a defamation lawsuit—they see them all the time, and often wear them like a badge of honor. But for an individual whose reputation is wrecked by a story, who wants to move on and hopes the story eventually goes away, the

publicity of a lawsuit does not make the story go away; it often publicizes it further.

10. The one thing that *can* work for a plaintiff in a media lawsuit is the jury. Getting in front of a panel of men and women who care about individuals, not corporations with deep pockets, shifts the balance of power. Our Florida jury in the Hulk Hogan case proved this is true. But getting to the point where you can present your case to a jury requires a huge amount of time, money and built-in resources—all of which media companies have in spades, and most individuals cannot afford.

* * *

CRITICS HAVE SUGGESTED that the private financial backing of the Hulk Hogan case is a dangerous sign that anyone with deep enough pockets and an agenda can bankroll the destruction of a news organization. I will admit that billionaires with agendas can pose risks to anyone—including media companies, but certainly not limited to them. Media companies just happen to be the most vocal about it, because they "buy ink by the barrel." But to be clear: Thiel only leveled the playing field. The financial disadvantage for Bollea was neutralized.

Thiel's funding did not cause all of the factors listed above to suddenly swing in Bollea's favor. Far from it. Gawker still had most of the advantages enjoyed by media companies in a lawsuit over a publication. The reason you don't read many articles about the tremendously unfair advantage of media companies in lawsuits is because the media companies write the articles! They control the narrative. How many journalists are going to write stories, or media companies are going to publish those stories, about how journalists and media companies have tremendous, unfair advantage over individuals harmed by their irresponsible coverage? I've yet to see one, and I read everything I can on this subject. The stories swing in the other direction because of who writes and publishes them.

These concepts certainly did not start with Peter Thiel, and the fact that he leveled the *financial* playing field for Bollea should not be a realistic cause for concern among media companies. He's the only one who ever did it, and to my knowledge no one has done it since the *Bollea v. Gawker* case ended in 2016.

Also worth noting: Gawker did not consider itself to be a journalistic enterprise—at least not until it was a defendant in a lawsuit. Then suddenly they saw the tremendous advantage of being journalists, and sought to wrap themselves in the First Amendment, demanded coverage by their insurance carriers, hired some of the best media defense lawyers in the world, and launched a media blitz against Bollea right before the trial, claiming his suit was a threat to journalists' right to report the news, which then generated scores of articles about how Bollea's case was a threat to journalism and the First Amendment.

In an open letter to Thiel, after Gawker lost the case, Nick Denton called his adversary a "thin-skinned billionaire" who had pursued a "diabolical decade-long scheme for revenge." I don't see it that way at all. I see Peter Thiel as a hero. He saw the world's largest cyberbully terrorizing people every day, and he had the guts—and the generosity —to spend his money to see if that reign of terror could be put to an end. And it was. Gawker had unfettered power to destroy reputations that people had built over the course of many years, and decades, with the click of a mouse—by posting the story. Gawker was, in Thiel's words, a "singularly terrible bully." With his help, we punched the bully in the nose so hard, it never hurt anyone again.

The jury, the judge, Bollea, Thiel, and the legal team were all heroes in this story. Gawker stopped terrorizing people when it went dark on Aug. 22, 2016. Its days of merciless cyberbullying without consequence were over. Ding-dong. The wicked witch was dead.

* * *

I MET Thiel twice over lunch in his former office in San Francisco shortly after Gawker had filed for bankruptcy. He's a brilliant, tenacious guy who does not give up, and finds a way. We celebrated Gawker's demise a year later in Los Angeles, at Thiel's incredible home in the hills of West Hollywood. He threw a dinner party, and flew Bollea and David Houston in for the celebration. Our victory in the long war against Gawker was a testament to Thiel's vision and strategy. As a thank you, he gave me a really nice chess set.

6

THE IMPORTANCE OF
BOLLEA V. GAWKER

D uring the *Bollea v. Gawker* case, the *Tampa Bay Times* ran a front-page story about the CFO of a Tampa facility maintenance company who installed a hidden camera in the women's changing room, and secretly filmed over 100 female employees undressing and showering, in nearly 200 separate recordings. His perverse scheme was uncovered when a tech support worker happened upon the disturbing images while working on the executive's computer.

Florida law enforcement got involved, charging the man with 123 counts of video voyeurism. During the deposition of Gawker.com's managing editor, Emma Carmichael, who helped to edit and publish the Hulk Hogan sex tape video, I asked her about the incident. She testified under oath that the footage of the women employees should not be posted by a website like Gawker without the consent of the women depicted, even though the story about their employer filming them was most certainly newsworthy.

But she also testified that footage of Terry Bollea, secretly recorded in a bedroom naked and having sex, was fair game for Gawker to publish, without his permission, because the story was newsworthy. It was a clear double standard.

Surreptitious recordings of people in private places are *not* fair game for others to watch, whether or not the stories about the recordings are newsworthy. They are a violation of the right to privacy. Period.

All of this—our protective stance when it comes to our own privacy, and attempts by outside forces, including the media, to stretch the definition of what is private—is not a new concept. The notion that people are guaranteed their own space, safe from prying eyes, has been the subject of fierce debate dating all the way back to the days of so-called "yellow journalism" and new inventions like the telephone and the mass-market camera.

* * *

ALEXANDER GRAHAM BELL won the first U.S. patent for the telephone in 1876, the same year he made the first telephone call, to his assistant Thomas Watson, from the next room in their Boston laboratory. (It was an anticlimactic way to kick off a new era in communication; Bell's inaugural sentence was, "Mr. Watson, come here—I want to see you.") In 1888, George Eastman's Kodak camera hit the market with the slogan "You press the button, we do the rest." Within a few years, photography was available to the masses.

This also was the heyday of "yellow journalism." The term was born during the competition over the New York City newspaper market between publishers Joseph Pulitzer, who founded Columbia Journalism School and established the Pulitzer Prize, and William Randolph Hearst, the legendary media mogul who built Hearst Castle in California and on whom the classic film *Citizen Kane* was based.

Yellow journalism came to describe the sensationalist style both publishers used in their profit-driven coverage of world events. The peak of yellow journalism was in 1898, when Hearst and Pulitzer—who sold many papers by fanning anti-Spanish public opinion in the U.S.—published rumors of plots to sink a U.S. battleship, the *Maine*, that had sunk in a harbor in Havana, Cuba, after an explosion. Calls for war, inflamed by the papers' coverage, escalated. Within months, the Spanish-American War had begun.

Against this backdrop, in 1890, Boston lawyers Samuel Warren and Louis Brandeis published an article, "The Right to Privacy," in the *Harvard Law Review*. Although the Fourth Amendment to the U.S. Constitution—which guarantees freedom from unreasonable searches and seizures—has often been interpreted as a broad protection of individuals' privacy against government intrusion, this landmark article was the first explicit declaration of a citizen's right to privacy in the United States.

Warren and his partner Brandeis, who would go on to become a U.S. Supreme Court justice in 1916, described a society being frayed by intrusive journalists and modern technology. Sound familiar?

"Instantaneous photographs and newspaper enterprise have invaded the sacred precincts of private and domestic life; and numerous mechanical devices threaten to make good the prediction that 'what is whispered in the closet shall be proclaimed from the house-tops,'" they wrote. "The press is overstepping in every direction the obvious bounds of propriety and of decency. Gossip is no longer the resource of the idle and of the vicious, but has become a trade, which is pursued with industry as well as effrontery."

Brandeis and Warren argued that the "intensity and complexity" of modern life had made an expectation of privacy all the more essential, and that invasions of that sacred space caused "mental pain and distress" even more destructive than bodily harm. This article was published in 1890—more than 130 years ago! It is just as true and relevant today.

* * *

IN 1972, PRIVACY BECAME AN "INALIENABLE RIGHT" in Article I, Section 1 of the California Constitution, on par with five other inalienable rights: life, liberty, property, safety and happiness.[1] That's a big deal.

Around the country, laws are trying to keep up with technology. At least 46 out of 50 states now have revenge porn laws, which prohibit the distribution of sexually explicit images of someone without their consent. It's applied unevenly, but it's a promising start.

In Florida, video voyeurism is a crime, but the state refused to prosecute Gawker for it—possibly because the state court of appeal wrote that it believed Hulk Hogan was behind the release of the sex video, which he wasn't. There is no civil component to the video voyeurism law, so if law enforcement doesn't prosecute, then the law is worthless.

That executive in Tampa who was busted secretly making nearly 200 recordings of female employees in his company's changing room? He was arrested under the state's video voyeurism law, but because the one-year statute of limitations had run out by the time the authorities learned of the invasion of these women's privacy, the charges—123 of them in total—were all dropped.

* * *

THIRTY YEARS after Brandeis and Warren's law review article changed the national discourse on privacy, Brandeis offered another landmark opinion on the topic.

"The makers of our Constitution undertook to secure conditions favorable to the pursuit of happiness. They recognized the significance of man's spiritual nature, of his feelings, and of his intellect," Justice Brandeis wrote in his dissenting opinion in *Olmstead v. United States*, a case stemming from a bootlegger's conviction based on FBI wiretap evidence—the first wiretapping case to come before the nation's highest court.

"They sought to protect Americans in their beliefs, their thoughts, their emotions and their sensations. They conferred, as against the Government, the right to be let alone—the most comprehensive of rights, and the right most valued by civilized men."

The right to be let alone.

It is an essential right. And it is still under assault. That assault didn't begin with Gawker, or the internet, or a paparazzi culture that profits from stepping over the line into the "sacred precincts of private and domestic life," as Brandeis and Warren so presciently described. No, the juggling act between the public's "need" to know, the media's duty to share what it deems newsworthy, and the right to privacy you and I expect when we're doing private things in private places, like using a public restroom or changing room, visiting a doctor's office, or relaxing in our homes, is as old as our democracy itself.

But the unregulated power of a hungry and irresponsible press— and the breakneck pace of technological advancement in the era of blogs, YouTube, Twitter, Instagram, Snapchat and TikTok—means it is more important than ever to constantly evolve, innovate and find new ways to protect our fundamental and inalienable right to privacy, the right to be let alone.

7

STRONG FOUNDATIONS

"Things turn out best for the people who make the best of the way things turn out." —Coach John Wooden

I've been asked if there was a pivotal moment in my life that made me want to fight against oppressors and punch bullies like Gawker in the nose. I had a pretty comfortable, happy childhood. But from an early age, I was aware of the difference between good and evil, and wanted good to always triumph.

Around the age of 5, I attended a children's production of *Annie*. A family friend was performing in it. I was very moved. I was left with a sense that children were being oppressed and, going to bed that night, I felt that I needed to save all the children in the orphanages.

My childhood involved a lot of Disney movies, with their classic good vs. evil plots. Naturally, I wanted good to win each time. In 1977, at the age of 7, I saw *Star Wars*, and then watched it 10 more times in as many months. That film, and the next two installments in later years, introduced me to the concept of the Dark Side and those who fight against it, seemingly against all odds, like the Rebel Alliance against the Galactic Empire.

My childhood reality was a far cry from Annie's orphanage or the

Galactic Empire. I was born in late 1969. My brother was nearly 2 years old when I was born. My father was a business manager; my mother stayed at home to raise their sons. Our first home was a small two-bedroom, one-bathroom house on the same hill as Universal Studios. When I was nearly 2, my parents moved us to a four-bedroom, ranch-style house built in 1939 in the L.A. suburb of Encino. Because the selling market was so terrible in 1971, they held on to the little Studio City house, and it's been a rental ever since.

Random story: Sometime around 1973, when I was about 3, Barry Williams—the actor who played Greg Brady—was around 18 at the time and looking for a small house to rent. He came to my parents' rental in Studio City to take a look. My brother and I were there that day with my dad. *The Brady Bunch* was the hottest show on TV for families. My brother and I instantly recognized him and were giggling uncontrollably and pointing at him, saying, "It's Greg Brady!" (He didn't rent the house.)

In Encino, we had a small yard with a pool and diving board. Practically my entire childhood was spent in that swimming pool, with my brother and our friends who came over—swimming, diving, playing, eating, and even napping by the pool. The pool was life.

* * *

MY FATHER WORKED Monday to Friday, and went into the office most Saturday afternoons too. Sundays were my brother's day and mine with our dad. He would take us to Winchell's for donuts in the morning. John Wooden was there often. We'd get our donuts and head home and my father would always say, "He's the greatest basketball coach in the world." For dinner we'd order in: Italian, Chinese, whatever. Sundays were my mother's day off.

My mother was Super Woman. She took care of two sons, a husband and a bustling household: cooking and cleaning, scheduling and organizing, shuttling boys to school and sports, all of the shopping, all of the errands, all of the appointments. She got everything done—far more responsibility and work than any "full-time" job.

My mother also taught me to be independent and self-sufficient by showing me how to do things myself like cook basic meals (French toast for breakfast or English muffin pizzas for a snack), do laundry, iron clothes and even sew. If I ever asked her to do those things, she'd say, "You can do it, remember: I showed you how." Now that I'm a parent I can see that my learning these skills made her life easier, but it was great for me because I gained independence.

Life was pretty laid-back in our home. My dad loved sports, so I played baseball, basketball, soccer, and later tennis on the high school varsity team. I wasn't great at anything, but I was fairly good at everything. I also was a very rule-oriented child: When there was a rule, I followed it.

I attended Encino Elementary School. When I was 5, one day my carpool accidentally left school without me, and so I walked home. My house was about a mile away, and I had to cross a huge boulevard called Ventura. My mother almost had a heart attack when I arrived home late and told her that I'd walked home by myself.

In the fourth grade, one of my best friends was Joey Ueberroth, whose father is Peter Ueberroth. It was around 1978, and Peter had just been selected to be the president of the U.S. Olympics for the 1984 games in Los Angeles. I would hang out with Joey at his house when his dad was bringing high-quality sports equipment into the backyard, so that his children (and their friends) could try out the real equipment used by the Olympic athletes. I remember shooting arrows in his backyard, with Peter showing us how to use the Olympic bow. We were not very far from the target, and I was hitting bull's-eyes. I loved the feel of the arrow flying out of the bow and the "thump" of hitting the target.

I liked my teacher that year: Miss Eich. She was very young, super nice, energetic, pretty, great with kids. She made the whole year so fun. Almost 20 years later, during my last year of law school, I was at a memorial service for a friend's mom, who had been a teacher at the same school, and Miss Eich attended. I hadn't talked to her since the last day of fourth grade, and told her she had been my teacher decades ago. I was so excited to see her and talk to her—it was like a dream come true. She looked at me and said very matter-of-factly, "I don't remember you." I told her I was the president of the class, and it was the year Joey Ueberroth was her student (she *had* to remember Ueberroth). She just looked at me like I had two heads. I was sad that my teacher, who I thought the world of, had *zero recollection*, and didn't even want to *try* to remember. But I assume she had other things on her mind, being at a memorial service.

In the fifth grade, I was bused to Van Nuys Elementary School. My classmates were far more ethnically diverse than at Encino. Busing was great, and the Van Nuys area and student population were a melting pot: Latino, Black, Asian, Middle-Eastern, and more. My favorite classmate was Alvin Quon. His parents owned and ran a Chinese restaurant in Van Nuys. A few months into the school year, after my parents had heard me talk *nonstop* about Alvin, they said: "Well, let's go have dinner at their restaurant." So we went. When we entered, my parents told his parents that I was his classmate. I think he was home at the time, but a few minutes into our dinner, Alvin was there: "What are you doing here?" he said over and over, with a huge grin on his face that I will never forget. It was such a fun moment for both of us.

* * *

OUR TEACHER that year was the best teacher I ever had: Nancy Grade. I absolutely loved her. She was full of life, and had so much experience as a teacher—she knew just what to say to get the entire class silent and completely intrigued by whatever she was talking about. We hung on her every sentence. We all loved her, and I think she loved everyone in the class. There was something about her that made everyone love everyone and everything. I loved all my classmates too. On the last day of school, a girl in the class, my best friend in school that year, kissed me on the cheek. It was the only time that ever happened. I never saw her again. Still, it was a great school year —best one I ever had.

One extremely random footnote to fifth grade: Ms. Grade's longtime boyfriend was a man named Bill Foster, also known as "The Fox," who I think held records for how fast a person could chug a glass of beer. He literally could drink a glass in about one second. Unreal. If you look him up on YouTube, there are videos of him on various TV shows. I remember he came to class one day—he did not drink beer there, of course—and was a very nice guy. Naturally the students made lots of beer jokes.

The next year I was back at Encino Elementary for sixth grade, and several of my classmates from Van Nuys were bused to Encino. Alvin was in my class that year again, and we were both very excited. That year, he and I memorized every word to "Rapper's Delight" (the four-minute version for the radio with clean language, not the seven-minute risqué version), and we performed it for the class. Our teacher, Mrs. Palmer, was in love with Ronald Reagan and had a picture of herself with him when he was governor of California. During my sixth-grade year he was running for president and won. She was thrilled. Mrs. Palmer also was *huge* into recycling. She made me *huge* into recycling too, and it's stuck with me to this day. The school had "paper drives": recycling as many newspapers and aluminum cans as possible. Our class won, and set records for the school.

Mrs. Palmer inspired us. She made me want to collect every newspaper and aluminum can in my whole neighborhood. I was collecting paper grocery sacks full of newspapers from all of my parents' friends, and I would spend hours riding my bike around the neighborhood, fishing aluminum cans out of people's trash bins. I loved it! Once I was at the basketball court at Encino Park, across the street from my school, and a bunch of guys playing basketball had just drunk a 12-pack of beer. To me, it was like hitting the mother lode: I fished their cans out of the trash, poured the excess beer into the trash can, squashed the empty cans with my foot and put them into the sacks on both sides of my bike handles. I was happy as could be to get so many cans, though the smell of beer and garbage was quite strong. My father was less thrilled: "Don't get *those!*" he said. But there was no stopping me—I was on a mission.

* * *

IN SIXTH GRADE, I made friends with a classmate named Tony Andrews. We were on the same AYSO soccer team that year. Our team, the Cheetahs, won the league. Then our coaches required us to run a mile every day, and have our parents sign to verify. A month or two later we started playoff games against other teams who had won *their* leagues. We beat one, then another, then another. We won seven playoff games in a row, and then faced a team for the regional championship of all of Southern California. The Cheetahs won: 1 to 0. Of course we went berserk. There was a trophy ceremony, and Erin Moran, the pretty young actress who played Joanie on *Happy Days* and *Joanie Loves Chachi*, handed out the trophies. She handed me mine, and I was over the moon. It seemed like life could not get better.

Tony's father was Tiger (Tige) Andrews, co-star of TV's *The Mod Squad* in the late '60s and early '70s. I never watched the show, so to me he was just "Tony's dad." One of Tiger's best friends was the actor who played Sam the butcher (Alice's boyfriend) on *The Brady Bunch*. Tony's mother was my "mom away from home" in sixth, seventh and eighth grades. I spent practically an entire summer at their house, sleeping over almost every night. Tony and I were inseparable and his mom was the greatest. She loved Yosemite National Park, and would take us camping there every summer. Some years she took us there in the winter too, and we'd ski at Badger Pass and ice skate at Curry Village with the iconic Half Dome in the background. We had the time of our lives in Yosemite. It's the most beautiful place in the world. One summer we visited three national parks: Bryce, Zion and Yosemite. What an amazing trip.

* * *

I ATTENDED Montclair Prep School for grades seven through 12. It was a small, academically rigorous school in Van Nuys. I had gotten used to the public school system in L.A., and made straight A's every year. Then I tested for Montclair and they required me to spend the summer before seventh grade taking classes to prepare me for their classes in the fall. "How hard could it be?" I wondered. Then seventh grade started, and I was *struggling*. I eventually figured out how to study and learn, and it became not quite as overbearing. I had at least two hours of homework every school day from seventh through 11th grades. Senior year was easy; I think they wanted to give us a break before college.

I liked the teachers at Montclair, but many of the students were materialistic and catty. They didn't bully, but they were overly interested in their possessions. When students started turning 16, their parents gave them brand-new BMWs and other luxury vehicles. The unfortunate "car bra" was popular at the time, so students whose parents clearly had lots of disposable income were buying and talking about car bras and other ridiculous features of their new luxury cars. I was turned off to that group. My father gave me his seven-year-old Oldsmobile Cutlass Supreme, the least cool car imaginable, but I was overjoyed. It was comfortable, roomy, a nice shade of light blue, and I had the freedom to drive anywhere I wanted.

Looking back at my comfortable and happy childhood, I can't help but wonder if my early fascination with Disney villains and *Star Wars* heroes (and my strong desire to help Annie and her fellow orphans) were signs of my innate sensitivity to right and wrong, my need to see justice done. To this day, the thing that makes me angriest is when someone takes advantage of another, especially when the victim is in a vulnerable class like the very old, very young, poor, too kind, or too trustworthy. As an adult, helping people is the essence of my profession. I've realized that in the real-life struggle between good and evil, I can make a difference.

8

THE HALLE EFFECT

"The freedom of the press works in such a way that there is not much freedom from it." —Grace Kelly

In early 2013, about two months after my then-partners and I started our law firm, Academy Award-winning actor Halle Berry and her business manager, Jeff Wolman, came to our new office for a meeting. Part of the purpose was to let Berry know the types of services we provided. She hired us for a few matters that were standard fare for our firm—getting her name and image removed from some websites and social media posts, and pursuing a lawsuit against a commercial infringer. But Berry wanted to talk to us about something else—something we'd never done before, and have not done since. With the help of a team of people that would include Berry's daughter, Nahla, and an 8-year-old girl named Violet Affleck, and with a large dose of Berry's natural superhero qualities, we pulled it off. It was a "mission impossible" that became possible, because we didn't give up and found a way.

Halle Berry had a paparazzi problem. It was similar to a cockroach problem, but much worse. At least you can poison roaches. Lowlife photographers would literally camp on her front lawn before the sun came up, waiting for her to leave the house, usually to drive her daughter to school. Once Berry and her then-5-year-old, Nahla, emerged from the house, the paps would spring into action, pull out their cameras and snap photos. The sun was barely up, and they were stalking and shooting their prey. But they did not stop at the front lawn—that was just the beginning.

The paps would leap into their cars and follow Berry and Nahla to school, running red lights if necessary to stay with their targets. When Berry was pregnant with Nahla, a paparazzo ran them off the road. Berry and her unborn child were uninjured, but Berry felt the pain of that day every time she stepped behind the wheel followed by her relentless pursuers.

Berry was surprisingly understanding about their focus on her: "I'm fair game," she told us during our meeting. "But Nahla is not. She did not choose this—she should be left alone. They can follow me around all they want, but they should not be allowed to stalk my daughter."

Her story became more intense as we spoke. "If we stop anywhere, they stop too. If we get out of the car, they get out too. They put their cameras in our faces. And shout the meanest things you can imagine." Berry was simply telling us her life, and it was intense. "Nahla: How do you feel that your mom is trying to take you away from your dad forever?" was one of the questions she relayed that the paps liked to shout at her little girl. If they could get a shot of both mom and daughter frowning, it's money in the bank. A photo like that gets a front-page story and a headline like "Halle Berry: Unfit Mother." Of course the story doesn't mention that it was the paper's own photographer who made them frown—or that, other than the paparazzi stalking them, they are generally happy all day.

Berry told us she tried to move to France to get her daughter away from the paparazzi. France allows a person to be photographed *while working*—like during any press interview, or on a red carpet, or film set. But if they are walking down the street, or in a public park, or at a restaurant, photos are against the law. Berry had primary custody, but her ex had partial custody, and an L.A. family law judge would not let her move outside of L.A. So Berry wanted us to change the laws to be like France.

* * *

MY THEN-PARTNER DOUG MIRELL, a First Amendment expert, explained how our laws are based on the First Amendment news gathering privilege, which allows photographers to take photos in any public place, and allows them to get very close to their subjects. The Constitution cannot be changed without an amendment passed by two-thirds of the 50 state legislatures, plus a majority vote in the U.S. Congress. And if the purpose of such an endeavor is to protect celebrity children from photographs, there's no way it would happen.

"But the paparazzi are engaged in harassment," Berry implored. "How could that possibly be legal?" I agreed: Legitimate news gathering is one thing, but intentionally causing Berry and her daughter emotional distress crosses the line and needed to be stopped.

We resolved to research the current laws and find a way to do that.

Doug did some research and found a law on the books in California prohibiting anyone from harassing or threatening the child of an abortion doctor. Apparently in the past, pro-life activists were harassing the children of these doctors. What if we amended that law to apply to *all* children targeted because of the profession of their parent, not just abortion doctors? Also relevant at that time was a rampage by a former LAPD officer who killed multiple people, including a child of a fellow LAPD officer. Our strategy was to create legislation that benefited children of all professions, including law enforcement, and enlist their support for the bill. It was the beginning of our legislative project.

I should mention that my firm, unlike many our size, actually had a fair amount of state legislative experience. I had worked for a California state senator 20 years earlier. Doug had worked for a different California state senator 34 years earlier. He spearheaded the project. We also had a first-year attorney who had worked in the California

Assembly for a year, just before law school, about four years earlier. Collectively, we had some solid legislative experience—not common for an L.A. media litigation firm.

Our first move was hiring one of the best lobbyists in Sacramento: Jennifer Wada. She reached out to some of the more effective legislators, and the No. 2 senator in the California State Senate, Kevin de Leon of Los Angeles, accepted the challenge.

Senator de Leon and his staff wrote and introduced the Senate bill—numbered S.B. 606—and with Wada's help, it was backed by law enforcement: the California Police Officers Association, the California Sheriffs Association, and others. With that backing, no mention of celebrities, and the influence of Senator de Leon, S.B. 606 sailed through the State Senate without a single "no" vote. It took only two months.

But then we got the call we dreaded. Wada told us that the bill, now heading to the State Assembly, was picking up opposition from the media lobby: the newspapers, the photojournalists and the mass-media interests, like Comcast, who own news organizations. The bill's first stop was the Assembly Public Safety Committee, and its chairman was a big supporter of the media lobby. The bill was likely to be killed in his committee on June 25, Wada told us, if we didn't act fast and pull out all the stops. Whatever we had, she said, we had to bring it. "You mean, bring Halle to Sacramento?" we asked. "Yes," she answered.

* * *

ON JUNE 25, 2013, before sunrise, I drove through the gate of Van Nuys airport—a private airport where, ironically enough, I used to appear at local hearings 20 years earlier as an aide to the local state senator to advocate against airport noise. We achieved a big victory after two years of fighting the airplane operators who had previously lobbied to water down or eliminate the noise restrictions at that airport. We helped residents win responsible noise restrictions. Twenty years later, I was climbing into a private jet with a world-famous movie star to zoom up to Sacramento to discuss with state legislators why we needed to pass a new child protection law.

I was not aware that Berry was pregnant when she first met with us in our new office. A few months had passed since then, and she was definitely showing. Berry, her business manager, Jeff, Doug, and I climbed into a small four-seat private jet, facing each other. I was across from Berry. The jet shot into the sky like a rocket, and we were in Sacramento very quickly—about 40 minutes' time. The sun was just coming up as our black Suburban entered the underground parking garage of the State Capitol building—the building where I used to work bills through committees to get them passed and signed into law.

We first met in Senator de Leon's office, and then went straight to the office of the chairman of the Assembly Public Safety Committee: the man who, we were told, was about to kill our bill. He was friendly, and mentioned up front that one of his favorite films was *Bulworth*, a 1998 political satire comedy written, directed and starring Warren Beatty, and co-starring a 32-year-old Halle Berry. They talked for a few minutes about the film, and the chairman's guard was dropping quickly. Berry then segued to the purpose for her visit, and explained what she and her daughter experienced on a daily basis at the hands of paparazzi with no regard for their peace or safety. Jeff, Doug and I chimed in rarely—only when necessary to answer a question—but it was Berry who converted him: To our huge relief and excitement, the chairman said he'd support the bill.

We then went into the offices of every Democrat on the Public Safety Committee—and mentioned each time that we had the chairman's support. Berry gave her pitch; Jeff, Doug and I again spoke only when necessary to answer a question. Each time we left a new office, we had another "yes" vote. We met with the lead Republican on the committee: She was a mom herself, connected with Berry, and expressed her strong sympathy toward Berry and Nahla's plight. But she said she could not support the bill because of the interests (the media lobbies, presumably) opposing the bill.

Berry then appeared at a press conference with Senator de Leon in a large room in the Capitol, where there were 20 to 30 video and still cameras and several times the usual number of reporters. After that, we proceeded to the Assembly Public Safety Committee meeting. Its meetings are usually held in a small room, but that day it was held in the largest committee room in the Capitol—large enough for about 100 audience members, and 20 cameras circling behind the committee members in a horseshoe. The room was packed, with several people standing in the aisles. Berry and Senator de Leon gave short statements and then fielded questions from the committee members.

"My daughter doesn't want to go to school because she knows 'the men' are watching for her," Berry told the members. "They jump out of the bushes and from behind cars and who knows where else, besieging these children just to get a photo." She added, "I have to yell, 'She's a child. Leave my child alone. Leave my child alone.' We get into the car, and my daughter is now sobbing, and she says to me, 'Are they going to kill us?'"

* * *

AFTER BERRY and Senator de Leon spoke, lobbyists gave short statements, in favor and against, and the committee members then cast their votes: With mostly "yes" votes and a few abstentions, the bill passed without a single "no" vote. It was a big victory, and we were on our way. But there were still three more obstacles to passage: the Assembly Judiciary Committee, the Assembly Floor (all members), and then the governor.

By 2:30 p.m., we were back in Senator de Leon's office, and someone was finally getting Berry a sandwich. She was five months pregnant, had not eaten since before the sun came up, ascended and descended at least 20 flights of stairs—in heels—to meet with the committee members, spoke at a press conference, then the committee meeting, and then attended a lunch meeting where she spoke to a couple of dozen senators, but didn't get to eat. Forget X-Men, Berry was a real-life superhero.

Meanwhile, Jeff, Doug and I were tired. We'd all woken up at 4 a.m. The day was long, arduous and stressful. We were ready to jump in the plane and head home. But one member of our L.A. team wanted more: "Is there anyone else we can meet with while we're here?" asked Berry, finishing her half sandwich. Wada and the senator's staff said we could probably meet with some members of the Assembly Judiciary Committee—the bill's next stop—though it was not scheduled for that committee meeting for another month. "Let's do it," Berry said.

While those meetings were being scheduled, Senator de Leon took her to meet privately with the very powerful Speaker of the Assembly, John Pérez. I was not in the room. It was just Berry, the senator, and the speaker. But she told us what happened when she returned. The speaker had a wall of yellow rubber ducks. When a famous person visits, the speaker asks them to sign one. So Berry of course signed one, and gave him the standard pitch about why our bill was necessary.

Berry was the talk of Sacramento that day. As our group walked down the hallways, Assembly and Senate members' doors were open. We'd see their staff notice us, their eyes would bulge, and they'd run to the doorway to catch a glimpse of our fast-walking group. "There she is!" we'd hear. Before our plane took off, we squeezed in meetings with the top Democrat and the top Republican of the Assembly Judiciary Committee. We still had work to do, but we were making great progress.

When Berry returned home, she purchased a yellow rubber duck, just like the kind on the speaker's wall. She wanted another special person to sign it. She and Nahla decorated this duck to the nines: makeup, jewelry and a handbag. On the bottom, Nahla wrote: "Thank you for helping me. Nahla." The duck was delivered to my office in Los Angeles. We packed and shipped the duck to Senator de Leon, who then personally delivered it to the speaker.

* * *

A MONTH LATER, Berry returned with Jennifer Garner, and they met with Assembly Judiciary Committee members and testified before the committee. "We're moms here who are just trying to protect our children," Berry told lawmakers. Garner choked back tears as she gave a detailed account of what it's like to be a celebrity whose children are constantly hounded by photographers. "Being stalked," she told them, "is hard for me, but it's beyond what a child should have to endure."

Both women did a stellar job, and our bill passed the Judiciary Committee, again without a "no" vote. It was then on its way to the Assembly floor, with the strong support of Speaker Pérez—the recipient of Nahla's decorated duck—who controlled the majority party in the Assembly. With his help, our bill passed the Assembly floor, again without a single "no" vote. It then was sent to the governor's desk.

Our lobbyist, Jennifer Wada, informed us that the state was under an order from a federal judge to lower prison populations. All legislation with any potential to add to the prison population was being vetoed by the governor for that reason alone. We needed the governor's signature, or all our efforts would be lost. Never ceasing to amaze us, Berry turned to a secret weapon: her former *Bulworth* co-star. Warren Beatty and Gov. Jerry Brown were very close friends, going back decades. Berry called Beatty, and in less than a minute he completely understood: "I have children," he said. "It's a great bill." The fact that the bill passed both houses of the Legislature without a single "no" vote helped as well. Beatty called his powerful pal in the Capitol, and within days, our bill had the governor's signature. Our little S.B. 606 made it. It was the law of the land.

* * *

THERE WAS some celebration and relief, but I was not convinced. I said to our group: "We need law enforcement to enforce this new law. If they don't, this whole exercise was a big waste of time and money. We need to *meet* with law enforcement, tell them what it's about and get their commitment to enforce it. They need to hear from celebrity parents who experience aggressive paparazzi, so that law enforcement can formulate a plan to stop them."

Our team decided to have one big meeting with our core group and every top person from L.A. law enforcement that we could get in the room. Jennifer Garner offered to host the meeting at her house. (She was married to Ben Affleck at the time.) That provided some added incentive for top members of law enforcement to attend. The meeting included police captains and top lieutenants from the police departments of L.A., Beverly Hills, Santa Monica, and Culver City, plus the L.A. Airport Police and L.A. County Sheriff's Office. The L.A. city attorney himself, Mike Feuer, came with his staff, and the L.A. County district attorney herself, Jackie Lacey, came with two of her top people. Berry and Garner were there, of course, along with Jeff, Doug and me. Ben Affleck was on set filming *Gone Girl*, but in his place was a family member far more persuasive—and I'm not referring to Garner.

Garner welcomed the guests to her home and everyone in the room took turns saying their name and title. It was an impressive array of L.A.'s "top brass," plus our team. Berry spoke briefly with her usual (and very effective) account of how the paparazzi stalk and harass her daughter, Nahla. Garner then introduced the single most effective speaker that night, and we all could have gone home after her presentation. It was Jennifer and Ben's daughter Violet, who was a few days away from turning 8.

At the time, I had two 8-year-olds myself, and could not imagine either of them being in a room packed with uniformed officers and middle-aged people in business suits, let alone making a presentation to all of them. But Violet did it, and boy did she deliver. Violet had written on a single sheet of lined paper things that she experiences every day from paparazzi. Garner told us before the meeting that she'd glanced at the sheet to make sure it was OK, but had no part in writing it, nor did Affleck, who had been working 16-hour days and nights on set.

Violet spoke about the photographers who camp outside of her house every morning, follow her in their cars everywhere she goes, jump out of their cars when she gets out, get as close as possible, shout at her, put their cameras in her face, take pictures, and do this every day of her life, and won't back off or leave her alone, even when she tells them to. She described how it makes her feel. Though her little hands were shaking, her voice was strong, and she delivered this two-minute statement like the most powerful eyewitness account one could ever deliver. Courtroom dramas are based on this kind of testimony.

As Violet spoke, I looked around the room. Everyone was focused like a laser beam, hanging on her every word. When she finished, there was not a dry eye in the room. Literally. You'd have to be a robot not to feel for this perfect little child whose life is being ripped apart by evil photographers who try to upset her because it means an extra $100 for the photos they sell.

* * *

Doug and I then led a discussion with law enforcement on what they needed from us—from celebrity parents whose children were the subject of a legal violation of our new law. The law enforcement, largely the D.A. and city attorney, explained what they needed to get a conviction: evidence, preferably video, of photographers getting too close and upsetting children. The law still allowed paps to take photos and videos of children, but because of our S.B. 606, they had to do so at a *distance*, and without shouting at or upsetting the child.

That meeting was followed a month later by another gathering in the same room at Garner's house. It was attended by dozens of celebrity parents who had signed on as supporters of the bill, and wanted to know what they could do to help enforce the new law and protect their children. Matt Damon was first to arrive for the meeting and said, "Please tell me I'm not the first one here." We smiled and said, "Uh, yeah. You are, actually." He then made a beeline to the bar not far away. Gwyneth Paltrow (*sans* her then-husband, Chris Martin, my favorite rock/pop star), Kristen Bell and husband Dax Shepard, a pregnant Emily Blunt, Gwen Stefani, Brian Austin Green and his then-wife, Megan Fox, Heidi Klum, Alyssa Milano, Rita Wilson (wife of Tom Hanks—her husband showed up later and entertained us with paparazzi stories), Sacha Baron Cohen with his wife, Isla Fisher, and others, all attended.

D.A. Lacey and City Attorney Feuer also were there, and a few of the top cops from the previous meeting. Garner again thanked everyone for coming, and we soon launched into the purpose of the bill, what it says, what it does, what it doesn't do, and how the parents and their assistants could help to enforce it. I made the initial presentation and led the discussion, including a Q&A with our celebrity guests. Doug chimed in as well.

Word got out to the media that celebrity parents were joining forces with L.A. law enforcement and things were going to be very different from now on. They got the message: Paparazzi kept their distance from the children.

* * *

A FEW MONTHS after that meeting, Kristen Bell took the initiative to launch a "No Child Policy" campaign to get media outlets to stop buying paparazzi photos of children. Her husband, actor-writer Dax Shepard, penned a really funny and poignant essay for the Huffington Post on Jan. 30, 2014, titled "Why Our Children Should Be Off Limits to the Paparazzi." (Easily found on Google and worth a read.) He begged people to stop consuming content that included photos of celebrity children. "So long as people pay good money to buy magazines featuring famous people's children, there will be men popping out of bushes and lurking around playgrounds to get those pics. Those are just the facts. The consumer is the only one who can put an end to this. They are the only ones with real power."

A long list of media outlets, including industry leaders like *People* and *Entertainment Tonight,* signed on to the No Child Policy, agreeing not to buy or publish photos of stars' children unless they were in a public place that clearly signaled their parents' permission, like a red-carpet event, or a snap shared by the celebrity on social media. But a trip to the farmer's market or a walk down the street—off limits.

The No Child campaign was another big victory for children like Nahla and Violet.

That one-two punch of Berry/Garner and Bell/Shepard caused a sea change in the lives of the children of celebrity parents (and of course the lives of the parents themselves). Along the way, I learned that the "Halle Effect" is real: Injustice and evil can inspire a superhero response. Hard work, strategic thinking, never giving up, and finding a way, not to mention a 5-year-old's hand-painted rubber duck and a handwritten statement delivered by a fearless and determined 8-year-old, really *can* change the world.

9

PATRIARCH AND PATRIOT

O n June 4, 2020, while I was writing this book, my father died. He was 92. He grew up in Northampton, Pennsylvania, a small town near Allentown and Bethlehem, in the heart of American industry. He was the youngest of four children born to Ukrainian immigrant parents. His father, Ignatz (nickname: *John*), worked at the cement factory in Northampton. My father attended Northampton High School, whose mascot was (and still is) the Konkrete Kid. I always chuckle when I hear that mascot name. Many mornings, my father told me, a thin layer of concrete dust covered the town: coating the houses, cars, sidewalks, school and everything else. His father, my grandfather, inhaled that dust every workday at the cement factory and died at the age of 52.

In 1944, our country was neck deep in World War II. My father—then 17—volunteered for the war. He joined the Navy, went to boot-camp and then radar school. By the time he left radar school, the war (thankfully) had ended. He was deployed to sea just as the world was at peace, and traveled far and wide on his destroyer: a lot of time in England and Scotland, and trips to France, Germany, Belgium, Portugal, Morocco and Denmark, among other places. He returned home on Dec. 16, 1946, the day *after* his father's funeral, completely unaware that his father had just passed.

My father's mother, Paranka (nickname: *Pauline*), was a homemaker. In 1912, she crossed the Atlantic, from Austria to New York, at the young age of 16—by herself—in the steerage class of a passenger ship. Her parents wanted a better life for her. My mother gets emotional when she recounts this story. She moved to the Ukrainian section of eastern Pennsylvania, where she probably lived with relatives or friends of relatives, became immersed in the Ukrainian culture centered around the Ukrainian Orthodox Church, met my grandfather, married at age 20, and bore four children, the youngest being my father.

When my dad returned from the Navy in 1946, he got a job working the graveyard shift at a steel mill in Bethlehem. He started work at midnight and scraped steel remnants off the boiler until 8 a.m. It was an inferno. He earned a union wage, and took pride in it.

He actually worked two jobs. At 8 a.m., right after working the eight-hour midnight shift at the steel mill, he worked eight more hours at a small grocery store owned and run by his mother and older brother, John. He helped the family business, without pay. After 16 hours of work, my father didn't complain. He ate a meal, went to sleep, and repeated the same routine again the next day, five consecutive days a week, 50 weeks a year.

Dad did well in high school (as a Konkrete Kid—*chuckle*), receiving mostly A's and B's on his report cards. His sister, Kate—nine years his senior—encouraged him to become a businessman, and to not get stuck working in the steel mill all his life. It was great career advice, which he later followed.

During his naval service, my father was sent on a train from the East Coast to San Diego for radar school. It was the dead of winter, and during a stop in Nevada, the snow was piled higher than the train. He awoke the next morning in San Bernardino, California, to clear blue skies and 70-degree weather. He pledged to himself at that moment: "I will move to Southern California when I get out of the Navy." And he did.

* * *

IN 1952, at the age of 25, after his naval service and after five years of working 16-hour days in the steel mill and then his family's grocery store—which had to close shortly after a supermarket opened up down the street, killing their business—my father left the freezing winters of eastern Pennsylvania and moved to sunny Los Angeles forever. With his meager savings from the steel mill, my father bought a tiny car wash in L.A. at the corner of Fairfax and Clinton. He washed and dried cars alongside his two employees, and greeted the customers, returned their keys and handled the money—all with a smile, I'm sure, because that was his way.

He took night school business classes at L.A. City College, later sold the car wash and landed a job selling P.A. (public address) sound systems to local schools. He earned a commission from each sale and did very well, because the schools didn't have them and all were buying. He told me all he needed to do was walk in the schoolhouse door, and he would make a sale. Until, of course, all the schools had bought one, and then he was out of a job.

He became a bookkeeper with the help of his college business classes, eventually received a bachelor's degree and then an MBA from USC, and became a business manager. He met a talented commercial photographer with a huge smile and gregarious personality named Gerald Trafficanda, and became the business manager for his studio—Trafficanda Studios—which did the photography for print ads: the images you see in magazines, billboards, product packaging, and so on. After a decade or two, they expanded into producing TV commercials. They shot a lot of ads for cars and toys in particular.

* * *

I MET MY PATERNAL GRANDMOTHER, Pauline, only once. She was about 74; I was 1. My parents flew my brother and me from Los Angeles to New York City, and she and my uncle John (my middle name is John, after him) drove the two hours from eastern Pennsylvania to New York City to meet us. My grandmother passed two years later, so I have no memory of her. My uncle passed when I was 16, but I never saw him other than that one time. My father had a fear of flying so he never flew East other than that one time, for my uncle John's funeral.

My uncle John was a union leader in Allentown for many years before his death, and his funeral was attended by all of the dignitaries in the city, including the mayor and the councilmembers. He also was a war hero: In World War II he served in the Army's 8th Air Force, flew more than 30 bombing missions, and received the Distinguished Flying Cross and Air Medal with three oak leaf clusters. Though he and I only met once, when I was 1, my uncle sent me birthday cards—with $10 in them—throughout my childhood. He also saved $15,000 for my college education, which paid for the first two years of tuition, room and board. It was very generous of him and my aunt Margaret to do that for me. They didn't have children of their own, so they saved money for my brother's college education and mine. When I was younger, I didn't think a lot about any of this. Now that I'm older, and a father, I realize the significance of my uncle's tremendous service to his country, literally facing death on each of those 30-plus missions, and also his great generosity toward my brother and me. Fifteen thousand dollars times two was a lot of money for them to save for us, and they didn't even know us. I wish two things: that my uncle John had flown over to L.A. to see us once in a while, because my father would not fly East, and also that I could tell him how proud I am of his service to his country, and say thank you.

* * *

I'VE MENTIONED a few times in this book my father's mantra. "Never give up!" he would say to me and my brother—usually when a real-life example presented itself and he could make the point. He also would tell us: "Find a way!" Eventually the first mantra fused with the second one, and it became: "Never give up, and find a way!" In other words, if you want something, stay at it, be creative, try everything you can, and you'll get it.

The *Bollea v. Gawker* case—that's how we won it. We never gave up, and found a way. All my other cases as well. I am persistent, think creatively, try different things, think some more, try some more, refuse to give up, and have a successful track record because of it.

My father was a very positive person. He believed in positivity. He was rarely negative, and if he was, he would catch himself, stop, and change it around. It made for a pleasant person to be around.

I do that myself. This book is an example: I've tried to be positive throughout. Who wants to read a book of negative thoughts or comments? I certainly don't. I often think, and sometimes say, that I live on the absolute best planet in the universe: the one with life on it! And on that planet, I live in the best country: the USA. And in that country, I live in the best state: sunny California. And in that state, I live in the best city: L.A. And in that city, I live in one of the best parts of town: the Westside. We have our health and enough money to pay for what we need. So I often remind myself how fortunate and blessed we are.

My father was the ultimate provider and family man. He worked into his 80s, and he and my mother reached their 54th wedding anniversary just a couple of weeks before he died. He was rarely without a kind word and a friendly smile. Even at 92. He never gave up, and he always found a way. That's how he lived his life. And because of him, that's how I live mine.

10

WHEN WORDS BECOME WEAPONS

"Sticks and stones may break my bones
But words will never hurt me."

This children's rhyme is meant to help children steel themselves against schoolyard taunts. But in the grown-up world, words *can* hurt. They can do worse: They can quickly destroy reputations, careers and businesses built up over the course of decades. They can ruin people's lives.

Take the infamous case of Richard Jewell.

When a bomb went off at the 1996 Summer Olympics in Atlanta, Jewell was a local security guard who was thrilled to be working the high-profile venue. At first, he was hailed as a hero. He had spotted an abandoned green backpack, notified police and started helping to move visitors to safety when the device exploded, killing one person and injuring more than 100. Three days later, Jewell picked up the local paper and read that *he* was the prime suspect.

The *Atlanta Journal-Constitution* published a front-page article identifying him as the focus of the federal investigation. Citing unnamed law enforcement sources, it said the soft-spoken man "fits the profile of a lone bomber." A CNN reporter read the article verbatim on the air. This set off a frenzy of reporters who set upon him, Jewell would later say, "like piranha on a bleeding cow."

Three months later, Jewell was officially cleared of any involvement in the bombing. (In 2005, a North Carolina man named Eric Rudolph pleaded guilty to the Atlanta Olympics attack. He's serving a life sentence.) But Jewell's treatment by law enforcement and the media stuck to him and his family like tar, and he could never outrun his notoriety.

Jewell sued several major media outlets and won settlements from NBC and CNN. But as he told Larry King in 1997, "Money can't buy your name back." Jewell's libel case against Cox Enterprises, the parent company of the Atlanta newspaper, made its way through the courts for a decade without final resolution, and much of it was dismissed along the way. On Aug. 29, 2007, Jewell died of diabetes complications at the young age of 44. He will be remembered not as the Atlanta Olympics bombing suspect, but as the hero who saved lives during the Atlanta Olympics bombing and then had his life turned upside down by irresponsible journalists with massive power and no oversight.

* * *

THE "PETER PARKER PRINCIPLE" known to all Spider-Man fans is: With great power comes great responsibility. That principle applies to journalists and media outlets. Millions of people read their stories, and believe them. A person's reputation, career or business, built over the course of a lifetime, can be vaporized in a matter of minutes. Thus, the media must do everything they can to ensure their stories are accurate and fair. People's lives literally hang in the balance.

The press has a duty to the people it covers *and* the people who consume the news. All too often, it fails on both fronts. This is as true today as ever. Modern technology in an increasingly competitive industry means that information—true, false or somewhere in between—can spread so fast that it can become impossible to contain.

A young man named Brandon Gonzales was accused, wrongfully, of killing two people in a shooting at a homecoming party in Greenville, Texas, in October 2016. He sat in jail, charged with capital murder, wondering why he stood accused when he'd left the event before the shooting even took place.

A week later, as abruptly as he'd been arrested, all charges against Gonzales were dropped. Authorities blamed the error on a mistaken witness identification in the chaos of the shooting's aftermath. He was free, but his life would never be the same.

Gonzales, who had worked at a car dealership, moved away from his hometown to live with relatives in Florida because of all the unwanted attention. He was unable to find steady work. A Google search still brings up his mug shot and articles calling him a suspect in a brutal killing. In a 2019 interview with *The New York Times*, he lamented: "My kids, their kids, can always look up and they can see, oh, he was arrested for capital murder."

* * *

ANOTHER REASON why it's easy for innocent people like Jewell and Gonzales to get flattened by a fast-moving locomotive of bad information: The media often shapes content to appeal to its intended audience. A recent example is the case of Nicholas Sandmann, a student at Covington Catholic High School in Kentucky.

The teenager was drawn into a social media firestorm in 2019 when he was filmed at a demonstration in Washington, D.C., standing close to an older Native American man named Nathan Phillips. A video shows Sandmann smiling at Phillips, an Omaha Nation tribal elder, who is playing a drum. (Their paths crossed because Sandmann was there on a school trip for the March for Life, and Phillips was attending the Indigenous Peoples March.)

Sandmann was wearing a red cap with the slogan "Make America Great Again." This open declaration of support for President Trump added fuel to the fire, or maybe a stick of dynamite is a more apt description. The video went viral. Outrage, debate and public shaming ensued, and Sandmann said he received death threats over social media.

The irresponsible press pounced. Left-leaning outlets, including CNN, ran *edited* video of the encounter that portrayed the teenager as a smug, menacing, racist bully. A more complete video, which emerged later, showed that Phillips had approached the teen and his classmates, and begun drumming in their faces.

Sandmann's attorney, L. Lin Wood, tweeted several months later: "History & media will never forget what was done on the steps of Lincoln Memorial in January of 2019 to a 16-year-old boy who exhibited grace & dignity under fire," as he took to task some of the outlets that had painted Sandmann unfairly. Wood had also represented Jewell in his cases against the media. "[Sandmann] will not now go quietly. He is a young man of courage. Like Richard Jewell, Nicholas Sandmann is a hero."

In early 2020, a libel suit that Sandmann brought against CNN was settled on undisclosed terms. That July, Sandmann's suit against *The Washington Post* was settled, also on undisclosed terms. Sandmann announced the settlement via Twitter on July 24, the same day he turned 18.

The media attempted to destroy a teenager—and in the process severely damaged him, simply because they don't like the president, and the boy was wearing his campaign hat. The media twisted reality, simply to carry out their left-wing political agenda, and had no regard for the young man they were making a casualty of their recklessness. Wood told the *Chicago Tribune*: "They didn't care what they said or did to Nicholas. They just saw him as an object to use to attack President Trump."

News outlets should focus on reporting the facts, and getting them right. "Just the facts, ma'am," as Joe Friday used to say on *Dragnet*. Facts presented fairly and accurately. People can make their own conclusions, based on the true facts. But no one can reach a conclusion on anything if they are being fed lies and spin, like we see from major news outlets like CNN. No one needs a reporter, editor, newspaper or cable TV owner telling them how to think—least of all a group that is on the outer fringe of one political philosophy or the other.

News propaganda, or what some call "fake news," causes people to reach false conclusions, and develop mistrust in the media at large. Americans *need* journalism. We need to know what's going on. If there is corruption in government, we need to know it. But if we can't trust it, then the words of journalists are meaningless. I don't know the percentages of how often journalists get it wrong, but *any* amount is unacceptable, because any amount—and it seems to be quite frequent—breeds mistrust in the media by consumers. That mistrust undermines the very purpose of journalism, which is to inform. If people are inherently skeptical of what they read or hear, the media are failing in their mission to inform.

Studies have shown that media outlets which demonize one side or another—anyone with a different viewpoint than that of the outlet or its target audience—contribute to a more polarized, less unified, less civil population. Most news outlets seem to lean heavily to one side. CNN, *The New York Times*, *The Washington Post*, NBC and MSNBC lean heavily to the left, while Fox News leans heavily to the right. They omit some important information and skew other information to pander to their audience. This "red meat" for the loyalists, as I call it, does have a place in our society's marketplace of ideas: It's called *opinion*, and should be clearly labeled as such, and written or read to appear like it's an opinion, as opposed to a cold, hard fact. In my view, nearly all of CNN's content is opinion or spin. The network should have a permanent caption at the bottom reading: "Everything on this network is opinion, and not necessarily facts." Fox News should post one as well. When opinion becomes the primary source of "news," especially amid so much tumult and disharmony in our country, it becomes dangerous.

Richard Jewell and Brandon Gonzales were innocent men, and Nicholas Sandmann was an innocent boy. All of them got caught in the gears of an American media machine whose great power *requires* great responsibility. But there was no responsibility at all. Unfortunately, these scenarios have become a regular occurrence in today's media. It needs to change—either through publishers and editors taking action to enforce ethics guidelines, or by the American people taking action to inform these outlets of their displeasure, or through legal action by the daily victims of countless fake news stories.

11

A CODE TO LIVE BY

One of our expert witnesses at the Gawker trial was a journalism professor at the University of Florida School of Journalism named Mike Foley. Foley previously had been a longtime editor at the *St. Petersburg Times* (later renamed the *Tampa Bay Times*), and he testified that the Society of Professional Journalists' ("SPJ") Code of Ethics is commonly accepted as authoritative on ethical issues in the profession. The Code is not a set of rules, but rather a guide—written by journalists, for journalists—that encourages all who engage in journalism to take responsibility for the information they provide.

The entire code is printed at the end of this chapter for you to read, and also is available at *www.SPJ.org/EthicsCode.asp*. But its four main themes are worth a mention here. They are so simple. They also can be applied to more than just journalistic practices. They are basic pillars of being good human beings, the kind of stuff that we learn from our parents and teachers, and that we teach our own children:

- **Seek Truth and Report It**
- *Ethical journalism should be accurate and fair. Journalists should be honest and courageous in gathering, reporting and interpreting information.*
- **Minimize Harm**
- *Ethical journalism treats sources, subjects, colleagues and members of the public as human beings deserving of respect.*
- **Act Independently**
- *The highest and primary obligation of ethical journalism is to serve the public.*
- **Be Accountable and Transparent**
- *Ethical journalism means taking responsibility for one's work and explaining one's decisions to the public.*

Section 2 of the Code, titled "Minimize Harm," includes some of the following points:

Journalists should:

- *Balance the public's need for information against potential harm or discomfort. Pursuit of the news is not a license for arrogance or undue intrusiveness.*
- *Show compassion for those who may be affected by news coverage...*
- *Recognize that legal access to information differs from an ethical justification to publish or broadcast.*
- *...Weigh the consequences of publishing or broadcasting personal information.*
- *Avoid pandering to lurid curiosity, even if others do...*
- *Consider the long-term implications of the extended reach and permanence of publication. Provide updated and more complete information as appropriate.*

Professor Foley stripped away the confusing layers of modern-day journalism and focused on the people doing the job. "Journalists don't check their humanity at the door when they enter the profession. They don't have to have cold hearts or lack sympathy or eliminate their empathy," Foley explained. "In fact, just the opposite is true. A journalist is sensitive and understands the power he or she has—tremendous power to help or harm."

"Real journalists," he added, "are ethical. Journalism has standards and values. The First Amendment is a privilege, not a license."

The SPJ Code of Ethics (which you can find by going to https://www.spj.org/pdf/spj-code-of-ethics.pdf or googling "SPJ Code") was my single favorite page in the more than 100,000 pages of documents in the *Terry Bollea (Hulk Hogan) v. Gawker* lawsuit. It is one of my favorite pages of writing in the world. I'm sometimes cast by reporters as an "enemy" of the press, but the opposite is true, and my love for this Code is proof. I don't understand why journalists and publishers don't love this document as much as I do. If they did, and if everyone who writes, edits and publishes information followed it, journalism would have exponentially better quality, and the public would trust and appreciate the news so much more than it does today.

12

TRUTH UNDER SIEGE

"Freedom of the press is essential to the preservation of a democracy; but there is a difference between freedom and license. Editorialists who tell downright lies in order to advance their own agendas do more to discredit the press than all the censors in the world."
—President Franklin D. Roosevelt

Would you go to a doctor not licensed to practice medicine?

Would you hire a lawyer not licensed to practice law?

Would you build a house using someone who is not a licensed contractor?

Of course you wouldn't. Nor would I.

Many professions involve a special set of skills and knowledge, and require licensing and the regulation that comes with it because practitioners have the power to impact the safety or well-being of others. Some 1,100 different professions are subject to licensing and regulation in this country. They vary by state, though some are predictably universal: doctor, lawyer, contractor, certified public accountant, teacher, pharmacist, real estate agent. My state, California, also regulates professions that include locksmith, electrologist (permanent hair removal), embalmer, private investigator, architect, barber, plumber, smog check inspector and horseracing stable worker/groomer. Talent agents also need to be licensed.

More than 20 states require a license for travel guides. So in Nevada, if you want to make a living showing people Great Basin National Park or Hoover Dam, you must put in 733 days of training and pay $1,500 for a license. In Louisiana, you need a license to be a florist. To be a nail technician, and give people manicures and pedicures, you need 600 hours of training in some states before you can even *apply* for a license.

The profession of journalism requires no license. No fee is paid. No training is required. No rules or regulations are required to be followed, other than the standard civil and criminal laws that apply to everyone. There is no supervision, regulation or oversight by any agency: not federal, nor state, nor county, nor city. Yet a journalist has the power to destroy a person's personal and professional reputation —including their career and business, which often are built over the course of decades—with a single false or misleading story or post, disseminated widely on the internet, where it can live forever, often becoming the No. 1 search result on Google under that person's name.

Words carry immense power—far more than an emery board or a bouquet of flowers. Journalists literally have people's lives hanging in the balance every day, based on what they report, how they gather information, and who they choose to quote as a "source."

Am I suggesting that journalists should be required to take classes and pass exams like attorneys or CPAs are required to do? Or that reporters and editors be required to obtain a license, and periodically renew it, to show they meet a set of state standards? Or that the media should be subject to government oversight like most other industries? No. But the absence of regulation and oversight means the pressure to behave responsibly and ethically is that much greater for those who choose journalism as a profession.

I have said many times, and will continue to say it: I value greatly the press and media—but *responsible* press and media. First Amendment protections to gather and report news, and to express oneself in speech, are essential to democracy, and essential to freedom. Without it, there is oppression and tyranny. Let's not forget the famous adage: "I may not agree with what you say, but I will defend to the death your right to say it."

But defamation is not protected free speech. The U.S. Supreme Court has held many times that there is no First Amendment protection for false speech. Many other forms of speech also receive no protection under the law. Copyright or trademark infringement. Using speech to defraud someone. Using speech to incite immediate violence. Hate speech. Child pornography. Revenge porn. Shouting "fire" in a crowded theater when there is no fire. These are just some of the many examples of speech that receive no protection under the law.

Legal speech—responsible speech, including responsible news gathering and reporting—is essential to our democracy and our free society. I am exercising my free speech rights right now in writing this book, and I am grateful to our Founding Fathers for ensuring that I, and everyone else in America, have this crucial right.

But free speech and freedom of the press are too often used as convenient shields by irresponsible media whose primary goal is to make money by writing and publishing clickbait or "hit piece" stories about people and companies, packed with false and misleading information. This causes substantial harm to the subject of the story. Too often, the writer and publisher place a low value on the truth, or the impact that the article will have on the subject. Very often, a reporter and publisher who print false or misleading facts about someone—which causes harm—refuse to take responsibility, refuse to correct the story, refuse to retract or apologize for it, and refuse to compensate the subject for the harm caused, absent a jury verdict and the exhaustion of all appeals. The law does not protect such conduct. The defamation laws exist to allow the victim of such an article—or rather hit piece—to seek redress in court and pursue both damages and an injunction requiring the correction or removal of the defamatory speech.

* * *

"The press was to serve the governed, not the governors," U.S.
Supreme Court Justice Hugo Black famously declared in *New York
Times Co. v. United States*, the landmark Pentagon Papers case of 1971.
Indeed, freedom of the press—the right to report news or share
opinion without intervention or censorship from the government—
was considered "one of the great bulwarks of liberty" by the
Founding Fathers.

The First Amendment, which among other things protects
freedom of the press, was adopted on Dec. 15, 1791, as part of the Bill
of Rights. It reads, in its entirety (with emphasis added):

Congress shall make no law respecting an establishment of reli-
gion, or prohibiting the free exercise thereof; or **abridging the
freedom of speech**, or **of the press**; or the right of the people peace-
ably to assemble, and to petition the Government for a redress of
grievances.

In its purest form, a free press was intended to protect the public's
right to a media that functions as a watchdog, with the power to
investigate and report on government wrongdoing. It was meant to
ensure America could be a vibrant marketplace of ideas where ordinary citizens could express themselves and be exposed to all kinds of
information and opinions.

Before the 13 colonies declared independence from Great Britain,
the British government tried to censor the American media by
prohibiting newspapers from publishing unfavorable information
and opinions. One of the first court cases involving freedom of the
press in America was in 1734. British governor William Cosby (for a
completely different case involving his modern-day namesake, see
Chapter 16) brought a libel case against the publisher of *The New York
Weekly Journal*, John Peter Zenger, for publishing commentary critical
of Cosby's government. Zenger was acquitted.

A free press is crucial for a democracy in which the government is
accountable to the people. As Walter Cronkite put it: "Freedom of the
press is not just important to democracy, it *is* democracy."

* * *

I GREW up with an unconscious appreciation for the media. Journalism was embedded in the fabric of my family's life in simple ways. The *Los Angeles Times* was delivered to our doorstep every morning, seven days a week. My father would always start with the sports section and then read the front page and the metro section. As a child, I read the cartoon page almost every day. Though I hate to admit it, even in high school I picked up the paper mostly for the cartoons. Once I got to college, things changed. I started reading newspapers every day. I read *The New York Times,* the *Santa Cruz Sentinel*, and the *Los Angeles Times* fairly regularly. I also became managing editor of a student-run weekly called the *Santa Cruz Independent* for three months. It was a fun job and great learning experience. (More about that adventure in Chapter 17.)

Since then—as an observant adult and attorney with an all-access pass to the world of media misdeeds—I've seen the news industry transform itself from what appeared to be a genuine desire to inform people of local, national and world events, into something whose stated ideals no longer square with its conduct. Worse, I've watched as journalists hurt both famous and ordinary people with impunity, and then try to wrap themselves in the First Amendment like it's a cloak of invincibility that allows them to avoid ethics, responsibility, libel laws, or basic notions of right and wrong.

Yellow journalism in the late 1800s paved the way for tabloid journalism in the 1920s and '30s, which has mutated into the various forms of sensational, slanted, scapegoat-seeking articles throughout the internet today.

* * *

THE "MAINSTREAM MEDIA"—OUTLETS like *The New York Times, Washington Post* and NBC—have become increasingly like the tabloids: trying to shock readers with headlines and skewed stories to get you to look. Meanwhile, the openly biased media like CNN, MSNBC and

Fox News have become even more polarizing. With these changes, the public's trust in *all* media has eroded.

When Gallup first measured trust in the mass media in a 1972 survey, 68 percent of Americans said they trusted it. A 2019 Gallup poll found that only 13 percent trust the media "a great deal" and only 28 percent "a fair amount." Meanwhile, 30 percent trust the media "not very much" and 28 percent report their trust level is "none at all." That's a whopping 58 percent majority of respondents with *little to no trust* in the media.

Who is to blame for these falling trust numbers? The media, of course. If they would only adhere to ethics and responsibility in reporting, and provide in-depth, detailed, "just the facts, ma'am" information, and let the reader, listener or viewer come to their own conclusions—without all the bias, spin and manipulation—the media would see their trust numbers rise considerably. In other words: Follow the SPJ Code!

The media's defense to their conduct is probably two-fold: (1) "freedom of the press—leave us alone and mind your own business" (in other words, they want to descend even further into the abyss of public mistrust), and (2) "we have to compete, and the public wants to be stimulated and entertained. They won't read, listen or watch if we don't have an 'edge.'"

If I can offer a contrary view—and the approach we took in college to compete against the other two weekly papers: News that is more in-depth, more accurate, more informative, but still presents the information in a way that is fun and interesting, but not sensationalized, can do wonders for ratings and revenue. The tabloidy tactics of the modern-day mass media are killing the industry, particularly the inaccurate reporting, superficial reporting, "made you look" headlines, and constant spin and manipulation within so-called hard news.

Sometimes I feel that reporters see their role as not to relay full, accurate information to the public, but almost the opposite: to persuade the audience of the reporter's personal political or sociological viewpoints. If the reporter wants people to vote for Trump, they report the news one way, and if they want people to vote for Biden, they report the news in the opposite way. But too little news today is plain, honest facts.

News today seems mostly about individual reporters writing and presenting based on their personal bias, and trying to perfect just the right type and amount of spin and manipulation of the reader to influence their votes, allegiances, and outlook on society and life, without the spin being so strong and obvious that the consumer recoils and says, "Stop—I'm not buying it." In other words, media today, even several "mainstream" outlets, seem to be engaged in the practice of *propaganda*. It's dangerous to the American people, the American systems, and the media themselves. The proof is in the falling trust numbers. If and when the media clean up their act and start to follow the rules of ethics and basic notions of responsibility, they will start to see their trust numbers return, along with the public respect, prestige and financial success that the media deserve.

* * *

JOURNALISM IS A NOBLE PROFESSION—VERY noble. Essential. When it is done responsibly and ethically. But when it's not, then it's no different from the doctor or lawyer who engages in malpractice and hurts people. The only difference is: Unethical or irresponsible doctors and lawyers have their licenses suspended or revoked. But unethical, irresponsible journalists survive and, in some instances, thrive.

Over the past few decades, the traditional style of reporting—neutral and objective presentation of facts—has become the exception; it is no longer the rule. The trend is away from "just the facts" and toward news *analysis*, notes the *Columbia Journalism Review* in a 2019 piece. I do feel that some outlets, like the Associated Press, Reuters, *USA Today*, ABC and CBS, continue to do a good job of providing accurate information in a relatively neutral and balanced way. But news analysis, aka commentary, aka propaganda, once the purview of op-eds and editorial pages, is now the norm for organizations like CNN, NBC, MSNBC, Fox News, *The New York Times* and *The Washington Post*. They are all heavily slanted.

It's even more of a public disservice for a slanted news outlet to *pretend* to be neutral, or fair and balanced, when they aren't, and they know it. CNN is the classic example. Their anchors give speeches about how they are neutral, fair and balanced, unbiased—and then behind closed doors their executives and employees talk nonstop, and on the air their anchors talk nonstop, pro-Democrat/liberal, and anti-Republican/conservative.

Fox News is just as biased to the right, but at least it dropped its longtime "Fair and Balanced" slogan in 2017 for a new one: "Most Watched, Most Trusted." Not a whole lot better. Meanwhile, CNN calls itself "The most trusted name in news." Equally misleading. Give me a break, Fox News and CNN: Neither of you is very trusted by a large chunk of the American news market—because at least half of the public does not agree with your heavily slanted politics. Instead, Fox News should call itself "The Most Republican Name in News" and CNN should call itself "The Most Liberal Name in News."

My challenge to news outlets is this: Do everyone a favor, and yourselves a favor. If you are biased, just be honest and up-front about it. Every hour or so, offer a reminder: "We here at CNN want Biden to win, and will say anything we need to say to convince you to vote for him." And at Fox News, the same disclaimer but replace "Biden" with "Trump" or "Republicans."

I have no problem with a news network that chooses a side, so long as they are honest about it, don't pretend they are neutral, and repeatedly remind the audience of their bias. Because believe it or not, a huge number of CNN and Fox News watchers think their network is truly fair and balanced. Scary. Be who you want to be, just wear it on your sleeve and don't apologize. But please don't insult people's intelligence, or attempt to fool them, with misleading claims and slogans.

* * *

THE NEW YORK TIMES seems to think of itself as the pinnacle of responsibility. But they get a lot of things wrong. And their Opinion pages are a disaster. They ran an op-ed about President Trump in March 2019 that was titled "The Real Trump-Russia Quid Pro Quo." It contained false statements. My firm filed a libel suit over that piece in February 2020.

In 2017, *The New York Times* ran an unsigned editorial from the senior editorial staff about former Alaska Gov. Sarah Palin that was outrageous. The piece said the man who shot Arizona Congress-woman Gabby Giffords in the head and nearly killed her, and did kill six people and injure 11 others at that same political event in 2011, was influenced by a Palin campaign mailer. The mailer featured a map of the U.S. and 20 congressional districts held by Democrats that were targeted for focused campaigning; there were "stylized crosshairs" over each of the 20 districts (not each member of Congress) within the mailer. However, law enforcement heavily investigated the connection between the shooter and political mailers. Turns out, the shooter was completely nuts and not influenced by anything political at all. There also was no evidence that he ever saw the mailer. Rather, he was diagnosed after his arrest as a paranoid schizophrenic and was said to nurse a grudge against Giffords for not responding suffi-ciently to a question he asked her at a 2007 event. Palin sued *The Times* for that editorial, and the Second Circuit held that the lawsuit could not be dismissed, but instead must proceed. On Aug. 28, 2020, the trial court scheduled the case for trial on Feb. 1, 2021.

Why would *The New York Times* say, in an editorial written by very senior people on staff—not outside freelancers paid per story—that Palin's mailer had caused that shooting? Simple. It's because they hate Palin. They also hate President Trump, and they also hate all or almost all Republicans. It's misleading and disappointing that *The New York Times*, which claims and acts like it's the model for ethics and responsibility, is not a responsible news organization.

The *Times*' editorial department is such a disaster that in June 2020 the head of the editorial page, James Bennet (who presided over the Palin fiasco and several other big missteps), resigned in the midst of yet another controversy. He oversaw the publication the prior week of a controversial opinion piece by a Republican senator, Tom Cotton, which suggested that federal troops should be deployed to end civil unrest sparked by the death of George Floyd in Minneapolis, and the piece apparently had a number of factual inaccuracies that should not have been allowed in a newspaper that touts itself as containing "all the news that's fit to print."

A week earlier, *Times* publisher A.G. Sulzberger cited "a significant breakdown in our editing process, not the first we've experienced in recent years," in a note to the staff announcing Bennet's departure. It's a start, but Sulzberger needs to look deeper than one editor who made some bad decisions.

Sulzberger and his senior staff should spend more time focused on fairness and accuracy, and stop carrying out a political agenda. To be fair, the paper is capable of really good work—like the May 24, 2020, front page, a stark and somber list of names marking the grim milestone of 100,000 American lives lost to Covid-19. There was no analysis, no spin, not even a single photo. Just the facts. And they were powerful.

* * *

THE CIVIL COURT SYSTEM IS, unfortunately, the place to address misbehavior by journalists via libel and defamation lawsuits. News organizations should offer: Tell us where we went wrong and if you're right, we'll fix it. But so many of my letters, pointing out in detail specific false and defamatory statements in articles, and providing substantial evidence in support, all too often are brushed away. An individual with no representation is not likely to have greater success.

As illustrated by the Gawker case, it is so expensive and burdensome to litigate against the media that only wealthy people and companies can afford a case against a major media company without incredible strain. (See Chapter 5.) The average Joe or Jane rarely has a chance. Few law firms take defamation cases on a contingency fee basis. It's too expensive, too time-consuming, the cases drag on too long, and often a First Amendment defense is used to defeat the case, either in the trial court or an appellate court.

I often think about alternatives to the court system. There are so many instances of defamation and other unlawful or irresponsible journalism, and it is so expensive and time-consuming to fully litigate each of them. It seems to make more sense to have a small-claims type of court to handle the volume. I would call it "media court." It would be kept relatively streamlined, fast-moving and affordable. It would hear nothing but cases involving the media. The essence of such an invention is that it would not require a personal fortune to pursue a complaint and get it resolved. The billion-dollar media conglomerates easily can afford long-term litigation in the current system, but average folks cannot.

Media court could quickly determine if a story is defamatory: If not, case dismissed. If so, injunction and damages. The appellate process should be quick and streamlined as well. It would be a huge benefit to the country to have a place *everyone* can go to have cases decided quickly, efficiently, fairly and relatively inexpensively—where no billionaires are required to help anyone to level the playing field.

13

MELANIA VERSUS THE MAIL

"Fake news is the cancer of our time."
—Dr. Patrick Soon-Shiong, owner of the *Los Angeles Times*

I n late 2016, I had not yet represented anyone named Trump, and the presidential election between Donald Trump and Hillary Clinton was less than three months away. Trump and Clinton were dominating all news stories and headlines at the time. I was visiting with my father when my phone chimed, alerting me to a new voicemail. We'd won the Gawker case earlier that year, and my phone was ringing more often, particularly from people who wanted to take on the media. I read the voicemail transcription that auto-generates the message in text format (usually with lots of typos) and I told my father, "It says it's a call from Melania Trump." "Listen to the message!" he said. "It's probably someone just playing a joke," I told him. "I'll listen to it later." But he insisted that I listen to it right then, so I did, and it was her. I could tell. He wanted me to call her back right then, but I told him that I'd do it when I got back home. It was a weekend.

When I called, Mrs. Trump explained that the *Daily Mail* had written a horrible and completely false story about her. She asked if I would sue them immediately for $150 million. After reading the article, I told her yes, I would, and then got to work.

The U.K.-based *Daily Mail* newspaper, and its worldwide digital publication, Mail Online, had published a story with the headline: "Racy Photos and Troubling Questions About His Wife's Past That Could Derail Trump." The story claimed that the professional modeling agency where Mrs. Trump had worked in the 1990s had also been a high-end escort service, and that she had engaged in that profession, as well as modeling.

It's customary to send a letter demanding that the publication retract and apologize. I did, and the company refused. Next, we prepared a complaint to file in court.

* * *

IN THE PROCESS of reviewing numerous other articles reporting on the same subject, I came across a Maryland blogger who repeated the same allegations as the *Daily Mail*, and then added several more false allegations, including claims that Mrs. Trump had suffered a "nervous breakdown" over the *Daily Mail* supposedly "outing" her. She was equally appalled by the blogger, and so we sued him too.

We filed one suit against both defendants in state court in Rockville, Maryland. Mrs. Trump turned out to be the ideal client. She was determined to move the case forward, fully committed, available whenever I needed her, would get me information quickly whenever I asked, was aggressive but not too aggressive, and overall was a thoughtful, calm, strategic and pleasant person. And the bills were paid on time. I could not have asked for a better mix of great qualities in a client; she literally set the bar for all others.

At one point, Mrs. Trump wanted to know what she could do to help with the case. I told her that we had a routine scheduling conference coming up, and clients *never* attend these procedural conferences, but are allowed to if they want. I expected her response to be, "Thank you, but I won't be able to." Instead, she asked me for the date and location. I told her, she glanced at her calendar and said, "I'll be there."

* * *

WHEN THE SCHEDULING conference was a week or two away, Mrs. Trump was the "first lady-elect," her official title during the transition. The Secret Service had to do multiple run-throughs on how they would get her into the courthouse, protect her while there, and get her safely out and back home. The courthouse already had lots of security, including metal detectors when you enter, and uniformed officers all around. We had to notify the courthouse that she would be coming, for security purposes, and the judge was alerted, but I didn't tell opposing counsel because I wanted to surprise them in the courtroom.

Before the court appearance, Mrs. Trump wanted me to meet her in the lobby of Trump Tower in New York and fly with her. I was happy to oblige. The original plan was to fly from New York to Washington, D.C., very early the morning of the court appearance, but fog was forecast the day before, so the plans changed. We would fly from New York to D.C. the night before, stay overnight at the Trump International Hotel in D.C., and then drive to the courthouse the next morning. I was fine with that too.

I'd never driven in a motorcade before, yet in a 24-hour period I was in four of them. I went to the lobby of Trump Tower on Fifth Avenue in NYC, walked through a metal detector, Secret Service dogs sniffed my luggage—the whole thing. Then Mrs. Trump and I, and a friend of hers, Stephanie Winston Wolkoff, who in 2020 wrote an unfortunate book about the first lady, drove to LaGuardia Airport with flashing lights and police cars in front and back. Traffic of course was jam-packed in Manhattan, but somehow cars found a way to scooch over just enough so we could slowly get through. We then took a Trump jet to Washington, and another motorcade to the hotel. Trump International Hotel in D.C. is a spectacular place. It previously was a huge turn-of-the-century U.S. Post Office (known for the past several decades in D.C. as the "Old Post Office") on Pennsylvania Avenue, five blocks from the White House. The lobby is huge, with a ceiling over 50 feet high, and the rooms are beautiful—like how I imagine guest bedrooms in the White House look, but I've never been in one.

My room at the hotel was adjacent to the first lady-elect's room, which was a bit surreal. Secret Service officers stood guard outside. We were e-mailing each other about the next day's court appearance, while she was just on the other side of the wall. In the morning, we were whisked away in a motorcade, during rush hour, from downtown D.C. to Rockville, Maryland. We parked in the garage where the judges park, took their elevators, used their private hallways, and arrived in a small, very cold room outside of the courtroom a full 45 minutes before the conference was scheduled to begin. It was expert planning by the Secret Service.

Opposing counsel did not let on that they were surprised—who knows what they were thinking when they saw the next first lady standing beside me, extending her hand to shake theirs. Their clients were not present—not even the blogger who lived just down the road.

The hearing was about 25 minutes long. We discussed a trial date and various pre-trial dates and deadlines, standard stuff at the beginning of a new case. The only thing Mrs. Trump said during the hearing was, "Thank you, your honor," when the judge ended the conference. And that was that.

Secret Service had us out of the building in less than five minutes. Something that I've learned from Gavin DeBecker & Associates, the company that handles the private security of Jeff Bezos, Bill Gates, Oprah Winfrey and many others: The exit is the most important part of security because while the celebrity is in a building, word travels fast. Anyone who might want to try something knows where she is. So in less than five minutes we went from courtroom to SUV— driving with police escorts and lights flashing—to the D.C. airport. My opposing counsel wanted to ask me a question in the courtroom, but when I saw my client and Secret Service leaving, I told him, "Call me," and quickly exited with my group. If I was a minute behind, I'd lose my ride back.

I knew that the *Daily Mail* was going to file a motion to dismiss the company out of Maryland, because they were based in New York, as was Mrs. Trump. We had good arguments for keeping the case in Maryland: Not only was the blogger based in Maryland (a separate defendant), but the *Daily Mail* reaches Maryland readers and places Maryland advertisements onto its website for those residents to see. But a month later, the judge dismissed the *Daily Mail* in favor of a New York forum, and we immediately re-filed the case in New York within days of the dismissal. The case against the Maryland blogger remained in Maryland.

* * *

THE CASE PROCEEDED to two mediations. By that point, Mrs. Trump was the first lady, and appeared in person at each one. The mediations were held at Trump Tower in New York, at the offices that had previously been occupied by the Trump for President campaign, but the campaign was over and the floor was abandoned. An executive from the *Daily Mail* traveled from London to appear at both mediations. The Maryland blogger appeared at the first mediation and agreed to a settlement: payment of a *substantial* amount of money, the specific amount of which is confidential, plus a full-throated public retraction and apology.

At the second mediation, we settled with the *Daily Mail*: payment to Mrs. Trump of $2.925 million plus an extensive retraction and apology in the newspaper in England, and on the home page of the worldwide Mail Online website, where it stayed within the top six stories for 24 hours. It was titled "Melania Trump—An Apology," featured a large photo of the first lady that she supplied herself, and read, in part: "We accept that these allegations about Mrs. Trump are not true and we retract and withdraw them. We apologize to Mrs. Trump for any distress that our publication caused her." The *Daily Mail*'s lawyers in London also read the apology in open court, where it was extensively reported on throughout the world.

Both the first lady and the new president were very pleased with the result, and told me so.

Melania Trump - An Apology

By DAILY MAIL and MAILONLINE
PUBLISHED: 05:52 EDT, 12 April 2017 | UPDATED: 05:52 EDT, 12 April 2017

The Mail Online website and the Daily Mail newspaper published an article on 20th August 2016 about Melania Trump which questioned the nature of her work as a professional model, and republished allegations that she provided services beyond simply modelling. The article included statements that Mrs. Trump denied the allegations and Paulo Zampolli, who ran the modelling agency, also denied the allegations, and the article also stated that there was no evidence to support the allegations. The article also claimed that Mr and Mrs Trump may have met three years before they actually met, and "staged" their actual meeting as a "ruse."

We accept that these allegations about Mrs Trump are not true and we retract and withdraw them. We apologise to Mrs Trump for any distress that our publication caused her. To settle Mrs Trump's two lawsuits against us, we have agreed to pay her damages and costs.

Melania Trump

The *Daily Mail* states publicly that it is the most read English-language publication in the world. Even so, many of its stories read like tabloid journalism. It was personally satisfying to me to have taught the *Daily Mail* a very expensive and very public lesson. I can only imagine that its reporting on people, including major celebrities, became more responsible after that settlement. I also was told by multiple top media lawyers in London that ours was by far the largest settlement that the *Daily Mail* had ever paid to a defamation plaintiff in its 121-year history.

Mission accomplished.

14

LESSONS FROM A SUPERMARKET PARKING LOT

My first job was during the summer of 1985. I was 15. I worked at Ralphs supermarket at Ventura and White Oak boulevards in Encino, California—about a mile from my house at the time. My duties were bagging groceries, helping people to their cars with their bags (and refusing all tips—company policy), putting back items that people would leave in the wrong place around the store (we called them "go backs"), cleaning the extremely gross check stands, and for one hour a day: cart duty—gathering and returning shopping carts from the parking lot.

I was the youngest employee in the store. Their normal policy was to hire 16 and up, but they hired me at 15. The store was in the San Fernando Valley, and it was easily hotter than 115 degrees every afternoon during the summer, which was when I worked. So guess who was given daily 2 p.m. shopping cart duty? We had to wear black pants, a white button-down shirt, a bow tie, and an apron. Cart duty was basically pushing shopping carts for one hour in the parking lot —a really hot place built on a blacktop which absorbed and radiated the direct sunshine. I think the person at 1 p.m. didn't collect any carts, because carts were everywhere by the time of my 2 p.m. shift. I remember toward the end of one of my cart duty shifts being covered in sweat from head to toe, and feeling woozy from the heat. I looked across the street to the bank, which had a digital screen that toggled between the time and the temperature. It read 118°. Mind you, that's the temperature in the shade; I was in the direct sun, on a blacktop surface, pushing 10 shopping carts at a time for an hour. I felt like I was melting.

I will never forget that moment of looking at that sign, and the feeling of being a walking inferno covered in both wet and sticky dried sweat, and craving water, juice, Gatorade, soda, a juicy peach, a piece of watermelon, *anything wet* that I could put in my mouth because I was so thirsty and dehydrated. This was my first real job. It was my introduction to the working world. To labor. And somehow ... I loved it.

I didn't love the job. Or the heat. Or the monotony of putting items into grocery bags or pushing shopping carts in the afternoon heat. I loved the fact that I was earning money: a whopping $4.25 per hour, and time and a half over 40 hours per week. On the Fourth of July, I made double pay, and worked an extra-long shift. I also appreciated the learning experience about the "real world." I was 15 and felt like an adult—working eight hours a day, answering to a boss, collecting a paycheck. It taught me the value of hard work: the value of that work to the customers, to my employer and to me. It taught me about being responsible, being relied upon, being part of a team, getting a job done so that important things could happen: People were able to get their food, and go home and prepare it and eat. That's important. The supermarket was able to function because of us, the workers; without us, it couldn't. It made money, it paid us, we made money. It was a whole economic ecosystem, and also *literally* an ecosystem for the shoppers who were buying their dinner for that night. The job taught me to follow orders, which I did *to a T*, and to be courteous to customers even when they were not very courteous back, which I also was very good at.

Shopping carts in the actual parking lot where I used to collect them at age 15.

The next year, when I was 16, I started the summer working at Universal Studios. On Day 1, I spent the first six hours of an eighthour shift working at a Mexican food stand, serving up burritos, nachos and drinks. There were about six people behind the counter, in a small space, bumping into each other constantly. It was open-air, with no AC, in the San Fernando Valley, in the summer, and it was hot as heck. Not quite as bad as the blacktop parking lot of Ralphs market the summer earlier, because at least there was a cover over us at Universal, but not far off. Just like at Ralphs, I had to wear a uniform at Universal that did not seem to take the heat into consideration. So everyone behind the counter was hot, packed into a small space, and colliding. Not exactly fun. Because I was not yet 18, one of the first things they told me was: Don't pour beer, you're too young. The second thing they told me was: Pour beer! The customers were ordering it, and we had limited people to serve them. One of the two things I learned in that job was how to gently pour beer into a tilted glass to avoid a glass full of foam.

Our customers had just spent half the day walking the studios in extreme heat with their children, who seemed to be driving them crazy. The patrons were hot, tired, thirsty, hungry and seemingly miserable, and they made their misery known to us food service workers. The register also did not tell you the change—we had to calculate it in our heads. I was good at math, but only 16, plus hot and distracted; every so often I was off by a few cents—sometimes in their favor, sometimes not. The customers sure were checking my math: "You shorted me 12 cents!" was an occasional complaint. Between the grouchy park guests, the cramped space, and the heat (and sweat), I just didn't want to be there.

When my six seemingly endless hours at the burrito stand were done, I was told to report to a different concession area for the last two hours of my shift, to learn the drill there. I didn't. I went to the personnel office instead, and said in a really nice way, "This is not the job for me." I still remember the supervisor, who I thought was going to be mad at me, but instead was super nice, ask if I wanted to work in the parking lot or somewhere else. I just said "no thank you" and left. I'd had enough. The union dues took my entire paycheck for my six-hour shift, so my labor that day went uncompensated. And just like that, I was looking for my next job.

The second thing I learned in that job was: If you're not working the right job, quit right then. Don't stick it out. Life's too short.

* * *

WITHIN A WEEK OR TWO, I was doing something that paid much better, was far more enjoyable, and also was much more meaningful: Greenpeace. They had a team "canvassing" neighborhoods, meaning that around 6 in the evening, we went door-to-door with a clipboard and materials, telling people about what Greenpeace was doing for the world and asking for donations. Most people politely said "no thank you," but enough said "yes" to make it worthwhile. Canvassers earned a small base salary plus a small commission on donations. People who were good at it did quite well. I was OK. I still made more than if I'd worked 40-hour weeks at Universal Studios. Plus, I only had to canvass about two and a half hours per day, walking around beautiful L.A. neighborhoods on warm (but not hot) summer evenings, telling people what great things Greenpeace was doing—

and it was true, they were. I was really nice about it, not pushy, and most of the residents were nice to me back, even if they didn't give. But that was fine because I viewed my job as giving *them* an opportunity to make a contribution to a great cause, not me trying to persuade them to do something they didn't really want to do. That lack of pressure made it much more pleasurable for me, and also for them, and if I made less or more money because of it, it was all good. At least I wasn't serving up burritos at a hot, crowded stand to unhappy theme park customers.

Though we canvassed solo, we all had dinner together as a group. That was a lot of fun. There were about 10 of us—the group was smart and lively, and everyone shared a love for the environment. It also was a very diverse group in terms of both age and race: The group was from all walks of life. My summer with Greenpeace was a great lesson in how to communicate one-on-one with someone, raise money for an important cause and do something good for the world. We were saving the whales and baby fur seals and opposing unsafe disposal of nuclear waste. What could be a better job at age 16?

* * *

RIGHT AFTER THAT SUMMER, I was applying to college. My career goal at the time—and since the eighth grade—was to become a zoo veterinarian. Not just any zoo veterinarian: I wanted to be the head veterinarian at the San Diego Zoo, and help care for tigers, giraffes, polar bears, elephants, and other majestic creatures. I loved animals of all types, especially the exotic ones, and enjoyed my biology and physiology classes in high school. But after I applied to college, in the second half of my senior year, my interests started to change quite a bit: away from science, and toward the social sciences. In 12th grade, my classes included physiology (human biology), but also government, speech, "Current American Problems" (CAP), advanced writing, film, and classical music. CAP was about problems in the U.S. and the world, but most of our time was spent reading two books and talking about them in class, in the context of American society: *1984* by George Orwell and *Cat's Cradle* by Kurt Vonnegut. Those books looked at society's future through a dark, dystopian lens—and they still resonate today.

Speech class that year was unforgettable. Our teacher, Mr. Halloran, was an energetic, positive, young, tall fellow with a beard, who really cared about everyone and their learning. We followed the rules of Toastmasters: Every time somebody said "uh," "like," "ya know," or other types of filler words or sounds, somebody would click a clicker to remind them (and us) that they were saying it. By the time we finished the class, *nobody* used words like that in their speech—we were cured! For the first time, it seemed, we miraculously were aware of the words we were saying *before* they came out of our mouths. It was amazing. (I wish my own children were offered a class like that today, because—being Californians—every fifth word they say is "like.")

Mr. Halloran also had each student submit a different index card *every day* with a quotation on it. He said it could be a quotation of any type: from an author, philosopher, world leader, or even a rock singer, a movie star, a friend, a teacher. He would read several of them every morning to start the class—all of the good ones, most of the passable ones, but not many of the garbage ones, except for laughs. Some students would put lame things on cards, quoting their friends saying nonsense. I took the assignment seriously and would think every day about what to quote. I found myself paying very close attention to all of the words around me: from teachers, parents, friends, everything I would read, everyone on TV, songs on the radio—I spent nearly the entire school year always in search of my next daily quote. That was the whole point of the project: to get us listening to speech and recognizing what is meaningful to us—and why. Class time was a mix of lectures, daily student presentations, and larger class projects. I remember going downtown to interview an LAPD sergeant for a video project on gun violence (yes, this was 1987, not modern day).

* * *

THE SUMMER between high school and college, I had a very enriching work experience. I'd applied to the Student Conservation Association to provide volunteer labor in a U.S. National Park. Only about 20 percent of applications were accepted due to the limited spots and high number of applicants. I made it in and was assigned to Rocky Mountain National Park in northern Colorado.

In summer 1987, just a few weeks after my high school graduation, volunteering on a trial maintenance program in Rocky Mountain National Park, Colorado.

For four weeks, my group of 12 high school students and two adult supervisors lived in tents in the breathtaking park, with soaring mountains, forest and alpine tundra. The first three weeks, we spent eight hours per day, six days a week, doing intense physical labor: digging ditches and installing logs and rocks into the trails, to help prevent the trails from eroding in heavy rains. It was literally back-breaking work—I was sore all day, every day, and for weeks even after I returned home. The fourth week was our reward: a group hike for the whole week throughout the 415-square-mile park. The entire program was one of the most unforgettable and rewarding experiences of my life.

The latter half of that same summer, in 1987, included my first trip to Europe. I went with my grandmother, mother, brother, his girlfriend (now wife), and my friend Ken. We started in London for a few days, then Ken and I ventured by ourselves by train to Belgium, Luxembourg, Switzerland, and Nice, France. Then we regrouped with everyone in Paris for a few days. I still had a week left on my Eurail pass and, with my mom's permission, I went solo for a week, at age 17. I wanted to see where Mozart and Beethoven had spent their lives—I was a superfan, and still am today. So I went to Salzburg, Austria, the beautiful town of Mozart's birth and early years, and then to Vienna, where they both lived most of their careers. In addition to visiting Mozart's birthplace and various museums, I also attended inexpensive classical music concerts (playing their music) that are popular in those cities in the summer. When I returned home, I had only a few days to unpack and then pack again for my biggest adventure yet: college.

15

JULIA CHILD'S KITCHEN

"Learn from your mistakes, be fearless,
and above all have fun." —Julia Child

I n the 1960s and early '70s, countless home chefs watched Julia
Child whip up meals on her wildly popular PBS show, *The*
French Chef. They included my mother, who would jot down
notes as fast as she could on a spiralbound pad in front of the TV, and
then cook Julia's dish the next day. So of course my brother and I—
both under 12 years old—had a great time poking fun at Julia,
imitating her distinctive voice and pretending to set fire to the kitchen
during a TV cooking demonstration. And we had full bellies the next
night, eating the dinner our mother had cooked from Julia's televised
cooking lesson.

It was therefore very exciting for me (as well as for my mom)
when I had the honor of representing the Julia Child Foundation—
the legacy that she created while still alive and the successor to her
name and image rights, as well as book royalties—in multiple
lawsuits regarding the commercial misappropriation of her name
and image. The most interesting of those cases involved Julia's oven.

My former partner Jeffrey Abrams was doing work for the Julia

Child Foundation in 2012 when they discovered a huge infringement by Thermador. On the homepage of the company's website, and in various other marketing materials, was a gigantic, black-and-white photo of Child in her kitchen. A company blog described Child as "one of Thermador's original brand champions."

The problem was that, throughout her entire life, Julia Child never, ever, *ever* endorsed any products or brands. Unlike today's celebrity chefs, who make money endorsing everything from frying pans to beer and heartburn medication, Child was adamant about selling *nothing* beyond her impressive 18 cookbooks. She considered herself a cooking teacher (not a chef) on a *public* broadcasting station, which did not run commercials. She earned her credibility the old-fashioned way, and she refused to compromise it so that someone else could make a buck.

* * *

WHEN SHE WAS ALIVE, and a company would use her name or image, Child's very kind and dapper attorney in Boston (I had lunch with him a few years before he passed away—a charming fellow, with a Brooks Brothers suit and classy bow tie) would send out a nice letter explaining the situation and requesting the immediate removal of the image. Sometimes Child would even handwrite a note herself, very politely informing the company of her policy to never allow her name or image to be used to market a product, and requesting they remove it.

Thermador's usage was a massive violation. Child had passed away eight years earlier, but the Julia Child Foundation carries on her mission and protects her name and image whenever necessary. They gave us the green light to demand that Thermador remove its many uses of her name and image immediately, and make a payment to the Foundation to compensate for it. To show the company we were very serious, we drafted a complaint for a potential federal lawsuit in Los Angeles, and sent the *draft* to Thermador, along with a cover letter which said that if they didn't immediately cease and desist, and pay damages, we'd file the complaint in court. Their response: They did not cease, nor desist, nor agree to a payment. Instead, Thermador sued the Julia Child Foundation first—in federal court in Boston.

Thermador asked the court to rule that it could continue to use Julia Child's name and image on its website and all other marketing and advertising materials—forever—without paying *any* compensation to the Foundation. The lawyers for Thermador claimed that Child's name and image rights did not transfer to the Foundation, but rather expired when she died, because (they claimed) she had been a Massachusetts resident for most of her career and the laws of the Commonwealth of Massachusetts did not recognize postmortem publicity rights (name and image).

But Thermador had its facts wrong, and presumably did so intentionally. While Child did live in Cambridge, Massachusetts, for many, many years, she donated her house in 2001 and moved permanently to Santa Barbara, California, where she had a second home for many years which then became her primary (and only) residence as of 2001. Child lived there for three years, paying California state taxes, until her death in 2004 at the age of 91. Under the law, she was a California resident and as such received the benefits of California's postmortem name and image rights—among the strongest in the United States.

On behalf of the Foundation, we filed suit in California seeking an injunction to prevent Thermador from mentioning Child in any of its marketing or advertising, including online and print, and asking for compensation "commensurate with the market value of such uses," which our expert calculated in the millions of dollars.

We also filed a motion to the federal court in Boston to move the case to California. It should not have been too much trouble, but our federal judge in Massachusetts had a reputation of loving high-profile cases. Perhaps he also even loved Julia Child, who lived in nearby Cambridge for decades. The judge denied our motion to transfer. We were surprised and confused. We had done the research and this was a clear case of "preemptive litigation" by Thermador—a move highly criticized by federal judges. In fact, our federal judge in Boston, who denied our motion to transfer, had written the single strongest opinion in U.S. history criticizing preemptive litigation. So we filed a new motion, and in it, we included an entire page, single-spaced quotation of our judge, from a different case, criticizing preemptive litigation, just like the move Thermador pulled on the Foundation by filing first after it had received a demand with a threat of litigation in Los Angeles. I flew out to Boston for the hearing.

The judge was nice, and probably realized that his prior ruling denying our first motion should have been granted based on his own very strong distaste for Thermador's tactics. Fortunately, he started the hearing by stating that the case needed to move to California. But it seemed like he didn't want to let go of it. In an unusual move, he offered to work up the case himself in Boston, and then transfer the case to the judge in Los Angeles shortly before the trial. I thanked the judge for his offer and suggested he call the judge in L.A. first. Having clerked for a federal judge in L.A., I knew that judges don't want other judges, particularly in another state, to make a series of rulings in the case that could decide important aspects of the case before it ever gets transferred. Inevitably, the new judge is going to disagree with some or all of those rulings and need to find a way to undo them. In other words: It would be a big mess. I doubt the Boston judge ever called the L.A. judge, and instead simply transferred the case to the federal court in L.A. During a mediation shortly after the transfer order, the parties settled the case for confidential terms.

* * *

IN A WILD FOOTNOTE, I learned a fascinating story about Julia Child from one of the Foundation's trustees, who was one of the cook's closest personal friends in Santa Barbara during her final years.

In 2001, Child was preparing for her new life in California and getting ready to donate her house in Cambridge to Smith College, her alma mater. In the process, she realized that perhaps the Smithsonian would like to have some of her cookware or other items. Two representatives from the Smithsonian flew up from Washington, D.C., to take a look at what she had. Child took them into the kitchen and said, "Anything you want is yours." They conferred for a moment and then asked her, "Can we have the entire kitchen?" She was floored by the request and responded: Yes, you may. Today, you can go to the National Museum of American History in the nation's capital and see her entire home kitchen: the walls, the appliances, the peg board with pots and pans, all of the cookware, and even her Thermador oven.

Child had a one-way plane ticket from Boston to Los Angeles to permanently relocate to California, but the flight happened to be on the same morning the Smithsonian was coming to physically remove her entire kitchen from the house (before the rest of the house would go to her college). Her initial plan was to leave Massachusetts forever that morning. But Child was concerned the Smithsonian might need her for something the day of the kitchen removal, so she changed her ticket and pushed her flight to California by a week.

Thank goodness she did. Julia Child's original seat was on a 7:59 a.m. American Airlines flight from Boston's Logan Airport to LAX. The date? Sept. 11, 2001. The plane that Julia Child was originally booked on flew into the World Trade Center. Had she not changed her flight to supervise the removal of her kitchen, Julia Child would have been a casualty in the worst terrorist attack in U.S. history.

KATHRINE MCKEE, BILL COSBY AND ACTUAL MALICE

I n 2018, I was honored to be asked by the Time's Up Foundation to take a case to the U.S. Supreme Court on behalf of one of Bill Cosby's accusers. The man known as "America's Dad" became a convicted felon in 2018 when a jury found him guilty of drugging and sexually assaulting a Temple University employee 14 years earlier. Cosby has maintained his innocence from state prison in Pennsylvania, where he is serving a three- to 10-year sentence at the time of this writing. But 59 other women have come forward and shared horrifying detailed accusations about their encounters with Cosby. Kathrine Mae McKee is one of them.

According to her lawsuit, McKee was victimized by Cosby twice: first, when he raped her in 1974, and second, four decades later, when he smeared her reputation and called her a liar after she went public with her claims. She sued him for defamation. Before my firm became involved, she had lost her case and the appeal that followed. But at the Time's Up Foundation's request, I agreed to prepare, on a *pro bono* basis, the petition for a *writ of certiorari*—Latin terms meaning that, free of charge, my firm would prepare and file a lengthy brief explaining to the U.S. Supreme Court why it should take on her case. Ninety-nine percent of these *cert* petitions are denied; only 1 percent are granted. It was a long shot. But I said yes because McKee's case was very important.

It all started, according to her lawsuit, when McKee went to a Detroit hotel room to pick up the comedian, whom she'd known for eight years, to take him to a yacht party. McKee, a former casting director and actress, was on tour at the time with her boyfriend, Sammy Davis Jr. She had picked up ribs from a local restaurant, as Cosby had requested. When she arrived, Cosby, dressed in a bathrobe and knit wool cap, grabbed the ribs, tossed them aside, and "immediately set upon and physically attacked her," McKee said in her lawsuit. "[He was] wild and aggressive, and was acting nothing like the man Ms. McKee had known professionally." Cosby "proceeded to forcibly rape Ms. McKee," her suit said, in an attack that was "shocking, scary and horrible."

Like many of the women who eventually would share similar stories, McKee did not report it to police at the time. "Imagine a girl in the early 1970s trying to make it in Hollywood and have a career," she once explained. "He was in his heyday when it happened. My common sense told me nobody would believe me."

In December 2014, comedian Hannibal Buress made what's been called "the joke heard around the world." Performing in Cosby's hometown of Philadelphia, Buress referenced the rape rumors, which were an open secret in Hollywood. This unleashed a torrent of accusations as woman after woman came forward claiming Cosby had assaulted them over many decades. It was the earliest rumblings of the #MeToo and #TimesUp movements, which would transform the nation—and the entertainment industry—three years later. But that month at the end of 2014, after Buress set the wheels in motion and more than 20 women had publicly accused Cosby of sexual assault, McKee shared her allegations of the rape during an interview with a reporter for the *New York Daily News*.

* * *

COSBY'S ATTORNEY Marty Singer (full disclosure: my former boss, though I never worked on any matters for Cosby) sent a response to the newspaper. In the Dec. 22, 2014, letter from Singer, Cosby denied that he raped McKee, and called her a liar. Two days later, the *Daily News* published an article with Cosby's denial of the rape allegation and also his assertion that McKee "had [done] a lot of lying." He said she "defied credibility." Those quotes were picked up by other news organizations.

McKee sued Cosby for defamation. In the December 2015 suit, filed in federal court in Massachusetts, she claimed that Cosby's intention was to defame her to the *Daily News* and the world at large, and that he used false information to discredit and "damage her reputation for truthfulness and honesty, and further to embarrass, harass, humiliate, intimidate, and shame" her.

The U.S. District Court rejected McKee's claim. The First Circuit U.S. Court of Appeals did the same, concluding that Cosby's words didn't defame McKee because she was a limited-purpose public figure: "By purposefully disclosing to the public her own rape accusation against Cosby via an interview with a reporter, McKee 'thrust' herself to the 'forefront' of this controversy, seeking to 'influence its outcome,'" the court of appeals ruled.

Let's take a short detour and review the basics of defamation law. A valid defamation claim requires the communication be a false statement of fact (you can't defame someone with true statements or opinions), and the burden of proof for the plaintiff varies wildly depending on what *type of person* has been defamed: a private figure or a public figure.

A *private* figure is one who has not sought out the spotlight. The burden of proof is *negligence*: The publisher didn't do his or her homework, that is, did not act with a "reasonable level of care." However, a defamation case is very different for a *public* figure: someone with significant influence or of great concern to the public. They must prove that the person who made the false statement acted with *actual malice*. This means the speaker either knew that the statement was false, or acted with reckless disregard for whether it was true or false. Actual malice must be proven by "clear and convincing evidence," rather than the much lower standard of "preponderance of the evidence" for negligence that is required for a private figure. The burden for a public figure is massively greater than the burden for a private figure.

There's a little more to it: The "public figure" category is broken into two types: an "all-purpose" public figure (think of a famous actor, professional athlete, or elected official) and a "limited-purpose public figure." The latter are individuals who are not famous but "have thrust themselves to the forefront of particular controversies in order to influence the resolution of the issues involved," the U.S. Supreme Court held in 1974 in the case *Gertz v. Robert Welch Inc.* Both types of public figures have the same very high burden of proving actual malice.

Cosby's lawyers argued that although McKee had been out of the limelight for decades, she was still a former actress whose status gave her access to national media outlets to publicly accuse Cosby of misconduct. But I, along with the Time's Up Foundation, saw it very differently: The court of appeals was penalizing McKee for saying "me too." Bravely coming forward and saying that you were the victim of a crime should not be considered "thrusting" yourself into a controversy.

The First Circuit U.S. Court of Appeals did a disservice to survivors like Kathrine McKee. If someone says "me too," and then suddenly goes from a private figure to limited-purpose public figure in the eyes of the law, the survivor has a far higher burden to shoulder as the plaintiff in a defamation lawsuit than if she had just remained silent.

No one should be penalized for publicly stating that they were the victim of a crime. The First Circuit did just that when it turned McKee from a private figure to a public figure, simply for speaking her truth.

* * *

In April 2018, we filed our petition to the highest court in the land. After 10 months of consideration by the U.S. Supreme Court, we unfortunately were part of the 99 percent, and not the 1 percent: We did not succeed. Of the 7,000 to 8,000 cert petitions filed each term, the court grants certiorari and hears oral arguments in only 80 or so.

Despite our inability to get McKee's case before the Supremes, something remarkable happened. Justice Clarence Thomas, currently the longest-serving justice on the high court (he started in 1991), filed a 14-page concurring opinion that strongly urged a reexamination of the actual malice standard in defamation cases. "Like many plaintiffs subject to this 'almost impossible' standard, McKee was unable to make that showing," Thomas wrote.

Thomas argued that the landmark 1964 decision that established the actual malice standard for public figures, *New York Times Co. v. Sullivan*, should get a fresh look because there is "little historical evidence" that those rules flow from the "original understanding" of the First or the 14th Amendments. "If the Constitution does not require public figures to satisfy an actual malice standard in state-law defamation suits, then neither should we."

Justice Thomas' opinion echoed Justice Byron White's concurring opinion in the 1985 case of *Dun & Bradstreet v. Greenmoss Builders*, in which Justice White acknowledged the flawed nature of the actual malice standard and said essentially that the Court (including himself) had made a mistake in creating that standard 21 years earlier in *New York Times Co. v. Sullivan*. Justice White urged that a person defamed should, at the very least, be able to prove the truth and falsity of a statement about them—for the purpose of restoring their harmed reputation from a lie—without having to satisfy a nearly impossible standard of reckless disregard for the truth by the speaker, with "clear and convincing" evidence. Damages to a public figure should be a different analysis, which Justice White did not venture to articulate.

* * *

I AGREE WITH BOTH JUSTICES. I certainly do not advocate the rewriting of the First Amendment. As I have said many times, and will continue to repeat: The First Amendment is an essential pillar of our democracy that makes our democracy possible in the first place. Without it, we might not have survived as a nation, nor would we in the future. However, as Justice Thomas pointed out: The actual malice standard is not the First Amendment. It was an experiment by the high court in 1964 which, according to at least two justices since then, is an extremely flawed standard. In my view, the actual malice standard undermines libel and slander laws passed by state legislatures, and makes it extremely difficult for a person to vindicate their reputation from a defamatory article, post or statement. It should be revised.

I agree with Justice White that a person should be allowed to disprove any false statement about them, and thus restore their reputation, based on a simple standard of preponderance of the evidence. With regard to damages, perhaps a public figure should have a higher (though certainly not "nearly insurmountable") burden. I'll leave that revised standard for the high court, if and when they have the foresight to rewrite the standard, so that it has the intended effect of protecting responsible or even marginally negligent journalists, *but also* protects victims of defamation. Because currently, only journalists are being protected, including highly irresponsible ones, at the expense of innocent people's reputations.

With regard to Kathrine McKee, it is horrible that she was penalized by the U.S. court system, simply because she had the courage to speak out about a sexual assault that she alleges was perpetrated by Bill Cosby. Someone who says "me too" (assuming of course she is telling the truth) should never be punished for it. Doing so could not be more wrong.

McKee's case unfortunately did not survive the flawed U.S. court system, but she remains an inspiration: Her courage, along with the other women who told their stories after so many years of silence, put a sexual predator behind bars.

17

MY LIFE AS A SLUG

I attended the University of California, Santa Cruz, famous for its mascot, the Banana Slugs. Funny story about the mascot: The school was founded in the 1960s and did not have any mascot for its first several years. The sports teams needed a mascot name for tournaments so they called themselves the "Banana Slugs," which are bright yellow slugs native to the redwood forest on campus. I saw them every once in a while when I was a student. The mascot name did not exactly stick. The school's top administrators, including the chancellor, did not care for the chosen mascot, and unilaterally determined the official school mascot would be the sea lion. (Sea lions inhabit the Santa Cruz Wharf three miles away, and their barks are heard on campus.) The students didn't like the administration interfering with their choice of mascot, so in 1986, the year before I enrolled, the students held a campus-wide election to decide the issue once and for all: Banana Slugs vs. Sea Lions. The vote was a landslide, and the rest is history.

The other iconic thing about UC Santa Cruz is its campus. It's like a national park—the campus is within a redwood forest, looking down on a great meadow, with a view of the Pacific Ocean. It's one of the most beautiful views anywhere in the world, and it's also beautiful looking up from the bottom of campus: the Great Meadow, the redwood trees, and the blue sky above.

The school's official photographer for its first six years was none other than the iconic nature photographer Ansel Adams[1]. Known for his sweeping black-and-white images of Yosemite and other national parks, Adams remarked, shortly before UC Santa Cruz was built, that the campus would be one of the most beautiful college campuses in all the world. I think his prediction was spot-on.

Ansel Adams' photo of the Great Meadow, UC Santa Cruz, November 1962.

When I applied, I had declared as a biology major: recall from Chapter 14 that my life's ambition from eighth to 11th grades was to be a zoo veterinarian. But once I arrived at college several months later, I changed my major to politics. I took a broad range of classes including sociology, law, mass communications, psychology, environmental science, statistics, Third World studies, American literature, advanced composition, art history (amazing professor: Jasper Rose), theater arts, classical music, and The American Musical taught by the famous '60s political satirist Tom Lehrer. Lehrer was my favorite professor—he was so much fun, witty, brimming with energy, and a walking encyclopedia of American musicals from the 1930s through the 1970s, like *Camelot, The Music Man, The Pajama Game* and *Of Thee I Sing.* He hated *Les Misérables, Phantom of the Opera,* and seemingly most musicals made after 1980—too melodramatic for him. He loved the funny, clever ones with catchy tunes.

I sang tenor in several classical singing groups from my first year through graduation. The first group was the Bach Society, which was part of a class on J.S. Bach; the second group was the UCSC Concert Choir, during my sophomore year, and the third group was the UCSC Chamber Singers, throughout my junior and senior years. Half of the members of Chamber Singers were music majors with a focus on voice. I had to try out for the group and barely made it. They had high standards and moved quickly through the challenging material. We toured Central California with Mozart's *Requiem* mass, and recorded two professional CDs: an opera by Alessandro Stradella and a collection of French songs (chansons) from the Renaissance. Chamber Singers was by *far* my favorite activity in college.

* * *

I ALSO WAS active in student government and eventually became a sort of liaison between the university and the town, where I got to know the mayor, city council members, county supervisors, the assemblyman and state senator. I also did a two-month internship for the assemblyman, and in my senior year got a part-time job with the county supervisor, paying a whopping $24 an hour (while my friends were making only $5 an hour).

I somewhat improbably became managing editor of the *Santa Cruz Independent*, one of three weekly campus newspapers, during my senior year. It was a fun group of people that worked there. The year before I worked on the paper, I often would spend time in the news-room, called the "A-frame": a one-room, wood structure shaped like a large tent. I was friends with some of the editors and the A-frame was in a main thoroughfare on campus, so I'd stop in and hang out on occasion. The staff sometimes referred to me as the "mascot" because I didn't have a role but would come around to socialize, chime in to suggest things, or answer questions when asked. The publisher/edi-tor-in-chief wanted me to have an official role the next year, and offered me managing editor, which I gladly accepted.

It was more fun having a real job on the paper than just social-izing with the staff. I helped manage things, of course, and made a pitch to the vice chancellor for funds, which was granted in full, and got the assemblyman I'd worked for to place an expensive full back-page ad right before his election, which brought in needed revenue for the paper. I also wrote an editorial or two, and a front-page news story on the boring issue of local transportation funding, which was a good experience. I also promoted the paper, including doing a radio interview on the campus station KZSC about some of the big stories at the moment and our goals for the year. But perhaps my biggest contribution was to set up a distribution network in every dorm on campus. The paper's motto was "Makin' friends every Thursday" and I set up dorm reps who would slip the paper under every student door on campus every single Thursday—reaching the 4,500 students living on campus. This distinguished our paper from the other two weeklies, and helped us to compete with them for ads, because only our paper distributed directly to students. The other two weeklies left stacks of papers all around campus, which we did as well. But we reached readers directly, and in a place convenient for them to read the paper: their rooms.

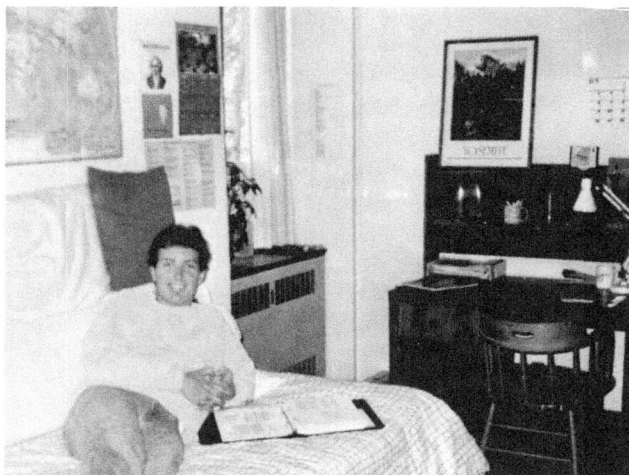

*In my dorm room, first year of college, with Beethoven
and Bach pictures on the wall and a Yosemite poster.
That little plant in the window is now in the ground of
my front yard—15 feet tall.*

Before I went to college, my mother told me several times: College is the most fun you'll ever have. She was right—about my last two years. I loved them. But the first two years were an adjustment for me. My freshman year I spent struggling to understand my professors, what they wanted from me, and to keep up with all of the work. My sophomore year was spent trying to fit in and get comfortable. But junior year is when it clicked. I was in Chamber Singers, having a blast. I was active in student government, and enjoying that. I had a group of friends and was socializing regularly. My required courses (less fun) were out of the way and I was taking classes because I enjoyed them, not because I had to. Life was great those last two years. So much so that my dream is to one day be a professor at UCSC, and even a provost of Merrill College (one of the 12 colleges of the campus, and the one that I belonged to). It's such an ideal place. UCSC's admission brochure in 1986, the year I applied, said on the front cover—accompanied by a huge, gorgeous photo of the campus —**"An ideal becoming real."** Maybe they didn't realize it yet, but the school was already there.

18

THE KISS THAT WASN'T

I t was a disturbing accusation: A worker on Donald Trump's 2016 presidential campaign claimed the candidate had forcibly kissed her in an RV at a Florida campaign stop.

She remained silent about it for three years, and then in early 2019, during the primary race before the 2020 election, out of the blue, the woman sued the president for battery in the U.S. District Court in Tampa, Florida. Her suit laid out, in vivid detail, her claims of "sexually predatory conduct" by the president of the United States. Ultimately I would find and reveal that the accusations were not true. But this case put me right inside the broken machinery of the American media.

Alva Johnson's dramatic tale was set in a recreational vehicle parked at the Tampa fairgrounds in August 2016 and filled with staff, volunteers and other supporters. Trump, who was set to take the stage at a rally, went inside the RV to get out of the rain, which had just started, and his supporters did the same. There were about 12 people in this fairly small space. At first he sat, signed campaign signs and spoke to everyone in the RV as a group. When it was time to head outside and move to the stage, a line formed to speak to the candidate as he was leaving the RV, and Johnson got in the line. When Trump reached Johnson is where her story diverges from the truth and becomes fiction.

Johnson, who is from Alabama, tells Trump she's been on the road and "away from my family for eight months for you." Her lawsuit claimed Trump "grasped her hand and did not let go. He told her he knew she had been on the road for a long time and that she had been doing a great job. He also told Ms. Johnson that he would not forget about her, and that he was going to take care of her." In truth: None of these things happened.

"He moved close enough that she could feel his breath on her skin," the lawsuit continues. "Ms. Johnson suddenly realized that Defendant Trump was trying to kiss her on the mouth, and attempted to avoid this by turning her head to the right. Defendant Trump kissed her anyway, and the kiss landed on the corner of her mouth." In truth: None of these things happened either.

* * *

THE PRESS POUNCED. Two years into the Trump presidency, the mainstream outlets had already dug in their heels and committed to an unspoken agenda of tearing down the president and his supporters, and propping up anyone who attacked him. On cable news, networks also had chosen sides but were more overt about it for the millions who tuned in daily to have their worldview rein-forced—rather than to learn the actual facts and decide for themselves.

The Washington Post broke the story about the lawsuit with details from the filing and an interview with Johnson. She went on MSNBC and did a prime-time interview in which she tearfully told her story again and called the president's mouth "gross and creepy." Johnson had eight lawyers—eight!—and they did a huge media push: a whopping 85 communications with the press and the public, within just 24 hours of filing the suit. There was an op-ed piece on NBC by one of Johnson's lawyers, multiple national interviews, numerous tweets, numerous Facebook posts and website pages. The media went bonkers relaying to readers and viewers all the horrific things the president supposedly had done to Johnson.

Many of the outlets that routinely attack President Trump dished every possible quote from Johnson and her lawyers, and the details of her claims. They gave a perfunctory line or two to the White House's straightforward denial: "This never happened and is directly contradicted by multiple highly credible eyewitness accounts." Some of the outlets (but hardly all) quoted a few of the eyewitnesses, including Florida's then-Attorney General Pam Bondi, who was in the RV at the time and unequivocally denied seeing what Johnson described.

Here's where I enter the picture. After being hired, I reviewed Johnson's lawsuit and the news articles, and made a list of witnesses. I obtained phone numbers of the witnesses and started to call them all: one by one. I identified myself, and they often had to contact someone at the campaign to verify that I was who I said I was. Everyone told me their own version of the same thing: "I was there and never saw anything like what Ms. Johnson describes. No one was upset, everyone was excited and happy." I asked all the witnesses who *else* was in the RV at that time, and I was told about some volunteers who were there and had not been identified by either the news media or the campaign. One of these volunteers had used his cellphone in the RV to record the candidate as he spoke to different people— including Alva Johnson. Meaning: *Their entire encounter was captured on video.*

The video was all of 15 seconds, and captured the entire exchange between the candidate and Johnson. I watched it 20 times in a row, normal speed, slow-mo, frame by frame, to make sure I saw and heard *everything*. If you want to see the video yourself, at both normal speed and slowed down to 25 percent speed, go to www. HarderLLP.com/JohnsonVideo.

Here is what the video depicts:

In an RV crowded with people, Johnson says to the candidate: "I left my family for eight months for you." She and Trump do a quick, innocent "hug"—the kind that candidates do 50 times per day on the campaign trail, as meaningful as a quick handshake or pat on the back. In the process, Johnson kisses Trump's cheek or the air next to his cheek, while he turns his face slightly *away* from her—he does not kiss her at all.

Trump then starts to walk away as she repeats, "Eight months for you." Then she *smiles* and says: "We're going to get you in the White House; I'll see you in February [the month after the inauguration]." There is no talk from Trump about not forgetting Johnson, taking care of her, or any of the other fabrications she included in her lawsuit. He also did not grab her hand and refuse to let go, or any of the other fictitious allegations that Johnson put in her lawsuit. This video fully exonerated the president, and confirmed that Johnson was never forcibly kissed. Her federal lawsuit against the president was based on a lie.

* * *

WE DIDN'T MENTION the video to anyone until her deposition—while she was under oath to tell the truth. We did produce the video with several other videos that Johnson had requested in discovery. None of her eight lawyers reviewed any of those videos before her deposition. Her lead counsel said at the deposition that the DVD drive on his laptop was not working, and he thought the DVD was blank. So at her deposition, Johnson was not prepared by her counsel to answer questions about the video.

I asked Johnson to explain exactly what happened in the RV. She stayed consistent with the words and details in her lawsuit—stating under oath the various things that actually did not happen at all. After a little while, I went back to the subject and showed her the 15-second video. Her lawyer threw a fit, accusing me of withholding the video, and when I told him I had, in fact, produced it in discovery along with several other videos his office had requested, he unilaterally announced a lunch break and left the building with his client, so that they could watch the video together during the break and prepare her to testify about it. This is not allowed in depositions, but I could not physically stop her and her lawyer from marching out the door; I could only state my objection on the record to the court reporter. They came back after an hour, and for more than an hour after their return I asked her questions unrelated to the video, so that perhaps she would forget what her lawyer had trained her to say about it.

Then I asked her about the video. She confirmed that it depicted what occurred in the RV, and that after their quick embrace she had smiled and said she would get him in the White House and see him in February. She admitted that some of the things she described in her complaint were inaccurate: For instance, he did not grab her hand and hold on as she alleged. But she still claimed that he kissed her on the cheek (though the video shows otherwise), and she denied that she gave him a kiss (again, the video suggests otherwise).

We filed a motion with the court to excuse the president from a deposition, and included with the motion the 15-second video (in both regular speed and 25 percent speed). The judge watched and then asked me to provide him with a full copy of Johnson's deposition transcript, which I did. He then ordered a conference call of all counsel in the afternoon.

When all this was happening, I was starting a European vacation with my wife, Kathleen, and two sons. Unfortunate timing for me. My family and I had just flown from Los Angeles to Madrid, and I was jet-lagged. I asked Kathleen to take the boys somewhere while I called into the court conference from my hotel room. The judge very calmly read the riot act to Johnson's lawyers: "Do you really think this video depicts a battery under Florida law?" he said. "Counsel [for Johnson], you are at an inflection point." The judge explained to her lawyers that sometimes a client does not tell the truth to their counsel, and counsel needs to do the right thing or they expose themselves to sanctions by the court. I had just sent Johnson's legal team a letter threatening Rule 11 sanctions against Johnson and all eight of her lawyers if they continued with the case. I sent the judge a copy of that letter, and he was all over the issue.

Johnson's lead lawyer told the judge they needed some time to review everything. The judge replied: Take all the time you need.

I expected the news outlets that had breathlessly covered the lawsuit to give the video the same level of coverage and exonerate the president. They didn't. Johnson's lawyer falsely claimed the video "confirmed" her accusations. I released a statement to reporters that the video exonerated him. Guess whose spin the fake news media followed? You guessed it. Even the so-called "mainstream" press claimed that it was "unclear" from the video whether the encounter was innocent or an attack. But the video could not be clearer—the encounter was mutual, innocent, and as far from an attack as possible. See for yourself (URL provided above) and draw your own conclusion. In addition, Johnson's false accusations, in my view, did a disservice to *real* victims of battery and assault who courageously come forward with their stories.

* * *

CNN, which seems to exist only to attack the president, ran a story with the headline: "Video of Trump kissing a campaign aide leaves both sides claiming vindication." See what they did there? Repeating in the headline that Trump was "kissing a campaign aide" reinforces Johnson's original claims. And then ostensibly giving air time to "both sides" (something CNN is well known for *not* doing) by suggesting the video could be seen as a victory for either side. It's a laughable example of biased journalism.

In that same story, CNN quotes Johnson's lawyers saying that "the video shows exactly what Ms. Johnson alleged happened to her: an unwanted kiss from Defendant Trump." They were so committed to the storyline that Trump had attacked Johnson, they just couldn't let it go.

In my opinion, Johnson and her lawyers were perpetuating a lie. But the news media covered it in a way that made Johnson look like a victim, without doing what the news media are *supposed* to do: fully investigate and accurately report the facts.

Two months after we released the video, Johnson dropped her case. She immediately issued a statement saying she stood by her story but that it was impossible to pursue "justice against a person with unlimited resources." (CNN's headline: "Former Trump campaign staffer drops lawsuit but stands by claims he forcibly kissed her.") Once again, another headline reminding the audience that Johnson supposedly was forcibly kissed.

It doesn't matter if you love or hate Trump, Obama, Bush or Clinton. The lawsuit should not be about politics—it's about what actually happened in that RV in August 2016. The truth won in court. But the news media failed and refused to tell it. It's a classic example of how the media push their political agenda on readers, at the expense of the truth. It should be disappointing to everyone how so many media outlets simply refuse to report the true facts if they are in favor of the president, and never pass up a chance to bury a dagger in his back.

The Johnson case is the shining example. I lived through every second of it. Her fabrications were gobbled up by the press like candy on Halloween. Vindicating the president was my goal, and I succeeded. But the case taught me some unfortunate lessons about the media: that false narratives are given unlimited oxygen by a press driven by profits and partisan motivations, and the truth is ignored if it doesn't fit the media's predetermined political agenda.

19

A BICYCLE RIDE ACROSS AMERICA

W hen I was 19, I rode an 18-speed bicycle across the United States. The year was 1989; it was the summer between my second and third years in college. I went on this adventure with a college friend, Greg. The year before, Greg and I wanted to do a trial run, to see if we liked biking for multiple days straight, sleeping in a tent and sleeping bags that we carried on our bikes, and cooking meals on a camp stove. So we went from Eureka, California, down to San Francisco. It took us six days, and we liked it. We decided to do the full trek the next year. In 1989, at the beginning of the summer, my mother was kind enough to drive me up to the Bay Area, where Greg lived. We grabbed him and his bike, and she then drove us up to Florence, Oregon, to start our trip. Florence is a small town on the Oregon coast, known for its large sand dunes and famous Shakespeare theater company. The whole drive up to Florence, my mom tried to convince us not to do the ride. She didn't stand a chance. Within a day, we had ridden to Eugene, home of the University of Oregon. I got a haircut, because my hair was really long, and I figured I'd just get a cheap cut when we started. It was nice and short, and lasted me the entire 75-day trip—all 4,445 miles of it. (My hair was *very* long by then.)

We followed an established transcontinental bike route created for the 1976 bicentennial of the United States, which went from Florence, Oregon, to Yorktown, Virginia. (The route is posted on Wikipedia under "Bikecentennial.") Greg and I did some training for the trip, but not a lot. UC Santa Cruz is on a hill, with a 1.5-mile bike trail through a giant meadow. So I rode my bike up that hill, then a quick downhill, then back up the hill. It's a beautiful ride, and I would do these ups and downs for about an hour a day, to get my legs conditioned, for about a month before we set out. That hour a day was nothing compared to the eight to 10 hours per day of much steeper uphill climbs, day after day.

The real training for the trip *was* the trip. Each day throughout the first six weeks our legs, backs and butts were sore, achy, stiff—you name it—along with the inevitable blisters, chafes and scrapes. But after about five or six weeks our muscles and skin grew accustomed to the ride, our bodies toughened up, and most of the pain and discomfort had vanished.

We brought sleeping bags, inflatable sleep pads, a camp stove, minimal cooking equipment, a small tarp, a two-person tent, and minimal clothes: I brought three bike shorts, three T-shirts, one pair of pants, one long-sleeved shirt, a waterproof windbreaker, and some socks and underwear. We left space in our packs for food, and had three water bottles mounted on each bike.

At the top of a mountain in Montana.

We slept most nights in designated campgrounds. In Kansas, we stayed mostly in the city parks in the middle of town—they allowed bikers to pitch a tent in the park. At first we cooked a lot of dinners ourselves but came to realize that, at the end of a day of biking eight to 10 hours, we were exhausted, and we were eating enormous quantities because of all the calories we were burning from riding. The process of finding a market, shopping for what we needed, preparing it on a small cookstove flame, with a small pot and pan, without a countertop or proper cooking equipment, cleaning up after, and having no refrigeration to store anything, was more of a hassle than it was worth. Early on, we mailed the stove home and found inexpensive places to eat along the way. Dinners were usually meals like cheeseburgers, fried chicken, spaghetti, all-you-can-eat salad bars, and other options with a high calorie-to-cost ratio.

We ate at least double our normal amount of calories. For breakfast, for example, we *each* would eat two large stacks of pancakes, both with eggs and bacon, lots of water, and maybe a large orange juice. For lunch, I tended to make two peanut butter, strawberry jam and banana sandwiches, and ate both between 1 p.m. and 2:30 p.m., again with lots of water.

We rarely stayed in motels—once every seven to nine days. We didn't have the budget for more. But when we did, it was amazing to sleep in a real bed and take a hot shower.

* * *

AFTER EUGENE, we headed east and north through Oregon. The town of Three Sisters was so picturesque. We entered the Cascade Mountain Range, which gave us our first taste of riding uphill all day long. I'll never forget the narrow roads with very wide logging trucks barreling by us. I thought about how one could easily knock us off the road into a ditch or over a cliff. Fortunately, the truckers were skilled at driving the narrow roads—with bikers on them—and avoided all hazards, including us.

We rolled into Idaho and next came the Rocky Mountain Range. These mountains were much larger and higher, and the air was thinner, than the Cascades. One mountain, called White Bird Hill, was a killer. It felt like we rode all day long, straight up, in our lowest possible "mountain" gear. Each long, steep uphill of an hour or more was matched with a super-quick downhill of about five minutes, followed immediately by another long, steep uphill of an hour or more. Repeat. Repeat. Repeat. It was grueling.

In the Rockies, we crossed the Continental Divide seven times— the line that divides watershed to the West from watershed to the East.

We stayed in the town of Grangeville, Idaho, for a few days because they were having their annual Fourth of July "Frontier Days" Rodeo. Residents came from small towns all around to compete in various events, including bull riding, bronco riding, barrel racing (where horses race around barrels), lassoing and other such events. It was very small-town and so much fun to watch. They also served up basic but very tasty burgers for something like a dollar each, and we were so hungry we ate them like they were potato chips.

We pressed on to Montana and eventually rode to Missoula, the state's second-largest city. One of my friends from the Rocky Mountain trail maintenance program two years earlier, Marianne, lived there at her parents' house. She invited us to stay with her for three days, so we took her up on it. It was great to see her, and a real treat was using her washing machine and dryer to wash everything we had —even my sleeping bag. Her parents were out of town, so we had a fun time seeing the city and hanging out at her house. We did local things like hiking "up to the M"—a huge, white, concrete "M" at the top of the hill overlooking the University of Montana.

* * *

THE NEXT FEW weeks were among the most beautiful. We rode through Yellowstone National Park, which straddles eastern Montana and western Wyoming. It is gorgeous country. Then we rode through Grand Teton National Park. It rivaled Yellowstone in its natural, majestic beauty.

I remember in the Tetons pulling to the side of the road to check my map and drink some water. It was a hot afternoon: mid-to-late July, and I'd been riding half the day. A young family in their minivan was pulled over near me, and I could see the couple had two young girls in the backseat, perhaps in the 3- to 6-year-old range. The young dad looked tired and a bit frustrated. He walked a few steps toward me to get into speaking range, and said three words: "I envy you." I was caught off-guard. I was tired, sweaty, sticky, dirty, hot, exhausted, some 1,500 miles from the start of my journey and nearly 3,000 miles from the finish. "Really?" I asked. "Yes," he said. "Thank you," I responded. And that was it. That was our entire conversation. I'll never forget that moment—it will live with me forever. I often think back to that moment, because he was right. I was in an enviable position: young, strong, free, and seeing the beautiful United States without a worry in the world beyond where to sleep, what to eat, are we on route and on schedule?

We stopped in Jackson, Wyoming, which is gorgeous and a quaint, fun town. I remember cute storefronts and gunfight reenactments in the streets, with authentic old Western clothes and really loud vintage guns.

We rode into Colorado and the ski town of Breckenridge. We stayed at a ski lodge with an all-cedar hot tub room. It was our first (and only) hot tub experience the whole trip. It was amazing. First, our muscles were always aching, so to put them into really hot water was a soothing treat. Second, inhaling the smell of cedar wood was unforgettable. The *entire room* was cedar. That tub soak was one of my favorite parts of the whole trip.

Soon the mountains were behind us for quite a while, and my body shouted: Hooray! We had the flats of eastern Colorado and the Plains of Kansas in front of us.

In Pueblo, Colorado, we stayed at a college dorm, and took a few days off to rest. We walked all around the town. We watched a live play on the campus: a comedy/murder mystery, staged in the round. It was a terrific production, so funny—we laughed our heads off.

* * *

AFTER COLORADO WAS KANSAS. There are five things I will always remember about Kansas: (1) Each town in Kansas has a city park in the middle and they let you pitch a tent and stay the night. So we took full advantage. (2) Kansas is so flat that you see each town 10 miles away, marked by a large grain elevator. We'd ride from one grain elevator town to the next, all day long. (3) We rode fast and were able to clock many miles per day. In the Rockies we were covering 50 to 65 miles per day. In Kansas, we were covering 100 to 120 miles per day. A 100-mile day is known as a "century," and we did a century each day in Kansas. (4) We were told by westbound bikers to visit Dan and Kathy Dirks in Kansas, who let all bikers stay at their property. They had an above-ground pool open to all cross-country bikers, and they cook burgers on the grill outside for everyone. What?! The couple even printed business cards with their name and phone number (the days before email and text), and asked their biker guests to hand them out to *other* bikers heading toward Kansas, so that every biker on the transcontinental route would stop in, stay, swim and eat. Unreal. And Dan and Kathy themselves were unreal—two of the nicest and most generous people that you could ever hope to meet. (5) Dan and Kathy exemplify all of the people we encountered in Kansas. The entire state has about the most friendly and thoughtful people I've ever met in my life. Every person, it seemed. Almost every driver we passed would wave to us as we rode, and we'd wave back. (In no other state did that occur.) At every restaurant, people would strike up a conversation: "Where are you coming from? Where are you heading? How do you like Kansas? Be sure to go to this place or that." They were beyond friendly.

We covered Kansas in about four days of riding. (We did take a day off at the Dirks' house to swim, rest and enjoy their meals hot off the grill.)

After Kansas was southern Missouri and southern Illinois. Missouri had lots of trees, lots of ups and downs in the Ozark Mountains, and it was extremely hot and humid in August. I don't know if it was the heat, or exhaustion, or if I caught a bug, but I got sick. We stayed in a hotel for two or three days while I recovered. I pretty much slept all of those days, and my bike partner, Greg, got very bored. That's all I remember of Missouri, unfortunately.

The highlight of southern Illinois was the Bike Surgeon in the college town of Carbondale. Just like Dan and Kathy in Kansas, the shop handed out business cards to other bikers to pass out to all transcontinental bikers—offering a *free* inspection, *free* labor, and all parts *at cost*. One day before getting to the Bike Surgeon, my chain was slipping in the chainring (the large metal circle with teeth that grips the chain and makes the bike go when you pedal). The shop inspected my bike, replaced the chainring and a few other worn-out parts with very high-quality parts—all at cost and with no labor charge. What would have cost me a *lot*, cost me almost nothing, and they were friendly as could be. That stop allowed me to finish the ride, because my bike would have broken down before the Atlantic Ocean, probably in the middle of nowhere, and I did not carry those spare parts with me: extra brake cables, brake pads, a chainring. The owner also let us sleep in the upstairs office of his business—he was very generous.

* * *

THE FINAL TWO states were Kentucky and Virginia. Kentucky had the Appalachian Mountains. While in Appalachia, in the middle of the day, a completely intoxicated man, skinny as could be and missing teeth, said, "Give me $20." When I shrugged and said "sorry," he tried to tackle me off my bike. Fortunately, I was able to speed away, untouched. I carried a metal hand pump with me with a spiny end that served as a weapon if I needed it, and I also carried a can of mace for dogs, which I used on a couple of dogs that attacked me—it was *very* effective. So if this drunk dude had tackled me, I had those weapons to fight back (plus some taekwondo and judo training from my younger days, along with the fact that the guy was so tanked he could barely walk).

Virginia had several major highlights. First, Damascus, which now has the nickname "Trail Town USA" because seven national trails intersect in that town, including the only place in America where the transcontinental bike route crosses the famous Appalachian Trail (the longest hiking-only footpath in the world, stretching 2,193 miles through 14 states). We stayed at a hostel in town that had both bikers and hikers. Apparently hostels like this dot the Appalachian Trail, and feature bins where hikers discard things they don't want anymore. One hiker we met, with a long beard and wild hair, said that everything he owned he got from those bins. His exact words were: "If I didn't get it for free, bro, I don't got it." He was a hoot —we enjoyed talking to him.

Three more highlights of Virginia were the beautiful, historic college towns that we rode through: Lexington (Washington & Lee University), Williamsburg (William & Mary) and Charlottesville (University of Virginia). We toured the UVA campus, as well as Monticello, the house that President Thomas Jefferson—author of the Declaration of Independence—built on the hill overlooking UVA and greater Charlottesville.

While assembling my two daily PB&J sandwiches one day on the side of a rural residential road at lunch time, a lady from a house just up the knoll by me walked down her lawn and asked me where I was from and where I was going. I talked to her for a while and she asked if I'd ever eaten okra. I said no, and she said, "Well, come on in and I'll make you some." I told her I would be happy to when my biking partner arrived. A few minutes later Greg was there, and the okra was just the start of a meal of Southern specialties she whipped up for us. She had a 17-year-old son, Lucas, and her husband, Larry, was the minister of the town's Baptist church. They were the Bollingers, and their Virginia town was called Rural Retreat. We stayed with them that night and also the next day. We played tackle football with Lucas and his friends—and were very achy the next morning.

The following day was Sunday, and they insisted we attend their church and then ride on the following day. We agreed. The minister had us stand up in church, and explained we were from California and had just ridden our bikes from the coast of Oregon and were only a few days from finishing our ride to the Atlantic. We were celebrities for a day. We attended a church ice cream social that night, and everyone was insisting we try their homemade cakes, cookies and other treats (as well as ice cream), and that we pack all the leftovers with us for our ride the next day. So we did, and ate it all over the next few days. It was a kind and sweet—literally—sendoff.

Finally we reached our final destination on the coast of Virginia: the town of Yorktown, where in October 1781, British General Charles Cornwallis surrendered his army of 8,000 men to General George Washington, effectively ending the American Revolutionary War and allowing the 13 British colonies and nearby territories to remain the United States of America. It was an accomplishment, and a relief, to roll our tires into the water and celebrate the end of a long, arduous and rewarding journey. I've never forgotten the beautiful country I saw that summer, or the genuinely good, friendly and caring people I met on my bicycle ride across America.

20

THE PORN STAR AND HER
CONVICTED FELON LAWYER

Until 2018, Stormy Daniels was known for her "performance" in 150 pornographic films. In February 2018, she made headlines by claiming she had an affair with the president of the United States a decade before he was elected.

Importantly, Daniels had emphatically *denied* at least six different times, in the years 2006, 2008, 2011, 2016 and 2018 (twice that year, in writing), ever having had an affair with Donald Trump. "I am not denying this affair because I was paid 'hush money' as has been reported in overseas-owned tabloids. I am denying this affair because it never happened," Daniels, whose real name is Stephanie Clifford, wrote in a signed statement she released in January 2018. Yet when Daniels saw an opportunity to try to cash in on making the very allegation that she had repeatedly denied, because it was the month before the 2016 presidential election, she went for it. But rather than "speaking her truth" at the time, whatever it was—because it had diametrically changed—she reportedly accepted a payment of $130,000 to keep her allegations to herself.

In my view, Daniels is a porn star looking to cash in wherever and however she can. She spent nearly 20 years making pornographic films. On the cover of her DVDs, she often has bodily fluids dripping from her face. She diametrically changed her story and sought a payment to keep quiet. To me, she had no credibility.

* * *

IN EARLY 2018, reports surfaced that author Michael Wolff was going to make "millions" from attacking the president in his book *Fire and Fury*. Immediately after those reports, Daniels no longer wanted to comply with the "agreement" she had signed—for which she was paid $130,000 to keep her (changed) allegations to herself. Instead, she wanted a book deal and the money that it could bring her. So she hired attorney and eventual convicted felon Michael Avenatti for a mere $100—plus an unspecified percentage of her future book advance—to file a lawsuit to try to get her out of her "agreement." She even said in her lawsuit that she would give back the $130,000, but of course she never did. She kept it *and* she released a book, which hardly anyone bought, probably because she had already released her (changed) allegations on *60 Minutes* some six months before the book's release.

The mainstream press didn't report that Daniels had denied six times, in five different years, her new allegations of an alleged affair. Why? Because they wanted the narrative to be that, according to this porn star, she'd had a one-time affair with the president at a 2006 golf tournament in Lake Tahoe. The media did not want the public to know that she had denied repeatedly that very allegation. Nor did Anderson Cooper, on *60 Minutes*, bother to press her about those many denials from 2006 through 2018. We filed a motion to dismiss Daniels' case. She and Avenatti vigorously opposed, trying to keep her case going. But they lost; the case was dismissed.

* * *

DANIELS AND AVENATTI also filed a second lawsuit against the president, one of the weakest defamation cases I've ever seen. They claimed the president had defamed Daniels in a tweet by calling one of her stories—that she'd been threatened by an alleged menacing stranger in 2011 not to go public with her allegations—a "total con job playing the Fake News media for fools. But they know it!" I won dismissal of that second lawsuit as well, and with it won a $293,000 award of legal fees and sanctions against Daniels and in favor of the president, issued by a federal judge.

On July 31, 2020, the Ninth Circuit U.S. Court of Appeals affirmed the lower court's order and rejected Daniels' appeal by a unanimous 3-0 ruling. The court ruled, fairly simply, that the tweet was not defamatory as a matter of law. The appellate ruling was not political: All three of the justices were appointed by Democratic presidents (two Clinton appointees and one Obama appointee). On Feb. 22, 2021, the U.S. Supreme Court denied cert review of Daniels' case against Trump, effectively ending her legal case and handing us a victory.

In 2019, the year after Daniels' two lawsuits against the president were dismissed over her strenuous objections, Avenatti was arrested for allegedly stealing $300,000 from Daniels. When I read about that one, I told my colleague, "They deserve each other."

In February 2020, Avenatti was convicted by a federal jury in New York of attempted extortion for trying to shake down Nike to pay him as much as $25 million or he would go public with alleged misdeeds in the company's college basketball division. At the time of this writing, Avenatti also was facing two more federal criminal trials in Los Angeles, one for allegedly stealing money from Daniels, and another for allegedly stealing millions of dollars from multiple other former clients. He is facing a total of up to 404 years in prison if convicted on all counts.

* * *

THAT'S NOT EVEN the whole story of Daniels' quest to profit off the president.

The lawyer who represented Daniels in negotiating the 2016 "agreement"—Keith Davidson—is notorious for demanding to celebrities that they pay him money, otherwise embarrassing secrets about them will become public. In 2012, he was arrested by the FBI for allegedly demanding a $1 million payment from Hulk Hogan for the sex tape that eventually brought down Gawker.

Daniels also used her lawsuits against the president to promote her 2018 national strip club tour, which she called "Make America Horny Again"—once again trying to cash in, in the cheapest, tackiest possible way. I suppose it was a step up from "performing" in 150 porno films, but not by a lot.

In person, Avenatti was annoying, conceited and comically over-confident. He was ineffective in court. He did not have a command of the law, could not stick to one subject at a time, and while he was arguing a point to the judge, he would turn 180 degrees to face the audience full of reporters to make a point, and then turn back to the judge to finish his argument. Federal judges hate showboaters like Avenatti, and it was obvious to me the damage he was doing to Daniels' case every time he showed up and opened his mouth. By contrast, we argued our case "by the book." We showed up prepared, answered the judge's questions directly, were respectful to the judge and his staff, and it all had an impact. Avenatti's strategy was to make headlines, and he did. Our strategy was to win the case, and we did.

21

FROM UNEMPLOYED TO MAKING LAWS

After college I applied to law school. My LSAT score was good but not great, and my "grades" from UCSC were terrific but instead of letter grades they were 19 pages of narrative evaluations. I received college honors, but only after I had already applied to law school. I was accepted to Vermont Law School, which had the No. 1 environmental law program in the country. I was rejected from other law schools. I flew out to Vermont, and found the campus very rural and remote: hardly any civilization around—just a few buildings where students lived and schooled, and where professors and administrators had offices. But that was it. That and lots of trees. A student there told me the place was buried in snow for five months out of the year. I'm a SoCal native—the sun is my life. Two months after the snow melted, I'd be off for the summer, only to return two months before snowfall. It was a beautiful place and a well-regarded law school, but being isolated and indoors all the time wasn't for me. I also wasn't feeling a strong draw to environmental law at that particular time, so I decided to pass.

I returned to L.A. with a college diploma and decided to postpone law school and work for a year. It was summer 1991 and the Southern California economy was struggling. There was a nationwide recession, and the region was getting hit extra hard because of cuts to defense contracts, a hiring freeze throughout the entertainment industry, and so on. I spent the summer applying for jobs, doing interviews and getting one rejection after another. Almost everyone said the same thing: "We're looking for someone with experience in this area." But I had just graduated from college with very little real work experience, and not much in the areas that I was applying for.

One of the jobs I had applied for was a part-time position with the local assemblyman. I had interned for an assemblyman during college—finally some relevant work experience! But the position was only 20 hours a week, paying $7 an hour. The decision came down to me and the president of a local homeowners' association. The assemblyman wanted to stay tight with homeowners, and gave her the job.

My father had his own business as a business manager and financial consultant, and he would frequently try new things to bring in new clients. Seeing that I was not having success in my job search, he hired me to go to particular offices, ask for specific people there, hand them a few pages of materials and tell them something quick about his business. I only did it for a week or two because, soon after, I finally landed a full-time position. But someone that I met when working for my father hired him for something, and I felt a sense of accomplishment and that my short job with my dad was worthwhile because of that.

* * *

MY NEW JOB was working for the local state senator as a full-time field representative getting $25,000 per year—*far better* than the part-time $7-an-hour Assembly job. The position was not advertised or posted anywhere. The Senate staff asked other elected offices in their area for recommendations, and the Assembly staff with whom I had interviewed a few weeks earlier recommended me.

Interesting story: I had met this state senator two or three years earlier. While on summer break from college, my parents went to the theater and sat next to the senator and his wife. They hit it off, and

my parents told the senator that their son (me) was in college
studying politics. He told them I could come to his office one day to
talk if I wanted. So I did, and we spoke for over an hour. Somehow I
had completely forgotten about our meeting when I was going to his
office to interview for a job. When I walked into his office, with
plaques and photos on the wall, I instantly thought: "This place looks
so familiar." Then I realized: Oh my—it's the state senator I met with
a few years ago. During my job interview with the senator, I reminded
him that we'd met in his office before, and he said, "Oh yes, I remember." The rest of the interview went great after that. I spent the next
two and a half years working for him, going around his district on the
Westside of Los Angeles talking to people on his behalf, and giving
statements about his views on issues like education, the environment
and transportation.

After the first year, I wanted to do more. I wanted to go to Sacramento, where the action was, and work to make an important state
law. But I enjoyed Los Angeles and didn't want to relocate. The
senator and his chief of staff were nice enough to put me in charge of
two important L.A.-centric bills and working them through the
legislative process. When the bills came up for committee, I would
hop on a one-hour flight to Sacramento to meet with the legislative
staff of committee members to inform them of the bill and persuade
their members to commit to a "yes" vote. One of the two bills
succeeded in getting passed and signed into law. The other fell short.

The bill that prevailed was the top legislative priority for Heal the
Bay, a well-known SoCal environmental group. They had made a list
of seven bills they wanted to get passed into law that year: Ours was
their No. 1 priority, and it was the *only* bill on their list that actually
got passed and enacted. Our bill gave a 5 percent price advantage to
the recycled versions of motor oil and paint, for all state government
contracts. The purpose was to kickstart the recycled oil and paint
industries, so they could dominate government contracts like the
motor oil in all state vehicles and the interior and exterior paint for
all state government buildings, and eventually become popular in the
private industry as well. The bill almost died in a committee by one

vote, but after an hour of intensive activity, an environmental lobbyist and I got the single vote we needed. With only minutes before the committee meeting closed, we found an assemblyman in a different committee, passed him a note to please go downstairs to vote for the bill, and he did. It passed by one vote, made it through the floor votes, and was signed into law by Republican Gov. Pete Wilson.

The bill that fell short was the top priority for the senator I worked for. It was also considered by everyone to be a long shot. The bill was to prohibit the SoCal regional Metropolitan Transit Authority from constructing a rail line on the 101 and 405 freeways that cut through West LA and the San Fernando Valley, the senator's district. There was a big movement to put the new rail lines on top of these freeways—the theory being that if people were snarled in traffic and looked up at a train shooting by, they would want to park their car in a lot by their house, and hop on the train to beat traffic. But the problem was that the freeways did not connect "trip generators." A trip generator is an area that generates a lot of people coming in and out, such as a university, a government center, a business center (tall commercial buildings) or a major shopping center. Our belief was that people would more likely take the train if it took them right to their destination, rather than a mile away. The 101 and 405 freeways got within a mile or so of several trip generators, but not *to* the corner block of the trip generator itself.

On the senator's behalf, I advocated for train stations *at* UCLA, Valley College, Pierce College, Warner Center (a major business and shopping area), and the Van Nuys Government Center (the single largest trip generator in the San Fernando Valley)—and a train route that would connect all of them together. The bill failed by one vote in a committee because a San Francisco state senator whose staff *assured me* he supported it, and would vote for it in committee, decided for some unexplained reason to vote against it. Even though we lost, in the process my senator and I had built a coalition of politicians throughout the SoCal region, including the powerful L.A. mayor, Tom Bradley. A few years after I left the senator's office, the MTA scrapped the concept of rails on the 101 and 405 freeways, and adopted the wisdom of connecting trip generators. And that's what we have today. I don't know if my work contributed to that decision by the MTA, but it was the right decision, and if something that I did helped carry the message to the powers that be, then it certainly was a worthwhile campaign that we waged.

When the senator hired me, he said: *If you work for me, you have to stay for two years. I don't want to train you, and then have you leave in a year for law school.* So I committed to him that I would stay for two years, and I fulfilled that commitment. Two years later, I was accepted to Loyola Law School in downtown Los Angeles.

* * *

I WON'T BORE you with a chapter on law school. Watch *The Paper Chase*, a famous 1973 film about a law student's first year at Harvard Law School: a perpetual state of stress and confusion. My first-year experience felt something like that, with a large helping of boredom thrown in. That said, Loyola is an excellent law school and I thought it was a terrific place: great professors and opportunities, a beautiful campus designed by Frank Gehry. I'm not the type who enjoys listening to lectures, which is what law school is all about, but I got through it, and earned good grades too: top 15 percent and dean's honor list.

There were a few highlights. I wrote an article for the *Entertainment Law Journal* about the FDA's regulations to stop the tobacco industry from advertising to children. I titled the article "Is it Curtains for Joe Camel?" Soon after it was published, the "smooth" cartoon camel, who always had a cigarette hanging from his mouth, was gone forever. (*The New York Times* wrote an "obituary" with the headline: "Joe Camel, a Giant in Tobacco Marketing, Is Dead at 23.") It was a nice feeling to be a low-level person on the journal and have my article published, and then republished by the prestigious *Advertising Law Anthology*.

Second highlight: I scored a post-graduate clerkship for a U.S. District Court judge, which is really hard to get. It's very competitive.

I think of my entire graduating class of more than 300, there were only two federal law clerks: the editor-in-chief of the *Loyola Law Review*, and me. When I started, a fellow clerk told me, "You'll never have as much power in your life." He might have been right. There I was, in my first year after law school, handling several major cases, some of them multibillion-dollar cases, including the second-largest environmental damages case in America at the time, second only to the *Exxon Valdez* oil spill. The case was *United States v. Montrose Chemical Corporation* regarding allegations of Montrose Chemical pumping the pesticide DDT into the Santa Monica Bay for two years.

Being a clerk for a U.S. District Court judge was an amazing experience. I would read briefs from some of the best attorneys in America, and decide which evidence and arguments were persuasive. I'd look up all the cases they cited, and do research beyond those cases. I'd apply the law to the evidence and facts, and make recommendations to the judge on what I felt he should do. He would ask me specific questions and challenge me on this point and that point— I'm not sure if his questions were to help him fully understand the case, or to help *me* with my skills fully analyzing a case and addressing a judge. Maybe both. While working up the papers, I would prepare an extensive memo on each motion and then, before the hearing, prepare a tentative ruling which the judge would read and the attorneys would use as a basis for their oral arguments. The judge almost always stuck with his tentative ruling, and I would convert it into the judge's final ruling.

The clerkship was a once-in-a-lifetime opportunity to spend a year interacting with a federal judge, who had over 30 years of experience, regarding the briefs, arguments and techniques that he found effective and ineffective. This and everything else about the experience helped prepare me for a career tangling with skilled counsel and seeking to persuade federal and state judges to rule in my clients' favor.

22

THE ITALIAN JOB

One of my most fascinating cases was a bitter dispute between an Italian film mogul and one of his most trusted top executives, who for decades was like a brother to him. They had a falling out. Then came a lawsuit, a countersuit, and finally a lengthy trial—all with such colorful characters and so much international intrigue that Martin Scorsese (who knew them) reportedly once said it would make a terrific movie.

The main players in this real-life drama were my client, 66-year-old Italian film mogul and former Italian Senator Vittorio Cecchi Gori, and his former close friend and former head of U.S. operations, 50-year-old Gianni Nunnari. A little background:

Vittorio Cecchi Gori is the son of Italian film pioneer Mario Cecchi Gori, founder of Cecchi Gori Group, based in Rome. Vittorio and his father produced more than 200 films together (and his father produced some 100 films before Vittorio came of age) including Academy Award winners *Il Postino* (*The Postman*), *La Vita e Bella* (*Life Is Beautiful*) and *Mediterraneo*. The Cecchi Gori family is legendary in the world of Italian cinema. At one point he reportedly was the third-richest man in Italy—before his empire crumbled.

Gianni Nunnari originally worked in Rome with father and son

Mario and Vittorio. Mario treated Nunnari like another son, and Vittorio treated him like a brother. Nunnari eventually asked to go to Los Angeles to head the company's U.S. operations, was given that position at age 37 and held it for 12 years: from 1996 to 2008. Nunnari also created his own personal production company, which he called Hollywood Gang Productions, also based in L.A. Nunnari's side business received film credits and revenue on films *300* and *Everybody's Fine*, and Nunnari received a producer credit on Scorsese's films *The Departed*, which won Best Picture and three other Oscars, as well as *Shutter Island,* both starring Leonardo DiCaprio.

That side business was the core of the problems between Vittorio and Nunnari. According to our lawsuit, during an unannounced visit to the office in 2006, Vittorio discovered Nunnari was running Hollywood Gang Productions out of Cecchi Gori Pictures' L.A. office and using the Cecchi Gori employees, offices, funds, assets and corporate opportunities to further Nunnari's own personal interests. In April 2008, Cecchi Gori ordered the L.A. office shuttered.

The lawsuit was filed the following month, when Nunnari sued Vittorio and his company, Cecchi Gori Pictures, for breach of Nunnari's employment contract and related claims. A month later, Vittorio and Cecchi Gori Pictures countersued Nunnari for breach of fiduciary duty, fraud, breach of contract and other claims. I entered the case 11 months after it was filed, replacing a law firm that had allowed Cecchi Gori to get hit like a punching bag, with hardly any effort to fight back or win the case. I litigated the case for nearly two more years, and represented Vittorio and company at a four-week trial in Los Angeles Superior Court in 2010.

* * *

WHEN I MET VITTORIO, he'd had a string of adverse court decisions and was considering switching attorneys. When someone comes to me looking to switch counsel, my first instinct is to assume they are being adequately represented but don't enjoy the process of litigation, which is inherently rough and tumble, or perhaps they need to communicate better with their counsel. Rarely do I recommend the person switch counsel. But in the case of Vittorio, I reviewed the court record the afternoon before my morning meeting with him, and I was convinced he needed new counsel—his case was very close to being dismissed, and Nunnari was about to win by default.

At the time, I had been an entertainment litigator for 12 years, and never had a judge order a client, or myself, to pay sanctions to the opposing party, opposing counsel, or the court. But Vittorio and his company had been ordered to pay sanctions to Nunnari *three times* in just the first 11 months of the case, and virtually every ruling in the case was against Vittorio, and in Nunnari's favor.

When I told Vittorio (through his interpreter, because he speaks Italian) about the sanctions orders, and the other orders in the case consistently against him, he had no idea—it was as if no one had informed him what was happening in the case. I told him, "You need to hire someone else. It doesn't have to be me—I can give you a list of the best entertainment attorneys in Los Angeles and you can meet with them while you're in town, but you can't stay with your current counsel, because you're at risk of losing the case in the near future." He said to me, "You're hired."

I soon realized the law firm representing the other side had represented Vittorio and his company in the past—a clear conflict of interest. I sent a letter notifying them of their conflict and the need to withdraw as counsel for Nunnari, or face consequences. Within days, they withdrew. It was an immediate game-changer, to knock out Nunnari's counsel that had been winning the case for 11 months straight, and force him to hire new counsel who knew nothing about the case. I was on the year-long case for less than a month, but suddenly knew more about it than Nunnari's next counsel.

I realized that Vittorio's prior counsel had not sent *any* discovery to Nunnari. I typically send a full set of written discovery within two months of the case being filed. So I prepared a comprehensive set of written discovery (interrogatories, document requests, deposition notices, and more) and served it—while Nunnari was in the process of hiring new counsel. His new counsel didn't respond to it; I demanded that they do so. They did not agree to my demands, so I filed three motions to compel. All went to a hearing, were granted in full, and then *Nunnari* was sanctioned by the court on each of my three motions—for a triple sanction order. I evened the sanctions score within a few months' time. Nunnari also was ordered to produce to me every shred of their documents, and there were some "smoking guns" among them.

* * *

I DEPOSED Nunnari for three days—sitting him in a conference room for 10-hour days, three days in a row, with a court reporter and videographer recording my every question and his every response. When Nunnari gets angry, he turns red and erupts—all while being filmed. That was not good for his case.

My client would get emotional as well. This became one of my biggest challenges in the case: controlling a very powerful, very wealthy, very passionate man who speaks very little English—while I speak virtually no Italian. Shortly before trial, we had three huge challenges:

Challenge No. 1: On the eve of trial, I told Vittorio that he had to be in L.A. on a certain date so that we had time to prepare. He arrived in L.A. a week late, literally the day before the jury trial was scheduled to begin. Hardly any time to prepare.

Challenge No. 2: When my partner Marc and I met with Vittorio to prepare for trial, we put our first document in front of him to discuss it. It was Nunnari's signed employment agreement, which all parties had agreed was his contract. Vittorio erupted: "That's not my signature! That's a forgery!" His face turned red and he was very upset. He just couldn't get past this contract, but its authenticity was undisputed. Marc and I took a break, left the room, looked at each other and said: *We have to waive jury trial.* The Nunnari side felt the same way: Two days earlier, they had filed a document in court waiving jury trial. Fortunately for us, our judge, Los Angeles County Superior Court Judge Amy Hogue, postponed our trial by two weeks in order to take two other, smaller cases to trial first. That allowed us the time we needed to prepare Vittorio for trial.

Challenge No. 3: Vittorio was distracted. He had booked a room at the famed Beverly Hills Hotel, but he wasn't happy there: His room was small and dark, and his personal assistant was booked at a different hotel a mile away. Vittorio complained, so his new head of U.S. operations rented him a small, modern house in Beverly Hills, up on a hill, with a nice swimming pool and gorgeous views.

I arrived at 10 a.m. and Vittorio was outside by the pool, having just had a swim and eaten breakfast. Vittorio was very calm and content—for the first time since arriving in Los Angeles. We sat outside, looking out to all of Beverly Hills, and through the interpreter (an excellent and calm interpreter), I told him: "Look around. Look at the beautiful view, feel the warm air, and the peaceful surroundings. When you are in court, and you take the stand to testify, I want you to feel just like this: *calm* and *relaxed*. Now let's talk about this case, but while we talk about it, I want you to maintain this feeling of calm that you have right now."

"At the trial," I told Vittorio, "we will tell your story. When you make movies, you tell stories—stories about other people. This time, you will be telling *your* story. The story about you and Gianni Nunnari, how you trusted him like a brother, and he took advantage of you."

* * *

I MET with Vittorio every other day. He would go for an hour at first, then two hours, then three, before he would get upset and start shouting. But he needed to be able to go the full court day, from 10 a.m. to 4:30 p.m., with a 90-minute lunch break. Once, when he got upset after a few hours of prep, I told him through our translator, "You're like milk—you have an expiration date." I told him he was expiring, and getting upset, too soon. He needed to last all day. He laughed and understood.

Also during our prep sessions, he wanted to veer off course and take over the storytelling, but it was turning a sympathetic story into one that became bitter and vindictive, because he felt so betrayed by Nunnari. I told him, "I can win your case for you, but you have to answer my questions and not go off on tangents. I'm the director and you're the actor. You have to do your job, but you cannot interfere with the director. That's my job." This was a man who produced 200 motion pictures, and was on the set of every single one of them. He knew the director calls the shots, and when an actor tries to interfere, it spells disaster for the film. He and I had gone over the materials so thoroughly—a very complex and detailed set of facts over the course of 12 years, and even decades earlier—that he practically had a script to follow. I told him to "stick to the script," and trust the director. With this analogy, he fully understood and did not interfere again. He also understood the point about his expiration date, and soon was routinely answering questions effectively for four-hour sessions without getting upset.

When Vittorio finally testified during trial, he was very good. Not perfect, but his imperfections made him human. He testified for the entire day, and came off as a man who was not caught up in money or power, as Nunnari and his counsel tried to portray him, but as a man who had been trusting and was taken advantage of—which was the truth.

* * *

IN STORYTELLING, I am always focused on where to *start* the story. My initial thought was to start it when Nunnari went to Los Angeles to run the company's U.S. operations in 1996. But there was important information dating back to when Mario Cecchi Gori, Vittorio's father, first took Nunnari under his wing back in Rome many years earlier. During our sessions, I asked Vittorio when he first started working with his father, and he said while he (Vittorio) was at university. So I brought the story back to there. But I still sensed there was more.

At one point, I asked Vittorio how his father, Mario, first started in the film business, and what he did *before* he was in the movie business. Vittorio told me: My father fought in the Italian Resistance against Mussolini and Hitler during World War II. After the war, he got a job as an assistant to a producer, carrying scripts and delivering film reels. He eventually started to produce small films himself.

That's where I decided to start Vittorio's direct examination at trial. My first question was: "What did your father do before he started working in the film business?" He answered (in Italian, which was translated by our terrific translator sitting next to him): "My father fought in the Italian Resistance during World War II." His testimony quickly discussed how his father produced 100 films, and then Vittorio, with his father, produced 200 more, and so on.

One of the issues in the case was whether Vittorio had won a particular Oscar award because he did not go on the stage to receive it or give an acceptance speech. It was the award for Best Foreign Language Film for *Mediterraneo*. Vittorio testified, through his interpreter: My father had a heart condition and was told by his doctor that he could not fly. He was in poor health and did not have long to live. So I went to the Academy Awards without him—though we had always gone together. The awards were held across the street (referring to the Dorothy Chandler Pavilion, which is across the street from the courthouse we were in). They announced that our film had won the award and my group started to pull me up from my chair to walk to the stage and accept the award. But I couldn't go, because my father was not with me—I could not bring myself to walk to the stage without him. So I told the director to go up and accept the award.

The judge was moved by Vittorio's testimony. He came off as he truly is: a generous and trusting man with a big heart who was taken advantage of by his head of U.S. operations, Nunnari, who used the company's money and personnel to develop projects. Right as a project was about to be "greenlit" for production, the film would miraculously switch from a Cecchi Gori title to a Hollywood Gang title, and all payments from the film would end up with Nunnari, not Vittorio or his company that was paying for everything—including Nunnari, all staff, the offices, funds to option or buy scripts and treatments, funds to pay writers to further develop them, and the rest.

* * *

AFTER A FOUR-WEEK TRIAL in downtown L.A., Judge Hogue issued a 50-page Statement of Decision detailing what the evidence showed had happened between Cecchi Gori and Nunnari. The decision discussed the history between the litigants: how Nunnari had idolized Mario Cecchi Gori, a legend in his native Italy. Nunnari's father, also in the film business, died when Nunnari was 23. Before he passed away, Mario Cecchi Gori made a promise to Nunnari's father that he would look after his son—and he made good on that promise by employing Nunnari in various positions at his movie empire.

After Mario's death years later, his son Vittorio continued to employ Nunnari. The men had developed a strong bond and were close friends. In the late 1980s, Vittorio sent Nunnari to Los Angeles to oversee operations there. Nunnari was a fluent, self-taught English speaker, which made him all the more valuable to the company.

Over time, Nunnari felt undercompensated, and began to work as a producer for hire. With the wide latitude and trust he was given by his boss, Nunnari's outside work—which Vittorio initially approved—grew to become a "direct conflict of interest," the judge wrote, as Nunnari obtained rights to material and developed projects that competed with Cecchi Gori Pictures. The judge found that Nunnari had improperly diverted all of the money generated from films like *300* and *Everybody's Fine* to his own personal company.

"In his testimony, [Vittorio] came across as a voluble, expansive, and sometimes emotional personality who focuses on the big picture and delegates as many details as possible to trusted advisors like Nunnari," Judge Hogue wrote. "[He] does not speak English and his trust was so unquestioning that, at Nunnari's request, he apparently signed his name on agreements and memoranda without translating them."

* * *

WE WON THE CASE. Judge Hogue awarded Vittorio and his company more than $13 million in damages, plus $2 million in attorneys' fees, plus $2 million in interest on top of that, as well as the rights to several films that the judge ruled were the property of Cecchi Gori Pictures and not Nunnari or his company Hollywood Gang. As far as Nunnari's claims against Vittorio and his company, for which Nunnari sought $5 million, Nunnari received nothing. It was a huge, resounding victory for Vittorio and Cecchi Gori Pictures, and a total defeat for Nunnari.

Looking back, the case was complex, time-consuming and often stressful—but also super interesting, rewarding and often fun. I saw the need to step into the role of "director" in order to wrangle a diffi-cult, yet likable "star." My leading man, an Italian film mogul and former Italian senator in his late 60s whose empire had fallen on hard times, was rewarded appropriately from the case because he focused on his true story and did not let his emotions get the better of him.

23

STARTING A NEW LAW FIRM

By mid-2012, I had been an attorney for 16 years, and was doing well. I was a partner (but not an owner) at a law firm with 45 attorneys in three offices in California and Nevada. In 2010, I was the largest rainmaker of that firm, meaning I generated more revenue to the firm than anyone else. By late 2012, I could see that 2013 was looking like another great year: I had the *Hulk Hogan v. Gawker* case generating solid hourly rates, and two contingency cases: one for Sandra Bullock, and another for George Clooney and Julia Roberts, which were going well, among several other cases and clients.

My biggest complaint about the firm, which I had joined in 2008, was that it was not honoring the compensation formula that I had been promised when I was hired. When I asked that it be honored, I was given B.S. reasons why it could not happen. The real reason, it seemed to me, was that the equity partners (i.e., the owners) wanted to keep more of the money that I brought in than they'd agreed to when I said "yes" to their offer to join the firm. I suggested to them other methods of compensation to make up for their shortfall, but my suggestions were turned down. I felt like the firm loved the business and revenue that I brought them, and the long hours and hard work that I put into the cases, but simply did not want to pay me *my end* of the bargain. Naturally I was feeling frustrated and unhappy with the situation.

One unique challenge with my practice at the time was that it was largely entertainment litigation on behalf of talent (like major actors and independent producers), who are typically averse to the major entertainment studios like Disney, Paramount, Sony, MGM, etc. So law firms choose sides: The vast majority of the firms represent studios, while a minority represent talent. I was on the talent side, and I was on my second law firm (and was not well-treated at the first firm either—seeing a pattern?). There weren't very many good talent-side law firms left to join, and there were a few that I was avoiding because of their reputations for being stingy or unpleasant to work for.

There was one large national law firm with a talent-side entertainment litigation practice. I knew a senior partner there, and talked to him about applying to his firm. He loved the idea, submitted my résumé to the right people, and set up the interviews. I had several rounds, they went great, and I was then asked to fly back East to meet the heads of the firm and receive an offer. But at that point, the partner who had brought me in took me aside and told me that he was leaving the firm, and explained why. I suddenly lost interest in going any further in the process. The partner said he was going to start his own firm and asked if I wanted to join forces with him. He is a very good attorney, but his personality was more aggressive than mine: I'm calmer and more laid-back. It was not the right fit.

I had been conferring with my friend and co-worker Jeffrey Abrams. He knew that I was interviewing at the big national firm, and I told him that I was withdrawing my application—and why. I also told him about the offer to join forces with the partner there who was leaving, but that we were not a match. I didn't want to stay where I was, but I was at a loss for what to do.

Jeff asked me, "Would you ever start your own firm?" He knew I had the clients to support it, but he also knew that I was good at my cases because I focused on them and not on distractions like law firm management: hiring attorneys and staff, locating office space, negotiating a lease, shopping for insurance, buying furniture, computers and other office necessities, selecting the right IT system and the many other nuts and bolts needed to set up and keep a firm running. Managing a start-up would take countless hours, and take needed focus away from my cases.

"I wouldn't do it alone," I told Jeff. "With other partners —maybe."

"What if we started a firm together?" Jeff asked. "I could manage it." I knew he had managed the L.A. office of a large national firm for years. He knew how to do it.

"Sounds interesting," I said. "But we'd need at least one other partner with a book of business. In case my business and yours slowed down at the same time. We'd need the extra business to keep things going."

Jeff started to get excited about this idea, and I could tell he was starting to think about it all the time. I wasn't. I had plenty on my plate with my case load, especially once we were hired by Hulk Hogan in early October to immediately sue Gawker, on top of all of my other cases.

* * *

A FEW DAYS LATER, Jeff came into my office. "Guess who I just had breakfast with?!" he asked, his eyes bright and his face lit up. I thought really hard for a minute, guessing it was someone related to our law firm idea, but no names came to mind. "Doug Mirell!" he shouted. "Who's that?" I asked.

Jeff explained that Doug was a partner at the national firm of Loeb & Loeb and did a lot of the same type of work that we did, but more on the defense side than the plaintiff side. He'd been practicing for 32 years (all at the same firm), which was double my total of 16 years in practice, and more than a decade longer than Jeff's experience. "Does he have business?" I asked. The whole point of the third partner was to have additional business (clients and revenues), in case mine and Jeff's were to temporarily hit the doldrums. "Yes, he told me he does," Jeff replied.

Jeff set up a breakfast meeting and the three of us met at John O'Groats, a very local, not fancy *at all* place for business breakfast meetings on weekdays, and family breakfasts on weekends. It's very close to my house, and not far from Jeff's and Doug's. ("John o'Groats" by the way, is a small town at the northernmost tip of Scotland. I was hoping it was a good sign: My maternal great-grandmother was full Scottish.)

Over breakfast, I found Doug to be a nice guy, very smart, with a lot of experience. His practice meshed with ours, and he seemed to have business. He checked all the boxes. Jeff's excitement was now in high gear. It was nice to see, because he's a guy who sometimes gets very excited about something, and other times is uninspired. It was great to see him excited.

Jeff had conversations with Doug separately, where they covered various issues in detail, including clients, cases, likelihood of bringing his various clients to a small new firm, projected workload and revenue in 2013, how much work Doug would do himself versus work performed by associates, and so on.

Jeff prepared a "pro-forma" with revenue, cost and profit projections based on his interviews with Doug, and separately with me, and Jeff's knowledge of his own clients and matters. Jeff projected Doug being the biggest rainmaker of the firm, then me, then himself, but Jeff also was going to manage the firm. They agreed that my name would come first in the firm name because I had the highest-profile cases and clients: active lawsuits for Sandra Bullock, George Clooney, Julia Roberts, Jude Law, *Hulk Hogan v. Gawker*, and several others.

Jeff proposed we have a "Mission Statement" and I volunteered to write the first draft. It had about 10 numbered points about our values, our goals, and our vision for the firm. The first two words that I wrote for point No. 1 were: "HAVE FUN." If we don't enjoy what we do, I wrote, nothing else makes any sense.

Jeff and I had both worked for multiple different law firms in the past, and Doug had spent 32 years at a large national firm. There is something fundamentally important to human beings that all of those law firm experiences lacked: a sense of fun. So I put it at the very top of our Mission Statement. My theory, which I wrote out in point No. 1, was that if we have fun, we'll be better at what we do, the people around us will enjoy what they do, and the quality of our work, and service to our clients, will be better as a result; we'll win our cases, and we'll stand out among the competition. Too many law firms in L.A., and all throughout the U.S., are just not fun. That was sad to me. What's the point of starting a new firm, I thought, if it's going to be the same unhappy place as everywhere else?

We signed the partnership papers for the new firm in late November 2012, but we were going to officially open our doors on Jan. 2, 2013. The head partner of our prior firm did not hand out bonus checks until the very end of December, so I needed to wait until my bonus check cleared my bank account before giving notice.

* * *

IN MID-DECEMBER, I took a business trip to England for a U.K.-based client that had hired me to sue a major U.S. company in federal court in Texas. The client wanted to have two full days of meetings with its senior executives, its London counsel and myself at its headquarters in Derby, England, which is way out in the countryside. After those meetings, the client's London lawyer wanted to introduce me to his colleagues at various other law firms in London that practiced the same area of law: media, entertainment and reputation protection cases. So before I left for England, I went to Staples and designed my own business cards with the name of our new law firm: "Harder Mirell Abrams." This would not be the long-term design; I made up a quick layout on the spot so that I would have something to hand out. I also told Jeff that I needed us to have an address, phone number, email address, URL, and a placeholder website, so that our new firm looked legitimate to the London attorneys who I was going to be meeting with.

The temporary business card I created for my trip to England, and the long-term design we updated to afterward.

THE TRIP to England went great. The two days of client meetings, at the company's headquarters two hours north of London, went really well. To get there we took a train to Nottingham and drove a car through Sherwood Forest—no lie, these places really do exist. After the two days of meetings in Derby, the meet-and-greets at the London law firms went amazingly well too. I met with the top solicitors and barristers in London who represent the royal family, J.K. Rowling, Sir Elton John, Madonna and many other major celebrities and high-net-worth individuals. Everyone had my new (temporary) business card with the ink barely dry. It felt great to hand them out, with my name at the top of the law firm name. I felt that I'd finally "arrived" in my career. No more working for other people. From now on, I was my own boss.

* * *

ON JAN. 2, 2013, our new law firm was officially open for business.

In the months preceding that day, we had toured several office suites to rent. Not a lot was available that matched our challenging list of specifications, and several spaces were outright rejects for any number of reasons. But one space stood out: It was love at first sight for me. We took it, but unfortunately the building was torn down the next year.

1801 Avenue of the Stars, Suite 1120, in Los Angeles was about 3,000 square feet and had been used a few years earlier as the private art gallery for Michael Ovitz, the founder of Creative Arts Agency (CAA), the No. 1 talent agency in the world. He later went on to become president of The Walt Disney Company.

The suite had six individual offices, a large conference room, and a large common area in the middle of the suite, on the 11th floor of a 14-story building with killer views from every room. We were looking for a one-year lease, in case our law firm experiment did not turn out to be successful—commercial landlords are known to go after your house and other personal assets if you bail out on a lease. We wanted to be careful and conservative about financial commitments.

The reason we could score a one-year lease, versus the standard three-year or five-year commercial lease, is because the building had a date with the wrecking ball one year later. Still, they were trying to bring whatever revenue they could in the year preceding demolition. Our new firm was one of the few takers in 2013, and we knew that we (and all other tenants of the building) would be evicted after one year —building management was very upfront about it. The rental rate also was cheap because of this—an added bonus.

The building was built in 1963, the very first building of "Century City"—a cutting-edge "city within a city" commercial residential project which, over time, became the hub for Hollywood financiers, business managers, talent agents and attorneys. The first two buildings were each 14 stories. By the early '70s, new buildings there were 44 stories tall. We were among the last occupants of the first building in Century City.

Outside of our suite, the common areas of the building needed a refurbish, which never came. But the inside of our office was very nice. First, the layout was great: plenty of offices, with a wide-open feel in the middle of the suite. Best of all, we had amazing views from every vantage point. Our entire suite overlooked the golf course of the Los Angeles Country Club. Every window office had a beautiful view of it from the 11th floor. My personal office was in a corner: Windows to the north looked onto the golf course, while windows to the west looked onto West L.A., Santa Monica, and the Pacific Ocean in the distance. I watched the sun set on the ocean every evening.

We had another corner office on the opposite side that was even larger than mine. It was a big rectangle, with all glass on two sides. I named it the "Sky Box" and we used it for multiple junior attorneys and law clerks (law students who worked for us part-time, temporarily). We could comfortably put three or four people in the Sky Box, but usually the most we had were two. The Sky Box had the best views of all: a full golf course view to the north, and to the east, a view straight up Santa Monica Boulevard for miles and miles— Century City, Beverly Hills, West Hollywood, eventually getting to the multicolored Pacific Design Center building, and then up to the Hollywood Hills with a very clear view of the iconic HOLLYWOOD sign.

That sign was a selling point for me because my wife, Kathleen, and I got engaged at the base of the first "O" of that famous sign. It was Dec. 29, 2000, and I took her on an afternoon hike up Beachwood Canyon, which leads to the front of the sign, and then around to the back of it. It was before 9/11 changed everything in 2001, so security was lax. There was a chain-link fence at the back of the sign, but a big gap at the bottom was large enough to easily crawl under, followed by a short walk down to the base of the letters.

The rear of the iconic Hollywood sign, where I popped the question to my future wife.

From the small backpack I brought, I spread a colorful blanket down on the concrete base, pulled out a portable CD player (it was the era before iPods and mp3 players), and some small speakers that I'd just bought that day, and played "Kiss of Life" by Sade, which then became "our song." I went down on one knee, opened the ring box, and popped the question. "Yes!" was the answer, and I popped the cork of a chilled bottle of nice Champagne, filled up two flutes, and we sipped bubbly and watched the sun sink slowly on the horizon of our beautiful home city of Los Angeles. I had timed the proposal just right for a perfect sunset. We were married the next year and will celebrate our 20th wedding anniversary in the spring of 2021.

* * *

WE HAD lots of blank walls that needed something on them. At first I considered posters—they would be cheap, but also cheap looking.

Next I looked online to see if any local museums rented art. They didn't. Then I Googled "rent art los angeles" and up came Artspace Warehouse. The owner, Claudia, came over with an iPad loaded with all of her art—terrific, affordable, contemporary originals—and a measuring tape. She measured our blank walls, flipped through the art on her iPad and gave us her recommendations. We said, "OK," and that was that. Within a week, an entire suite of original art was installed, and the suite was gorgeous. We had the choice of renting or buying the art. If we rented first, and later decided to buy the pieces, 75 percent of the rent paid would be credited toward the purchase price, at the original sale price—the price would not increase on us. It was a good deal, and we went with renting for a year. (A year later, we bought it all, and a few more pieces too.)

We also bought desks and chairs—modern and affordable, just like the art. Then we bought a living room set: two light gray couches, two side tables, side lamps, a coffee table, a tall standing lamp, and several colorful throw pillows. Everything was contemporary, yet also homey (and affordable) and made the open area in the middle of the suite look like a really nice living room, with big windows and gorgeous views. We were on our way!

All of the clients and cases that I wanted to move from the old firm to my new firm moved over quickly and seamlessly. There were one or two cases that I did *not* want to move over, because the clients were bad at paying the bill, or unpleasant to work with (or both). Those cases stayed at the old firm. Everything else moved with me to the new firm.

After only a few months, we were settling some contingency cases that I thought would take much longer, and the firm (and the clients) received some excellent payments from those cases. Within about five months' time, my partners and I had paid off our initial line of credit to get started, and also had enough cash to pay 100 percent of the firm's costs for the rest of 2013, and into 2014. It was a great start! We even threw a lavish party at the penthouse of Mastro's Steakhouse in Beverly Hills, and ordered a substantial amount of food and drink (thanks to a clever waitress who recommended a lot of great things to order), and it was worth it. We wanted to celebrate our early achievement as a firm—a successful first year, when we were only about five months old—and that's what we did.

* * *

But it wasn't all roses. While the numbers that I generated our first year were way above our projections, my partners' numbers were well below the projections. Many of the clients and cases that Doug said he would bring to the firm stayed with other partners at his prior firm. Jeff's cases also were not materializing as he had expected. By year end, revenues for our first year (2013) were 85 percent originated by me, with Doug and Jeff sharing the remaining 15 percent.

We expected those percentages to change in 2014 and get closer to one-third each, but they didn't really. The percentages also didn't change much in 2015 or 2016. With the Hulk Hogan victory in March 2016, revenues from my business went up even more. Theirs went up a little too, but the percentages did not change much.

In each of these years, the wide discrepancy in revenue origination made for an awkward year-end discussion regarding how to divide profits. In late 2013, Doug wanted us to split profits equally: one-third each. But he brought in less than 10 percent of the revenue, while I brought in 85 percent. I also felt that I was working the hardest of the three. The fact that Doug would even suggest that he receive one-third of the profits offended me, and Jeff agreed. In my view, Doug had not accurately represented his book of business, saying that he could move clients and cases to our new firm that were not even his clients to move—they apparently were the clients of other partners of his old law firm, and stayed there. Doug did not deserve one-third of the profits, or anything close.

* * *

Our late-2012 agreement regarding compensation, before the firm opened, was not a formula but rather an agreement to consider revenue origination primarily, and a variety of secondary factors, and to discuss and agree on compensation numbers at the end of each year. So that's what we did, which was not a fun discussion for the first couple of years. We reached a more definitive agreement later: a formula that we stayed with for the remainder of our partnership, which worked, and was based primarily on revenue origination to incentivize each partner to bring in new clients and cases.

In February 2018, just after our fifth anniversary as a law firm, Doug decided to leave the firm. It was a bit of a relief to me, because he was more or less a solo practitioner in our office, and being paid well above what other law firms in town would pay him for the revenue he was generating each year.

I was not totally surprised that Doug was leaving because politically he is extremely liberal: like Elizabeth Warren or Bernie Sanders on the political spectrum. Doug did not like the fact that we were doing work for President Trump, though he had voted in favor of accepting him as a client and each of the cases we worked on. Doug's wife and adult daughter, who are very outspoken people, likewise are very liberal—and I suspect they influenced his decision to leave. Doug also lost a minor client who felt the same way as Doug and his family about the president. Doug chose to leave the firm to chase after his one minor client who left. It was the right decision for him, given the circumstances, and thus also the right decision for all of us. Because of Doug, we started the law firm in the first place and it did well—we all did well. I have no regrets, and assume that Doug does not either.

The last hour of Doug's five-year tenure with the firm, unfortunately, was not a pleasant one. In the morning, Doug had suggested that we all agree to tell any reporter who calls that Doug left the firm because he had been feeling "increasingly uncomfortable" with some of the work the firm was doing, including for the president. I hit the roof at the idea and said, "Absolutely not!" The way it works when anyone leaves a position, I said, is that everyone says *good things* about each other, and that's it. Doug agreed.

That morning, however, Doug told a reporter who covers entertainment law firms that he had been feeling "increasingly uncomfortable" about the firm, and specifically mentioned our work for the president—work that Doug himself had approved. But Doug did not tell Jeff or me that he'd had this conversation with the reporter. We then, unwittingly, had an all-law-firm sendoff lunch for Doug, which generally went well except for a few comments by Doug during the lunch that rubbed a few people the wrong way. I didn't hear them at the time, but heard about them afterward.

After lunch, the reporter that Doug had already spoken to called me and said that she'd heard he was leaving the firm, and she asked me for a comment. She did *not* mention the "increasingly uncomfortable" statement that apparently Doug had already told her. So I gave the reporter our agreed-upon positive comment about Doug, praising him and wishing him the best at his next endeavor.

At around 5 p.m., the reporter posted her story, which was widely read in entertainment legal circles. Doug—on his last day—had spoken ill of some of our clients and the law firm that he had co-founded. I was personally offended by his words, and the underhanded way that he disparaged the firm to the reporter. It was beyond unprofessional and made me realize that it was the right time for him to leave. That was the last time I ever spoke to Doug Mirell.

* * *

I WAS UPSET with Doug for exactly a month after he left, but then decided to let it go. My time and energy were better spent on representing the firm's clients, helping to manage the firm, and maintaining point No. 1 of our Mission Statement ("Have Fun"), than on harboring ill will, which was of zero value to me.

Right after Doug left, we needed to change the firm's name, because it had been "Harder Mirell & Abrams" for the prior five years. I asked Jeff if he wanted to call the firm Harder & Abrams, or just Harder LLP. It was his choice. I sensed that the joy of starting a new firm was over for Jeff, and he was feeling disillusioned and burned out. I told him that if we changed the name to Harder &

Abrams, I did not want to have to change it again, if he was going to leave in the near future. He said, "Call it Harder LLP."

About eight months later (in October 2018), Jeff told me that he was going to leave the practice of law at the end of the year. On Dec. 31, 2018, Jeff left the firm. On the first day of 2019, I became the managing partner for the first time—something that I'd avoided for six years.

* * *

MANAGING the firm was not as difficult as I thought it would be. At first we hired an expensive consultant to assist, but after a few months we realized that we didn't need her. So my amazing CFO/office manager, Carla, who was our first hire even before we opened our doors, and I have proceeded to run the firm ever since. Management was a huge challenge during the Covid-19 shutdown in 2020, starting in mid-March and continuing for the rest of the year. But before that rough patch, managing the firm was fairly easy.

Looking back, co-founding the firm was by far the best career decision I ever made, other than the decision to go to law school and the decision to actually become an attorney. It has also been a relatively fun place to work, and our attorneys and staff seem to have generally enjoyed the place. I think that is just as important a gauge of the success of a law firm as revenue or profit.

Also looking back, I appreciate the role that both Jeff and Doug played in the co-founding of the firm, and their important contributions to it during its first five years. We all did well in those five years, and I hope they remember it as a fun and productive time for all of us. The firm would not have existed without both of them, and were it not for them I'd probably still be working for someone else, with a lot less freedom, compensation, clients, media attention and the rest.

24

REPRESENTING THE A-LIST

"Before he was a fearsome media slayer, Charles Harder was an attack dog for the stars." —GQ, November 2016

My celebrity clients of the past 10 years have included (in alphabetical order) Halle Berry, Sandra Bullock, George Clooney, Bradley Cooper, Cameron Diaz, Lena Dunham, Clint Eastwood, Amber Heard, Hulk Hogan, Kate Hudson, Diane Keaton, Jude Law, Mandy Moore, NFL quarterback Cam Newton, Michelle Pfeiffer, Julia Roberts, USA Olympic gold medalist Shaun White, Reese Witherspoon, producer Dick Wolf, and the estates of Humphrey Bogart, Marlon Brando and Julia Child, among many others.

I have handled nearly all aspects of entertainment law cases including right of publicity (name and image infringement), right of privacy, defamation, various types of breach of contract cases, royalty audits, cybersquatting, copyright and trademark infringement, Talent Agency Act proceedings, and many other legal areas that are particularly important and popular in Los Angeles—home of America's film and television industry.

When representing a celebrity, my practice is generally to leave them alone as much as possible while I do my job. If I can bring money into their bank accounts, while their representatives work with me, and the clients themselves are not bothered by the particulars, that is the ideal scenario. Litigation is not something that most people (celebrities included) find entertaining; most find it distracting and sometimes stressful.

After one of my celebrity cases made headlines, I was contacted by Oxford University Press around 2009, asking if I would be interested in writing a law book. The editor said that I could have others contribute chapters if I wanted. So I conceived of a law book that would cover the details of practicing in the 12 or so most active and popular areas of entertainment law practice, and discuss both the law that applies and best practices of attorneys who specialize in these areas. I assembled a "dream team" of chapter contributors, edited their chapters, and even contributed a chapter myself on Right of Publicity (name and image infringement). The book, currently titled *Entertainment Law & Litigation*, was first released in 2011, has been updated several times, is now published by LexisNexis, and is approaching its 10th year in publication. I was pleased to learn a few years ago that the book was being used as the textbook in a few law school classes.

* * *

OF THE A-LISTERS I've represented, a few made particularly strong impressions.

Sandra Bullock

She is a natural talent, plus smart, with excellent business instincts, and one of the most naturally funny people I've ever known. When I have met with her, she was mostly business, but some humor. I attended an awards dinner in 2018, honoring her transactional attorney of many years, Cliff Gilbert-Lurie, as "Entertainment Lawyer of the Year" and Bullock gave the keynote speech right after professional comedian Drew Carey. Carey was funny. But Bullock was so funny I couldn't breathe.

I represented her for nearly 10 years, including when she was the No. 1 celebrity in the world. She had just won the Academy Award for best actress for *The Blind Side*, then split from her husband (who stupidly cheated on her), then adopted a baby boy and did a record-breaking *People* cover interview, and then starred in *The Proposal* with Ryan Reynolds (very funny) and *Gravity* with George Clooney (awesome film). She was on top of the world at that point—as was Clooney when I represented him separately in a different lawsuit.

Many companies wanted to use their invaluable images and stellar reputations for their own profit, without having to pay them or ask for their permission. In March 2012, we filed a lawsuit against ToyWatch USA for using Bullock's name and image to promote a rhinestone diamond-encrusted plastic watch—after demanding many times they stop, and receiving assurances that they *had* stopped, but yet the marketing and sales continued.

At one point the case went to mediation, and Bullock arrived at the mediation offices. She arrived alone, with no entourage, and I immediately introduced her to the person talking to me: my opposing counsel, who was not expecting her to show up in person, and thus was in a bit of shock when she walked up and said hello. After Bullock and my team spent several hours talking to the mediator on and off, we all needed a restroom break. I showed her where the ladies' room was, while I went to the men's room next door, and then went back to wait for her in the hallway outside the ladies' room, to make sure no one from the other side spoke to her. She then walked out of the ladies' room *talking with opposing counsel!*

The lawyer was from Chicago and had brought her husband and toddler to L.A. on her work trip. Bullock had a young son at the time, so their conversation was all about "what to do with a 3-year-old in L.A." For no less than 20 minutes, Bullock, a world-famous, Oscar-winning actress, stood in the hallway with various people walking by (and me standing next to her), brainstorming with a stranger—who was fighting *against* her in her case—about the best activities in the city for a young family. Bullock was totally happy to have this conversation, mom to mom.

We didn't settle the case that day, but settled it shortly thereafter, and I consider that hallway conversation to be instrumental to the settlement. The terms are confidential, so I can't say anything more.

I was grateful for the opportunity to work with Bullock. She is an amazing talent, a hard worker and a genuinely caring person. When I visited her at her home for a meeting, I was impressed that she had high-quality framed photographs of civil rights leaders on the wall. At the time, I happened to know the personal photographer of Martin Luther King Jr. during his last two years, Bob Fitch. His son was my classmate and good friend in college.

As a holiday gift for Bullock and her family, I bought from Fitch a framed, signed photograph of Dr. King. Fitch gave a second one to me at the same time, *gratis*, and it has hung on the wall of my personal office ever since. (See Chapter 26 for more on MLK and my personal heroes.)

* * *

Reese Witherspoon

I represented the popular Oscar winner in a case that went on for over two years. We filed a lawsuit against Sears and several other online vendors selling jewelry that copied Witherspoon's engagement rings, and used her name as the product name to suggest she had created a cheap replica and was selling it on the sites.

Witherspoon is a focused person and hard worker. You can tell she is juggling a number of things at once. We met in her office in Beverly Hills, which is modern and gorgeous, occupying an entire floor of the building. She would give us 45 to 60 minutes at a time; we met three times at her office, and once at her house. We'd have her complete and undivided attention for at least 30 to 45 minutes, and then she'd start to get pulled in different directions.

She has a small business empire (a production company, a

popular book club, a clothing line, a brick-and-mortar store in Nashville, Tennessee, and much more—plus her incredible acting career) *and* she's a hands-on mother of three. So we knew when we went to visit that we needed to get down to business, and get out.

Reese Witherspoon and I leave the Santa Monica Courthouse during her case against several jewelry manufacturers.

Witherspoon is highly intelligent. We did three prep sessions for her deposition in the case, and then I defended her for two days in a room full of defense lawyers. I was a little concerned because depositions are inherently unpredictable—you never know what will be asked or how your client will respond to it in the moment.

She remembered everything from her prep sessions, had total command of the very detailed facts in her case, and gave answers from the heart that I could not script better myself. In short, she was spectacular. I believed that if we went to trial, the jury would give her everything she asked for—because she was entitled to it, and she was able to flawlessly articulate why.

We ended up reaching multiple confidential settlements in the case with the several defendants, the final one in early 2016—a few weeks before the *Hulk Hogan v. Gawker* case went to trial. If her case had not settled, I would have spent two weeks with Witherspoon in trial, followed immediately (with only a weekend in between) by the Hulk Hogan trial. Fortunately for me, we were able to settle Witherspoon's case, so I could fly to Tampa, Florida, for the Gawker trial a week in advance.

* * *

Cameron Diaz

I represented Diaz and a few other actresses in a 2009 lawsuit against CompUSA, Tiger Direct, Panasonic, Toshiba and 10 other electronics companies that had used the stars' images in online ads, print catalogs, email blasts and other extensive product marketing, all without their permission.

We had two mediations in the case. After nearly a year of litigation, the first mediation didn't resolve things, and the defendants replaced their counsel and hired a well-known, very large and ultra-aggressive law firm. We tangled with them for nearly a year more, and then came the second mediation. I put out an ask: Are any of our celebrity clients available for 30 to 60 minutes to appear at the mediation? Diaz's representative responded: "Cameron would love to."

Nobody at the mediation, including in my room of celebrity representatives, and particularly the other three rooms full of defense lawyers, had any idea that any of the celebrity plaintiffs were going to appear at the mediation. I kept even the mediator in the dark. Just Diaz's attorney and I knew. I had the arbitration offices set aside a small conference room, and I put a sign on the door reading: "Reserved."

Diaz came up the elevator and we walked straight into the small room—nobody saw us. I summarized the case, which she already was aware of, and prepared her to meet the mediator, who had a reputation for being tough as nails. After about 15 minutes she said, with her big signature smile and bright blue eyes, "OK, I'm ready."

I brought in the mediator, who was a well-dressed fellow with a colorful bow tie, a tweed suit with a stylish contrasting vest, and signature round glasses. "Judge Romero," I said, "Cameron Diaz." He was momentarily speechless. Then they had the cutest exchange. He said, "I'm sorry we're meeting under these circumstances." She said, without a second's delay, "That's OK. I like your bow tie." He said, "Well if you like that, then you'll like my socks."

He pulled up his cuffs and showed her his bright green socks, and pulled a little higher to reveal sock suspenders just above them, holding them up comfortably. Without missing a beat, Diaz said, "Those would look good with shorts." They both busted out laughing. Judge Romero was known as one of the toughest mediators in L.A., if not the country. I had prepared her that he could be fire-breathing, harsh, and tell her she's got a terrible case. He didn't do that with her.

He asked her: Why did you bring this case? She told him that what the defendants did to her is not OK. She'd been in show business for 20 years: She started as a model, went into acting, and had slowly built her career to the point where she could *finally* have control over her own name and image, rather than studios and producers having the control.

Then she opens this print catalog, and there is her image, that she never selected, advertising products that she never agreed to endorse, for which she was never given the choice to say "no," and was never paid a cent. She told the mediator, "This goes against everything I've been about for the past 20 years, and I'll be happy to explain all of this to the jury."

He thanked her and went into the main room for the defendants' lawyers and insurance carrier representatives. There were three rooms set aside for this large group, but they all packed into the one room to hear what the mediator had to say, as they all saw Diaz walking into our room. The case didn't settle that day, but within about two weeks it was over. A confidentiality provision prevents me from saying anything more, but I am confident that Diaz's meeting with the mediator went a long way toward resolving the case.

* * *

THESE ARE three examples of the sort of talented, intelligent and fearless actors I've represented who had been wronged by large companies that believed they could profit off stars' valuable names and images, at no cost, and with no penalty. They were just a few of my experiences during more than 50 public lawsuits on behalf of famous clients, which included numerous court appearances, mediations, meetings in their offices and homes, and the occasional trial.

My involvement in these various cases was not glamorous; it was business. I treat celebrities as I treat every client, whether a total unknown person with an important matter to be resolved, or the president or first lady of the United States: with courtesy, respect and laser-focused determination to win their case. It has always been my honor to stand in the long shadow of the A-list and quietly help them to make things right.

25

AMBER HEARD, JOHNNY DEPP
AND A MEDIA WAR

J ohnny Depp and Amber Heard were married for 15 months. I was Heard's civil litigation attorney in 2016, during the time of her divorce case. In the pantheon of acrimonious Hollywood divorces, theirs was particularly ugly. Heard claimed Depp had been physically and emotionally abusive, and in May of that year she obtained a temporary restraining order from the Los Angeles County Superior Court. Photos of Heard showing apparent facial injuries, reports of a violent argument in the couple's L.A. penthouse, and unflattering stories about both actors began circulating in the press.

Three months later, in August, they reached a marital settlement: Depp would pay Heard a reported $7 million. Heard stated she would donate the entire amount to charity. She did so because she didn't want anyone to think she went public with allegations of abuse as a means to obtain money. In announcing the settlement, the former couple released a joint statement saying their relationship was "intensely passionate and at times volatile, but always bound by love." At the time, it felt like the end of the story. Turns out, it was just the beginning.

Since then, Depp filed two lawsuits: a defamation suit in London against *The Sun*, a U.K. publication, for writing that he was a "wife-beater," and a second suit against Heard herself in Virginia state court for publishing an op-ed about domestic violence that did not mention Depp or state that he harmed her.

Depp's quest to clear his name and salvage his career has caused his war with his former wife to go on for more than twice as long as their union itself.

* * *

THE FORMER COUPLE'S fraught relationship took center stage in a London courthouse in July 2020, when Depp's lawsuit against *The Sun* went to trial. At issue: the paper's April 2018 article that called Depp a "wife-beater." Depp's suit claimed it was a lie and the newspaper should be punished for saying he was. His London barrister was David Sherborne, a hip, youngish, stylish, very smart and witty chap I've met several times and had dinner with at least twice during multiple trips to London over the years (completely unrelated to Heard or Depp). Sherborne told the London court: "This is not a case about money. It is about vindication."

To chase "vindication" and support his case against the news organization, Depp had to open his life up to intense scrutiny, while dragging Heard through the mud. To achieve a victory in his libel case, Depp needed to persuade the London court that *all* of Heard's accusations were false: She raised 14 in total at the U.K. trial. Depp strenuously denies he ever abused Heard; he has called her accusations a "hoax" and claimed that it was *she* who was physically and emotionally abusive to *him*.

In pursuing this defamation lawsuit, Depp gave the public a front-row seat to the alcohol- and drug-addled world and dysfunctional marriage of a man who used to be one of the most bankable stars in Hollywood. As the U.K. libel trial got under way, the *Hollywood Reporter* published a piece entitled "Dear Johnny Depp, Fire Your

Lawyers." (The article was aimed primarily at Depp's U.S. lawyer, Adam Waldman, who apparently was directing the legal team.) Senior Editor Eriq Gardner wrote: "At the end of it all, no matter the verdict, this trial will likely do nothing to tamp down the controversies that have tarnished [Depp's] career. He's elevated a tabloid columnist's random musing into something that's going to be covered by serious news outlets for weeks, months, years on end. For that, Johnny Depp should regain his senses and fire his lawyers. Vindication ain't possible. The damage is done."

Gardner makes a good point: Depp's very public trial, with another trial on the horizon, with constant screaming headlines of abuse allegations about Depp, and serious narcotics addiction admissions *by* Depp, seemed to be having the *opposite* of their intended effect.

* * *

THE 16-DAY TRIAL against *The Sun* at London's High Court aired an astonishing litany of disturbing allegations about Depp. If he set out to prove that he never hurt his ex-wife, the public record now contains unforgettable descriptions of his alleged behavior—some of it supported by witnesses, audio recordings and photographs. (Note: I was no longer Heard's attorney at the time of Depp's London trial against *The Sun,* or thereafter.)

Accusations included Depp, an admitted chronic abuser of alcohol and illegal drugs, throwing a decanter at Amber Heard's head; headbutting her (he admits he did this but says it was an accident); trying to strangle her; breaking a bed frame by throwing her on top of it and jumping on top of her; pulling out her hair; dangling her Yorkshire Terrier out of a car window, and also threatening to microwave the dog. These are Heard's or *The Sun's* accusations, mind you; I wasn't there and am not implying they did or did not happen.

At trial, *The Sun* called Heard as a witness who described how the couple often fought over Depp's heavy use of drugs and alcohol.

Depp admitted during the trial that he has blacked out at times during his heavy drug and alcohol use, but denies any acts of abuse of his then-wife: "I may have done things that I have no memory of [but] I am certainly not a violent person, especially with women.... There were blackouts, sure, but in any blackout there are snippets of memory."

Heard testified that Depp's heavy use of drugs and alcohol led to very serious physical and emotional abuse and violence toward her. "Some incidents were so severe that I was afraid he was going to kill me, either intentionally or just by losing control and going too far. He explicitly threatened to kill me many times, especially later in our relationship," she testified on July 20.

Most of Heard's allegations of 14 instances of physical abuse are omitted from this chapter for the sake of brevity,[1] but one of her most disturbing allegations revolves around a three-day incident in March 2015 when she was with Depp in Australia while he was filming the fifth *Pirates of the Caribbean* film. She testified that in an alcohol- and drug-fueled rage, Depp attacked her, trashed their rental home, severed the tip of his finger and admittedly wrote messages to Heard on mirrors and walls around the house with the bloody stump of his finger, and when the blood stopped, dipped his severed finger in paint and continued to write.

Heard testified that Depp had slapped her, grabbed her by the neck, smashed her head against a refrigerator, choked her, spat in her face, threw glass bottles at her, and more. At one point, she testified, Depp, in his rage, ripped off her nightgown: "I was against the bar, naked, bent over backwards, my back against the marble [of the bar]. He was pressing so hard on my neck I couldn't breathe. I remember thinking he was going to kill me in that moment." Her testimony included that Depp forced her onto a hard floor covered with broken glass and alcohol from bottles that he'd smashed, and her arms and feet sustained numerous cuts and bled.

She added, "The best way I can describe what happened in Australia is that it was like a three-day hostage situation."

Depp rejects Heard's description of the Australia incident. "I vehemently deny it and will go as far as to say it's pedestrian fiction," he testified at *The Sun* trial. He does, however, admit to acting erratically during a period when he was trying to kick drugs and alcohol, and sometimes relapsing.

At trial, Depp testified that he felt he was in a "constant tailspin" and recalled telling Heard several times, "We are a crime scene waiting to happen."

* * *

THE JUDGE PRESIDING over the London trial was Sir Andrew Nicol, Judge of the High Court of England and Wales, who has law degrees from both Cambridge University and Harvard Law School, and co-wrote the U.K. law book *Media Law*. On Nov. 1, 2020, Judge Nicol issued a 128-page ruling which dismissed Depp's lawsuit and held that *The Sun*'s article was "substantially true." He added that the incident in Australia, described above, "must have been terrifying [for Heard]," and wrote, "I accept that Mr. Depp put her in fear of her life."

Judge Nicol acknowledged the risk that Heard took in speaking out about her former husband, stating, "I also accept that Ms. Heard's allegations have had a negative effect on her career as an actor and activist."

Four years before the London trial, when I represented Heard at the time of her divorce case, Heard described to me one-on-one, and also to others in my presence (a mediator, opposing counsel, her full legal team, and during her sworn deposition, which I defended), the very same details that she told at the London trial, including the details of the incident in Australia. Her detailed factual account was consistent each of those four times in 2016, and also at the London trial four years later. Her account did not waver. In my experience, when a person is making something up, the details of their facts tend to change each time they tell it, and particularly years later. The details that Heard told me multiple times in 2016, and that she testified to in the London court in 2020, did not change at all. You can draw your own conclusions. I believed Heard in 2016, and believe her just as much today.

Obviously I was not there when Heard was with Depp during their marriage, and will never know with certainty what actually happened. I am not being paid by her, I'm not owed anything from her, and I have no expectation of working for her in the future—she has other counsel. I have no reason to spin this story one way or another. My only interest is the truth. That said, Judge Nicol reached his conclusion following a three-week trial with numerous witnesses (including both Depp and Heard) and numerous documents including emails, text messages, photographs and the like.

* * *

AT THE TIME of this writing, Depp still had a defamation lawsuit pending in Virginia against Heard regarding a December 2018 op-ed she wrote in *The Washington Post* about domestic violence. Her opinion piece, which was very articulate in my opinion (you can find it by Googling "Amber Heard Washington Post 2018"), talks about abuse against women generally—it does not make any specific reference to Depp.

"Two years ago, I became a public figure representing domestic abuse, and I felt the full force of our culture's wrath for women who speak out," Heard wrote. "Friends and advisers told me I would never again work as an actress—that I would be blacklisted. A movie I was attached to recast my role. I had just shot a two-year campaign as the face of a global fashion brand, and the company dropped me.... I had the rare vantage point of seeing, in real time, how institutions protect men accused of abuse."

Heard urged readers to support women who come forward with abuse allegations and elect politicians who will fight for "changes to laws and rules and social norms." Three months later, Depp filed his lawsuit. What exactly she said in this op-ed that was a false statement of fact about Depp (a requirement for a defamation claim) is still a mystery to me. Depp filed in Virginia, presumably because of its proximity to the *Post*'s printing plant in nearby Springfield, rather than in Los Angeles County, where he and Heard both live, and presumably also because Virginia had a very weak anti-SLAPP law at the time, while California's was and is one of the strongest in the nation. (For more about anti-SLAPP laws, see Chapter 5.) Heard could have anti-SLAPPed the lawsuit if it had been filed in Los Angeles, but at the time, she couldn't in Virginia. The case remains pending and, as of this writing, is scheduled for a jury trial on May 3, 2021. We'll see if Depp insists on dragging everyone through that case too. Hopefully the judge will determine that the article does not make specific reference to Depp, does not make a false statement of fact about him, is a classic example of a person (Heard) exercising her Constitutionally-protected right to free speech and free expression under the First Amendment, and will dismiss the case without the need for a trial.

* * *

IN LATE JUNE 2020, on the eve of the London trial, the *Pirates* franchise reportedly passed on Depp and announced an all-female cast for an upcoming film. At the conclusion of the London trial, Depp's London barrister, David Sherborne, called the "wife-beater" allegation by *The Sun* a "reputation-destroying, career-ending allegation."

Assuming Depp's career was hanging in the balance from 2018 through spring 2020, I don't see how his two lawsuits, against *The Sun* and Heard, could possibly help his prospects. They generated one shocking news story after another, hundreds of such articles in all, which is *not* something that a person would want while trying to revive their reputation and career.

Not all of the bad news stories were about alleged abuse of Heard. Some, for example, covered Depp's testimony at the London trial that he had once told his then-13-year-old daughter to ask him for marijuana when she was ready to try it. "It's a safety issue," Depp explained. He said she later came to him to say she was "ready," and he then supplied her with the drug, and was a "good father" for having done so.

Depp, who has acknowledged heavy use of a plethora of drugs including marijuana, cocaine, Ecstasy and magic mushrooms, and an addiction to opioid painkillers, testified: "You don't want your 13-year-old going into some paranoid tailspin.... I knew that the marijuana I had myself, that I smoke myself, is trustworthy, is a good quality and I was bound and determined not to have her try any drugs out there in the world because it's too dangerous."

The things that Depp has admitted to would cause a reasonable person to wonder what all he is capable of. He has admitted that he does large amounts of illicit drugs. That he is extremely jealous. That he has done extremely erratic things like writing in blood on mirrors and walls with a severed finger. He has admitted he gave his daughter marijuana when she was a very young teen, and says that he is a good father for doing it. He has admitted to sending a friend texts about killing his wife, Heard, and "f---ing her burnt corpse." And on and on.

This would certainly give any potential employer pause when considering him for a film—particularly a family-oriented studio like Disney, and for family-oriented movie franchises like *Pirates* and *Harry Potter*.

* * *

On Nov. 6, 2020, only five days after the Depp verdict by Judge Nicol, Warner Bros. dropped Johnny Depp from the high-budget film *Fantastic Beasts 3*. The move was not unexpected, and highlights Depp's lack of foresight and common sense in filing that U.K. lawsuit in the first place. Even after Heard's allegations of abuse in 2016, Depp's career was still alive, though damaged. He was still cast in a major *Harry Potter* franchise film; J.K. Rowling, author and creator of the *Harry Potter* franchise, was standing by him. If Depp had simply moved on from his acrimonious marriage to Heard (she certainly was not talking about him), Depp would still be working today, and likely would have eventually made it back into the *Pirates* franchise and many other films. But Depp, for some reason, felt it necessary to "go for broke" and sue *The Sun* as well as Heard. Or perhaps he could not resist lashing out once again at his ex. As a result, Depp lost the trial, and with it, what was left of his career.

26

HEROES

E very few months, someone will tell me that they're a "fan" of mine because of my work, or say or imply that I'm a "hero" for taking down Gawker. I don't consider myself a hero at all, but there are many people who inspire me. Here are *my* personal heroes, listed in no particular order because they are impossible for me to rank.

* * *

WOLFGANG AMADEUS MOZART and **Ludwig van Beethoven.** I group them together because they are two of the greatest musical geniuses the world has ever known. They worked around the clock to write some of the most spectacular music ever created, and that ever will be. My first introduction to these icons was in high school: a class on classical music, with a terrific teacher who broke it down to its most basic concept—*What is music?*—and went from there. I was hooked. So much so that in college I took several classical music classes and even petitioned to create my own major (something that occasionally happened at UC Santa Cruz), to study Austro-German humanities between 1700 and 1850 with a focus on history, music, literature, architecture and art of that time. My request was denied. I've wondered how my life might have turned out differently had it been granted. I might have gone on to graduate school in the area and become a professor.

People have been marveling at the music of Mozart and Beethoven for 200 years, and probably will be listening to it for another 500 years or more. How many of today's artists will still be remembered in 700 years?

* * *

Nancy Grade. She was my fifth-grade teacher. She was a really terrific person. I don't think I realized how terrific she was at the time. She had this way of educating her students that made them feel good about themselves, about their fellow classmates, and about learning. She was a natural leader. She could've been the leader of a city or even bigger, if she had decided to go in that direction. She had this rare natural ability to make people happy and do their best. (If only our politicians were as skilled.) I strive to emulate her every day.

* * *

Cesar Chavez. He is remembered mainly for his work to improve treatment, pay, and working conditions for farm workers. He organized migrant laborers who had no rights and were being treated horrendously. But Chavez was more than that. He was a civil rights leader who championed nonviolent social change, and also crusaded for the environment and consumer rights. He didn't just talk about it: He literally dedicated his life to his causes. Long before he co-founded the National Farm Workers Association, which later became the United Farm Workers labor union, Chavez knew firsthand the plight of these laborers. Born near Yuma, Arizona, in 1927, Chavez and his family toiled as migrant workers after losing their own farm during the Great Depression. As he worked in the fields, orchards, and vineyards of California during his youth, he was exposed to the injustices of the life of a farm worker.

Chavez led powerfully and didn't back down. He also didn't believe in violence: He organized marches, led boycotts, went on hunger strikes—including a 36-day fast, when he was 61 years old, to bring attention to the problem of pesticide poisoning of farm workers and their children. He turned down opportunities for a more comfortable life and remained in relative poverty with his wife and eight children until he died. None of it was easy. For a century, others with greater resources had tried to organize farm workers, and failed. Many believed it couldn't be done. His motto was *"Si se puede"* ("Yes, it can be done"). He's a true American hero.

One of my favorite books that I've ever read is *The Circuit: Stories From the Life of a Migrant Child* by Francisco Jiménez. He is now a professor at Santa Clara University in California. The book is about his childhood. My sons were assigned the book in middle school, and I picked it up and read it in a day, and then bought the next two books in the series (my sons were not assigned those) and I read them too. I don't read many books, and rarely get past chapter three in anything, but these books were simple and very compelling—they told the true story of a boy who grew up in a family of migrant farm workers in California, and covered both their struggles and their celebrations. Definitely worth a read.

* * *

RORION AND ROYCE GRACIE. These brothers (whose first names are pronounced "Horion" and "Hoyce") introduced Brazilian jujitsu to America. The martial art is based on the ancient Japanese art of jujitsu, developed by the samurai for when they were off their horse, without weapons, and fighting their enemy hand-to-hand. The Brazilian version was developed in Rio de Janeiro by Rorion and Royce's father and uncle. It is based on grappling and ground fighting, focusing on the skill of controlling an opponent through techniques that force him to submit. It is highly effective, as has been proven in no-holds-barred competitions like the UFC.

Rorion came to America in the mid-1970s with almost nothing. He began teaching his family's technique, which they had developed and perfected since the 1920s, out of his garage in Torrance, California. Rorion was an entrepreneur. He'd take his students to different martial arts studios in the area and challenge the owner of the studio —like a seventh-degree karate master or sixth-degree kung fu master —to a sparring match with no gloves and no rules. Rorion would routinely put the other master on his back and apply an inescapable chokehold within two minutes. Because of the technique, it looked ridiculously easy. He'd challenge masters of tai kwon do, hapkido, aikido—you name it—and beat them all, easily. He would have a student film these challenge sessions, make highlight tapes and sell them. He wanted to show that "Gracie jujitsu" was a grappling technique worth incorporating into any of the martial arts that relied primarily on kicking and punching. Rorion later co-founded the UFC (the Ultimate Fighting Championship) where masters of different fighting arts would go up against each other, with no gloves and virtually no rules. (The UFC later incorporated thin gloves and a few basic rules.) Rorion's brother, Royce, won several of the initial UFC competitions and was the first fighter inducted into the UFC Hall of Fame. I trained at the Gracie jujitsu academy in Torrance for two years starting around 1995. Most of the classes in my second year were taught by Royce Gracie himself.

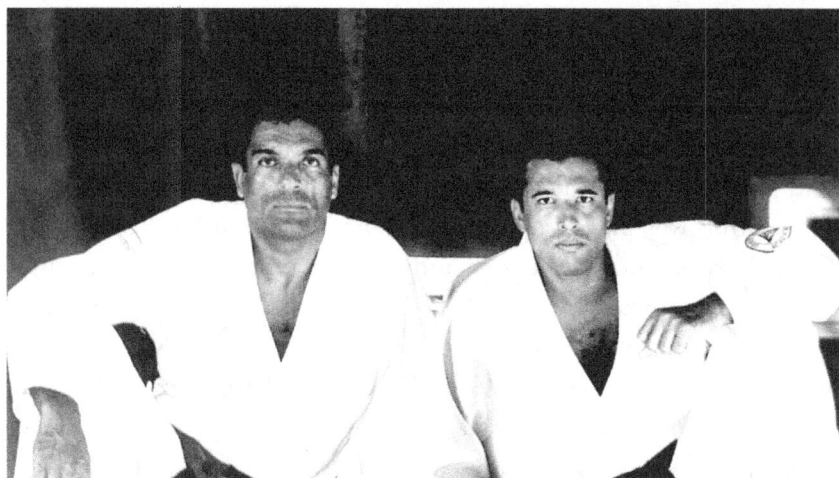

Brothers Rorion and Royce Gracie

These brothers were pioneers. They're brave and confident but not cocky. They're athletic but also smart and strategic. They are also extremely nice and humble. They started with virtually nothing and completely transformed the world of martial arts.

* * *

AMELIA EARHART. She's mostly known for her most famous feat: becoming the first woman (and the second person) to fly solo across the Atlantic. The mystery of her disappearance and death continue to make her the subject of fascination. I admire her fearlessness. She had great courage, which allowed her to become an aviation pioneer. But down on solid earth, she didn't follow the norms of the day. She didn't care about society's expectations of what a lady should be. She faced prejudice, doubt and disapproval from the time she was a little girl who loved climbing trees and hunting rodents with a .22 rifle. She went into a male-dominated field, put on a flight suit, and decided to take on world records and break down social barriers in the process.

* * *

THE MONTGOMERY BUS RIDERS. Rosa Parks was the *fourth* person in Montgomery, Alabama, in 1955 to be arrested for refusing to yield her seat on a bus to a white passenger. Three others before her, that same year and in that same city, two of them teenagers, were arrested for the same exact thing. Parks worked for the NAACP and they decided to generate publicity around her arrest and challenge the law, so Parks has the place in the history books. But I often think about the three others who preceded her. They did the same thing and should be recognized just as much:

1. **Claudette Colvin**, age 15, was arrested on March 2, 1955, nine months before the arrest of Rosa Parks. Colvin was on a field trip with her class from the segregated Booker T. Washington High School. Her class had been learning about the civil rights movement, and she wrote a paper that very day about how wrong it was that black people were prohibited from using dressing rooms at clothing stores. When her class was on the bus, returning from the field trip, new riders boarded at a stop. Three of her classmates complied with the bus driver's instructions (and the law) by yielding their seats to white passengers who wanted seats. Colvin didn't get up. "History kept me stuck to my seat," Colvin later explained. "I felt the hand of Harriet Tubman pushing down on one shoulder and Sojourner Truth pushing down on the other." The bus driver called the police, and two white male police officers boarded the bus, forcibly removed her, handcuffed her, and drove her to the police station—and made inappropriate comments about her body including trying to guess her bra size. Her minister bailed her out of jail and told her she had "just brought the revolution to Montgomery." Colvin wanted to become president of the United States one day. (I would have voted for her.)

2. **Aurelia S. Browder**, age 37, was arrested in Montgomery on April 29, 1955, seven months before Parks, for refusing to yield her seat on the bus to a white passenger and move to the back.

3. **Mary Louise Smith**, age 18, was arrested in Montgomery on Oct. 21, 1955, six weeks before Parks, for refusing to give up her seat on the bus to a white passenger and move to the back.

Colvin, Browder and Smith were plaintiffs in a 1956 federal lawsuit titled *Browder v. Gayle*, which challenged the constitutionality of state and local laws on bus segregation. When 15-year-old Colvin was being forcibly removed from the bus by two police officers, she shouted that her constitutional rights were being violated. She was 100 percent right. A three-judge panel of the U.S. District Court ruled 2-1 that the laws were unconstitutional, and in November 1956, the U.S. Supreme Court affirmed.

4. **Rosa Parks**, age 42, was arrested in Montgomery on Dec. 1, 1955, for refusing to yield her seat on the bus to a white passenger and move to the back.

All four were very brave. All four should be remembered equally as civil rights icons. Unfortunately, three of them remain largely unknown. All four of them are my heroes, starting with Claudette Colvin: the first one, the youngest one, and perhaps the bravest one.

* * *

JESUS CHRIST. I'm not a particularly religious person. But he left the most significant legacy in the history of the world. He'll be remembered for as long as humans are around. I think that's astounding. There's no TV footage of Jesus. He didn't write books; he didn't blog. There are no audio recordings, and he wasn't an influencer in the way we use that term today. But he must have been quite something to create such an impression on people.

In an era dominated by brutality, Jesus went against the norms of "eye for an eye" and taught instead to "turn the other cheek." Many people responded so massively to him. He was reacting to what was happening in the world, in a way that inspired and connected to people for 2,000 years. It's because of Jesus that we have people like Martin Luther King Jr., Mother Teresa, and many other courageous individuals who have made positive change in the world by standing up for what they believe. No one had a more profound, lasting impact on the human race than the original, one and only, J.C. himself.

* * *

Pastor Cash Luna. The founder and lead pastor of the Guatemala-based Casa de Dios church is one of my favorite living people. He's so impressive. He's a gentle person and cares about people in a way that's almost indescribable. His heart is the size of his whole body. That is what makes Univision's false stories about him so appalling. (For more on that case, turn to Chapter 30.) Pastor Luna embodies love, charity and goodness. He started with a congregation of three families that met in a living room, and turned it into one of the largest churches in Latin America. He uses his position and his church to help the poor, the sick, and those in need of spiritual guidance, and to speak out against corruption in his country and his region. Univision horribly defamed him, but I am blessed to have had the opportunity to meet him, get to know him, and represent him and his church in a righteous case.

* * *

Nurses. All nurses. They are, collectively, my hero. They're my favorite group of people in the world. As a group, they are spectacular human beings. It's incredible how kind, thoughtful and nurturing they are. They deal with some of the worst aspects of illness and aging—stuff that's not pretty. Doctors, of course, are heroes too. But the nature of the profession, from my observation, is that nurses spend far more time with patients, get them everything they need, help to ease their suffering, handle duties that are far less glamorous than doctors—things like changing bed pans and catheters. And they are paid a fraction of what doctors make.

Nurses launched even higher into the hero stratosphere during the Covid-19 pandemic. They put their lives on the line just by going to work each day. Many moved to the crisis zones to provide help where it was most needed, and many died while treating people suffering from the virus. Nurses took on a heart-wrenching new role amidst the horror: comforting the dying while loved ones were relegated to goodbyes on FaceTime or speakerphone. In the face of unimaginable suffering, nurses proved they are true modern heroes, as frontline as any soldier in active battle. I'm with the street artist Banksy, who put it this way:

* * *

DR. MARTIN LUTHER KING JR. The summer before I started college, I was assigned the book *Let the Trumpet Sound* to read for my first college course. What began as a forced reading assignment quickly became both a very enjoyable read and a transforming experience, before I even stepped foot in a college class. It was a lesson in the ultimate good vs. evil fight in America. The evil was racism, oppression, dehumanization, humiliation, injustice, poverty, suffering and murder. The good was the civil rights movement, all who participated in it, led by Dr. King, and the eternal hope of a better future. Dr. King was the ultimate champion: He kept fighting no matter how many times he was jailed, beaten, defamed or knocked down—physically, emotionally, professionally. He got back up, kept his eyes on the prize, and made huge positive change for everyone in this country and beyond. Everyone. A few days before I turned 50, I went on an eight-day road trip from New Orleans to Nashville. (See Chapter 34.) My No. 1 stop on this trip was the converted Lorraine Motel in Memphis, Tennessee, where MLK was gunned down on the second-floor balcony. It was an intensely moving experience.

Dr. King was in the eye of the storm. He was young and talented, and didn't need to devote his life to one cause, or put himself in danger. But he did, and went full bore. Ultimately he was killed by the evil, but it inspired millions to pick up the torch and carry on his movement.

The walls of my 6,500-square-foot office are decorated primarily with modern art. In the whole space, there is only one photo that hangs on any wall, and it hangs in my personal office. It's the iconic black-and-white image of Dr. King in his SCLC office with a framed picture of Mahatma Gandhi on the wall. It was given to me by Dr. King's personal photographer in the last two years of his life, Bob Fitch. (Fitch later became the personal photographer of Cesar Chavez.) Anytime I feel overwhelmed or just need some inspiration, I think about how whatever I'm going through is nothing compared to what Dr. King went through nearly every day of his adult life. Dr. King's famous quote from his 1963 Letter From Birmingham Jail has guided me through my career as an attorney: "Injustice anywhere is a threat to justice everywhere."

* * *

MOTHER TERESA AND MAGNUS MACFARLANE-BARROW. Everyone knows the iconic Mother Teresa, the Catholic nun who in 1950 founded the Missionaries of Charity in Calcutta, India, one of the poorest places in the world. It grew to include more than 4,500 nuns giving aid to the extremely sick and poor in 133 countries. The congregation continues to manage homes for terminally ill people, and runs orphanages, schools, soup kitchens, and mobile health clinics.

Mother Teresa was canonized by Pope Francis on Sept. 4, 2016, in Saint Peter's Square, Vatican City.

Magnus MacFarlane-Barrow was a fish farmer in Scotland who, with his brother Fergus, in 1992 decided to organize a local appeal for blankets and food to aid the residents of war-torn Bosnia. They drove 30 hours one way from Scotland to Bosnia to deliver the donated supplies and returned home to Scotland, expecting to return to work. Instead they found a shed chock full of donations that had poured in while they were gone—so they made a second trip to Bosnia. This led to a third trip, then a fourth, and on and on, until eventually they completed *23 trips* to deliver the donated goods.

Magnus decided to not return to work, and instead dedicated his life to charity. During a trip to Malawi in 2002, a light bulb went off: Incentivize hungry children to attend school by providing meals at the school. For many, it was their only meal of the day. His organization, Mary's Meals, went from feeding 200 children in schools in 2002, to feeding more than 1.5 million children every school day, in 13 different countries. MacFarlane-Barrow was featured as a CNN "Hero" in 2010 (this is how I first learned of him). In April 2015, he was named one of *Time* magazine's 100 most influential people in the world. His 2016 book, *The Shed That Fed a Million Children*, was a *New York Times* best-seller in the U.K. MacFarlane-Barrow is the exemplar of a person who leaves a career to spend the rest of his (or her) life helping the poorest and neediest in the world to be fed, receive an education and go from hopelessness to a chance at success in life.

27

WORKING WITH THE PRESIDENT AND
FIRST LADY

In 2017, my wife, Kathleen, and I were invited to a White House holiday party. I was really excited to receive the invitation and felt that I was part of a very small group of "dignitaries." Then I learned the White House has 16 holiday parties, each with around 300 guests, and my perception of my importance returned back to earth, where it belongs. Still, it was a thrill to receive the invitation and attend.

I had represented first lady Melania Trump earlier that year in a defamation case against the *Daily Mail,* aka the Mail Online. The British-based news outlet, which boasts that it is "the most visited English-language newspaper website in the world," had run a horrible false story about her, and Mrs. Trump and her husband were pleased with the outcome: a $2.925 million settlement payment to Mrs. Trump, plus a very extensive retraction and apology. (For more on the case, see Chapter 13.)

Kathleen and I flew to Washington the night before the party. We stayed at the historic Willard Hotel, a short block from the White House. During our flight, I had received a message from Jared Kushner, who is married to Ivanka Trump, the president's daughter; both were senior advisers to the president and worked in the West Wing. I was handling a minor matter for Kushner and he wanted to have a short discussion. Once out of the plane, I responded that I was in D.C. and could discuss with him in person the next day, before the White House holiday party, or by phone any time before the party. He said, let's meet in person.

So the next evening, after visiting two of my favorite museums—the American Art Museum and National Portrait Gallery—housed in the same building, Kathleen and I dressed up and went to the White House. Party guests normally line up outside, in the cold, to go through the East Entrance. We went straight in through the West Entrance, to go to the West Wing for my meeting. Kathleen was able to sit in a waiting area, with an enormous Christmas tree and a room full of beautiful holiday decorations, while I met with Kushner for about 20 minutes. My wife and I then were escorted by a West Wing staffer over to the Residence for the party. We exited to a covered outdoor walkway—the West Wing Colonnade—where the staffer pointed out the French doors leading into the iconic Oval Office just a few feet away, and then next to us was the equally iconic Rose Garden, where presidents for more than a hundred years have delivered important speeches to press and dignitaries. We then were led into the Residence, where the party was about to begin.

* * *

WE WERE EARLY. We were pretty much the *only* guests at the party when we arrived. But we weren't alone; the parties are staffed with White House staff who serve food and drinks, as well as a large number of members of the five branches of the military. Wearing their dress uniforms, these military volunteers help guests with anything they need: taking pictures of them with the guests' smartphones, offering to get them a drink or food, taking plates and glasses away, and the thing that I like the most: answering questions. The military volunteers are just as interested as I am about the building and its history, can answer almost any question, and also tell you stories about things that happened in the White House "just over there" (pointing). And they all are extremely nice as well as knowledgeable and helpful.

The holiday decorations that year were spectacular. The first lady and her staff worked on them, I assume for months in advance. They were gorgeous, classic, tasteful, colorful and sublime. You can see photos by going to Google Images and searching "White House Christmas Decorations 2017." And there were so many rooms to decorate! Here is a floorplan of the main floor of the Residence:

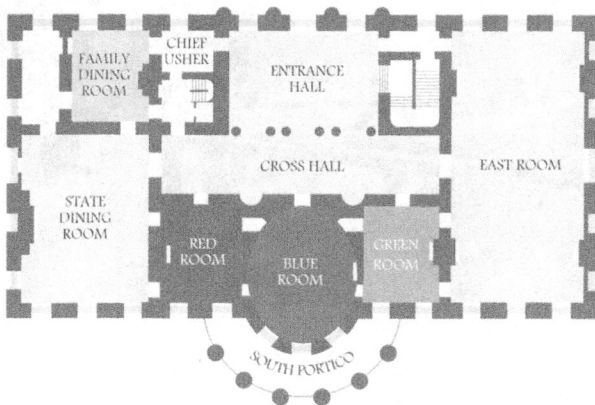

There also is a downstairs area just as large. The two main rooms of the main floor are the East Room and the State Dining Room where state dinners are held. Each of those rooms had a long table in the middle with lots of food: crudité, breads, cheeses, fried chicken, mac 'n' cheese, lamb chops, and many more items. There is a separate carving station, with roast beef and roast turkey. There also is a station with tons of supercute, homemade and decorated Christmas cookies, and bowls full of homemade eggnog: spiked and unspiked. A full bar in each room provides any drink you'd like, and trays of wine and Champagne are passed around as well.

White House holiday party 2017: the State Dining Room with a table full of holiday food, White House staff and an original portrait of Abraham Lincoln above the fireplace.

At the end of the party, guests are encouraged by White House staff to take the Christmas cookies home. Funny story: We also attended the 2019 White House holiday party, two years later, and while we were packing at home, Kathleen got out the purse she was going to bring, which she had not used since the 2017 White House holiday party. What was inside? A White House napkin with two Christmas cookies from the 2017 White House party! The cookies had lived in her purse, wrapped in a napkin, for two years! I immediately took a photo and texted it to the first lady. We had a laugh with her about it two days later at the 2019 holiday party.

*2017 White House Christmas cookies, discovered in my
wife's purse in December 2019 while packing to attend
that year's White House holiday party.*

The East Room and the State Dining Room are filled with decorations, including numerous Christmas trees and holiday displays. Some of the most memorable displays were a 350-pound gingerbread replica of the White House, and a wood-and-terra cotta nativity scene built in Naples, Italy, in the 18th century that has been a fixture at White House holiday parties since the 1960s.

Between the two large halls are the Red Room, the Blue Room and the Green Room. Each has a Christmas tree in the middle. Some rooms have a giant one, like the Blue Room—which was 18 feet tall—and some have a smaller one. Holiday decorations are all around the rooms. The rooms are a place to look around, mingle and take photos. Military volunteers are on hand to help guests by taking their photos and answering their questions. While the Red Room is very red, and the Green Room is very green, the Blue Room is actually very *yellow*. It has yellow walls, with blue drapes, and blue trim on the walls up near the ceiling. All three rooms are very beautiful, and the holiday decorations are gorgeous. The 18-foot Christmas tree in the large, oval Blue Room was particularly impressive.

One of my favorite parts of the White House Christmas party is the music. The Marine Band is made up of 17 to 20 instrumentalists playing strings (violins, cellos) and woodwinds. They play classic Christmas songs—instrumental only, no singers. The band is spot-on fantastic, and they perform in the Entrance Hall (see floorplan above), with marble floors and a high ceiling. The music fills the air throughout the entire main floor of the Residence.

Those with an invitation to take a photo with the president and first lady go downstairs. Photos are done in the Diplomatic Reception Room, a large oval-shaped room one floor directly below the Blue Room which is oval and the same dimensions. A long line forms in an adjacent room, and it can take an hour for guests to finally enter the photo room. Once inside, a person takes your name and that of your guest(s) and then announces out loud to the first couple the names, such as: "John Smith and wife Mary Jones." The president and first lady then say hello and exchange a few words with the guests. Men stand next to the first lady, and women stand next to the president for the photo. Handlers then usher you out to make way for the next guests to take their photo with the first couple. The photos turn out beautifully: the room, the lighting—it all looks spectacular. The 8-by-10 photo arrives in the mail a week or so after the party, in a large envelope with a piece of cardboard to prevent it from bending.

* * *

THE HOLIDAY PARTY photo in December 2017 was the first time I had met President Trump in person. I had spoken to him on the telephone, but it took over a year before I met him in person.

The holiday party we attended in 2017 was governors' night, so all or nearly all of the Republican governors from around the U.S. were in attendance with their spouses. I assume one of the holiday parties is U.S. senators' night, and a few of the parties might be U.S. representatives' night, for members of the House (who outnumber senators more than 4-to-1). In 2019, we attended the party for the Republican National Committee higher-ups. We never know which night is which group—we simply choose a night that works with our schedule, because holidays are such a busy time and we have to fly out for the party.

With my wife, Kathleen, at the 2019 White House holiday party, standing in the doorway to the Blue Room with its 18-foot Christmas tree.

In 2017, we spoke to the new governor of Indiana, Eric Holcomb, and his wife, Janet, who were super nice, as one would expect from Midwesterners. He had been lieutenant governor and was elevated when the governor he was serving under, Mike Pence, became vice president. In 2019, we sat with Kelly Loeffler, who had just been appointed by the governor of Georgia to be the next U.S. senator to represent Georgia. She had not yet been sworn in, and was going through her orientation. I asked her about what I called "Senate school," which sounded fascinating to me. We also sat with her husband, Jeffrey Sprecher, who was chairman of the New York Stock Exchange. They were in the process of moving from Atlanta to Washington, D.C., and it was fun to share, if just for a few minutes, that exciting time of their lives.

Back to 2017: After the party, Kathleen and I returned to the Willard Hotel. Charles Dickens, Buffalo Bill, Mark Twain, P.T. Barnum and Abraham Lincoln have all slept in this historic building. Julia Ward Howe wrote "The Battle Hymn of the Republic" in her room there early one morning, and Ulysses S. Grant, while staying at the hotel, frequented the beautiful lobby and coined the term "lobbyists" there. We were getting a drink after the holiday party in the hotel's famous Round Robin bar (where many political deals have been struck, going back over 100 years) when I received a text from the first lady. She asked if I could meet with the president the next morning in the Oval Office.

* * *

WE WERE SCHEDULED to fly back to Los Angeles the next morning. Kathleen said, "You stay and take the meeting, I'm going home to take care of our children." As I prepared to meet with the president, I realized that I had brought an extra dress shirt with me, but only one tie —the one that I had just worn to the holiday party and in our photo with the first couple. It was a really nice tie that Kathleen had bought just for the White House party. In fact, it was by far the most expensive tie that I have ever owned. But I couldn't wear the *same tie* to my meeting with the president the very next morning in the Oval Office. Most stores in the area were not open before my meeting. I checked the ties in the hotel lobby, but didn't care for them. The only store that was open was Marshall's, right behind the hotel. I quickly browsed the racks of the discount chain store and settled on a solid red tie. It was $6.99.

So getting ready for my first meeting ever with a president of the United States, I went from wearing the most expensive tie I've ever owned the night before, to the least expensive tie I've ever owned, and headed out the door for the Oval Office. It is a gorgeous room: super-high ceilings, magnificent light pouring in through the wall of windows by the president's desk. President Trump was very welcoming, had tons of energy, and was fun to listen to. I was not prepared for how funny he is. The president made me laugh out loud multiple times during the meeting—and I didn't do it out of politeness or deference to the leader of the free world. He has a genuine knack for humor and is a naturally gregarious and entertaining fellow. In the following two years, I would visit the President about four more times in the Oval Office, and once at the Trump Hotel in Las Vegas, to discuss the cases that I had with him. He preferred to discuss the cases in person, rather than over the phone, although I probably spoke to him 15 to 20 times over the phone as well.

I was also struck by Melania Trump's sense of humor when I worked with her on the *Daily Mail* case. Her humor usually does not come across in still photos and short video clips played on the news. She is naturally very beautiful, but in photos often looks steely and serious. During the *Daily Mail* case, we spent some 30 to 40 hours together in meetings or traveling. We would talk about the case, of course, but also chatted about our families. To give you a sense of our proximity in age: On the day in 2020 when she turned 50, my wife and I were both 50 too, and her son, Barron, was the same age as my two sons: 14. So we have a few things in common.

The first lady is very positive, very poised. A lovely person, with excellent manners. Pleasant to talk to, and naturally very funny. We spent as much as 10 hours per day in two different all-day mediation sessions, which typically have lots of down time. She kept me laughing with just small talk.

28

CDA 230: THE TRILLIONAIRES' PROTECTION ACT

Remember when the search for the perfect slice of pizza, a reliable house painter, a clean hotel room or a trustworthy dentist involved word-of-mouth recommendations, catchy ads, letting your fingers do the walking in the Yellow Pages, or (shudder!) taking a gamble and just trying something new? My children won't ever know that world. Yelp and other review websites have made information, photos and opinions from a multitude of strangers instantly available at the tap of a screen.

The upside, of course, is the trove of information you can peruse before ever making a choice. It is endless. There is a downside too, as a hard-working attorney named Dawn Hassell knows all too well. Hassell runs a small personal injury firm in San Francisco. She is great at her job, and acts ethically and responsibly. She and her firm had hundreds of consistent five-star reviews on Yelp when one day in January 2013 a former client gave the Hassell Law Group a one-star review on the site—and defamed Hassell in the process.

The former client, Ava Bird, did not simply share negative opinions, which—if truthful—would be perfectly acceptable. Writing under a pseudonym, Bird falsely stated, among many other things, that Hassell and her firm "didn't ever speak with the insurance company ... nor did they bother to communicate with me, the client or the insurance company AT ALL. then, she dropped the case because ... her mother [broke her leg]."

In reality, Hassell's firm *did* respond to all of the client's communications, *did* contact the insurance company, obtained a settlement offer from the insurance company, and communicated that offer to the client, who didn't want to accept it and then blew off communications by the firm's attorneys.

Bird's post contained numerous provably false statements that had the real potential of costing the firm business. Hassell responded with a detailed post on Yelp, addressing the incorrect claims and explaining that the negative review was likely retaliation for the firm withdrawing from representing Bird because of Bird's lack of cooperation—nothing to do with Hassell's mother.

Hassell also asked Bird to correct the review to make it accurate, or remove it, but Bird refused. Bird then posted two more times about Hassell's firm, stating in one of them:

"dawn hassell has lied about EVERYTHING! she can't seem to be able to see, understand, speak or write the truth. she is an extremely toxic and dangerous pathological liar. she has been unable, through her own greed, dishonesty and stupidity, to deliver the truth. NOTHING SHE HAS SAID IS TRUE! ... dawn hassell has continued to push her lies, deceit and crooked business practices to the total extreme.... SHE HERSELF CREATED THROUGH HER OWN OBVIOUS FAILURES AND REFUSAL TO DO HER JOB, OUTRIGHT INCOMPETENCE, GROSS NEGLIGENCE AND A FAILURE TO TELL THE TRUTH"

Hassell asked Yelp to remove the posts, pointing out that they were factually false and a violation of Yelp's own policies, but Yelp refused. Hassell was left with no other option but to sue Bird for defamation, and did so in April 2013.

Bird didn't respond to the complaint and was defaulted. At a later hearing, Hassell presented her evidence, and the judge found the posts to be defamatory and ordered Bird to remove the defamatory posts. Bird refused. The judge also awarded Hassell $558,000 in damages, which were never collected.

* * *

HASSELL THEN ASKED the court for an order requiring Yelp to take down the defamatory posts, and the court issued one. Yelp then entered the case and filed a motion for reconsideration so that it could be heard on the issue. The court denied Yelp's challenge to the take-down order. Yelp then took the ruling to the California Court of Appeal—where Yelp lost again. But the San Francisco-based company, which was valued at around $4 billion in 2013, steadfastly refused to comply with the court order to remove Bird's posts, which the court ruled were defamatory.

Yelp appealed to the California Supreme Court. Yelp claimed it was immune from any order of the California courts because of Section 230 of the Communications Decency Act. Section 230 states that "No provider or user of an interactive computer service shall be treated as the publisher or speaker of any information provided by another information content provider." That text has been interpreted by courts to mean that owners of websites and social media platforms cannot be held "liable" for user-generated content unless the site or platform actively creates or edits the content. But Hassell wasn't seeking to hold Yelp liable for money damages, only compliance with an earlier order to remove a post at Yelp that the trial judge had determined, based on evidence, was defamatory and thus illegal.

Hassell had her own counsel in the case, but when the issue headed to the California Supreme Court, it was important enough for my firm to weigh in. We filed an *amicus curiae* brief in support of Hassell's position. It's a type of brief filed in appellate courts for an outsider, like my firm, to express its views on an important issue. Ours was one of two *amicus* briefs filed for Hassell. For Yelp, *14 different law firms* filed *amicus* briefs representing a vast array of digital sites and platforms including Google, Twitter and Airbnb, among many others. We calculated the total market cap of the companies that filed *amicus* briefs in support of Yelp: It was over $3 trillion. That's a massive legal weight and corporate value going up against Dawn Hassell, a woman who owns a five-person law firm. This was a true David versus Goliath struggle.

Goliath won. In July 2018, the California Supreme Court ruled 4-3 in favor of Yelp. Three justices in the majority said Yelp was protected by Section 230, while the fourth justice, in a concurring opinion, said Yelp couldn't be forced to remove the content because it wasn't a party in the original lawsuit. Hassell's lawyer, Monique Olivier, called the decision and broad interpretation of Section 230 "an invitation to spread falsehoods on the internet without consequence." She was right.

The case didn't end there. Hassell asked if my firm would represent her in a *writ of certiorari* petition to the U.S. Supreme Court. We said yes, and represented her *pro bono*—free of charge—because we believed very strongly that a court order determining a social media post to be defamatory and ordering it removed needed to be followed, and that billion- and trillion-dollar digital platforms should not be above the law or out of reach of the American court system. I knew that the chances of the high court "granting *cert*" and hearing the case were slim. (See Chapter 16 discussing our *cert* petition for Kathrine McKee against Bill Cosby—another *pro bono* U.S. Supreme Court case that we took on.) The high court grants about 1 percent of all *cert* petitions filed. In January 2019, the Court denied our request, without comment, leaving the California Supreme Court decision in place.

* * *

THE UNFORTUNATE TAKEAWAY from Dawn Hassell's journey is this: Even if a person or company sues and wins a lawsuit against another person for defamation over a false online post, and the court orders the post to be removed, the platform (if in California) can refuse to comply with the court's order. Unless CDA 230 is repealed or amended, the platforms will continue to claim they are above the law and outside the reach of the American court system, and courts throughout the country could start to follow the California Supreme Court and let them.

The reason this is scary for you, me and everyone we know? If you are defamed online, and you want to do something about it, Section 230 might allow the website or platform you are complaining about to completely ignore you, and to automatically win any lawsuit you might file to seek the removal of the defamatory and harmful content. In that situation, you are powerless, while the billion- and trillion-dollar digital platforms like Yelp, Facebook, Twitter and Google can do anything they want. You can still pursue the individual who posts, but Hassell did that, obtained a court order against Bird to remove her posts and pay damages, and Bird ignored it. Forcing an individual to comply with such an order can be very challenging.

During the 2020 election *both* presidential contenders, President Trump and former Vice President Biden, called for revoking and retooling Section 230 in favor of a better system. It's not clear if President Biden will do anything about it during his term, but it was a major step that the two top presidential candidates were critical of CDA 230 because, for decades, hardly any politicians would say a word about it. In terms of changes, at the very least, the new system should require court orders to be followed. No one—including a billion- or trillion-dollar digital platform—should be above the law or outside the reach of the American court system.

There are other measures to be considered. Among them, platforms should at least temporarily remove content if the claimant presents reliable evidence of the information's falsity, to protect the claimant's reputation while the case makes its way through the legal process.

Platforms also should consider contributing to the creation and maintenance of a *private* tribunal—which is truly neutral—that reviews claims and has the power to award reasonable remedies such as temporary and permanent removal. It could be a win-win solution for everyone. A similar example is the ICANN process for challenging the ownership of a domain name: A claimant pays $1,500 for one arbitrator or $4,000 for three arbitrators, who review the complaint and all evidence provided with it (all in paper form—no live testimony) and renders a decision in 60 days. A dispute over a social media post could be that quick and easy—but should not have to be that expensive.

Dawn Hassell won against Yelp at several turns, but they were all Pyrrhic victories. She never received the relief she sought, which was simply the removal of *false and defamatory* Yelp posts regarding her and her business. Seven years after both the trial judge and court of appeal agreed the original post met the legal definition of defamation, Ava Bird's Yelp posts are still sitting there on the page. At least it's been pushed to the bottom by dozens of new five-star reviews. Perhaps in the future, the false garbage that is littering the internet will be cleaned up, and if so, everyone will benefit: people like you and me who search for responsible businesses, the responsible businesses who should not be falsely attacked, and the platforms that benefit from truthful reviews on their sites. False reviews benefit no one.

29

ALASKAN PORTRAITS
AND BARGING HOUSES

My maternal grandmother, Patricia Hamersley (or "Gam," as I called her), was quite a lady. I played a lot of baseball growing up, and early on I remember her playing at our local park with my brother, our neighborhood friends and me. She was quite a hitter and loved to have fun and laugh. "You're a good hitter, Gam," I told her, and she never forgot that.

Her mantra should have been: Never give up and find a way. Because that's what she did.

Gam's childhood was spent in the freezing tundra around Saskatchewan, Canada, and her family (thankfully) moved to the much more civilized and very picturesque small city of Victoria, British Columbia. In her 20s, in search of adventure, she moved to Juneau, Alaska. Around 1940, at the age of 28, she owned four small family portrait studios in four Alaskan cities: Juneau, Anchorage, Fairbanks and Ketchikan. She opened each studio one day of the week. She'd book appointments for each location on its designated day, and would hire a pilot to fly her to the city, where she'd open, take the portraits, close that shop for the next six days, and fly to the next city. The following day, she'd repeat the process, and at the end of the weekly tour, she'd fly back to Juneau. She followed this grueling schedule every week.

She later moved to Portland, Oregon, married my grandfather, had a daughter and son (my mother and uncle Cliff), divorced, remarried, had a second daughter (my aunt Vickie), divorced again, and found herself a single mom with three young children living in north Seattle.

In 1959, when my mother was 14, Gam found a large parcel of land on the waterfront of an island close to Seattle called Bainbridge Island. It is now a very desirable place to live, full of executives of Amazon, Microsoft, Starbucks, Boeing, Costco and other big companies based in the area. But at the time, it was middle class at best, and considered "out in the sticks"—hardly the in-demand enclave it would later become.

Gam found three houses in Northern Seattle, and hired someone to put these three houses onto barges and float them down Puget Sound, put them up onto the property on Bainbridge Island, and hook them up to utilities. She kept the largest house for herself—the one with the best location—and had her son, Cliff, sell off the other two.

Ferry boats still shuttle people and cars from the Seattle waterfront, out to the island and back, several times daily. It's a beautiful 25-minute ride each way, and the town of Winslow, on Bainbridge Island, is a terrific little place to visit. There are lots of cute shops, restaurants, a public house (aka pub) with terrific food, fun atmosphere and a gorgeous view of the harbor; great bakeries, coffee houses, ice creameries, and art galleries all around—a very cute, quaint, coastal Northwestern small town, full of trees and clean air, surrounded by water and with a view of the Seattle skyline.

One of my favorite stories about my grandmother and my mother is set in 1962. It was the World's Fair in Seattle, and the Space Needle was newly built and had just opened. My grandmother got a job working in the gift shop at the top of the Space Needle, in its first year of operation, during the World's Fair. She was friendly and gregarious, the customers loved her, and so did her managers. But the shop was overwhelmed with customers, and they needed help. She suggested hiring my mother, who was 17, and they did. So there they were—mother and daughter, working together at the very top of the brand new, soon-to-be-iconic Space Needle, during the 1962 World's Fair.

30

GOOD VS. EVIL: THE INCREDIBLE CASE OF PASTOR CASH LUNA

"The durability of free speech and free press rests on the simple concept that it search for the truth and tell the truth."
—President Herbert Hoover

I get calls and emails from a plethora of people from all over the globe looking for a top media attorney to take on a U.S. news outlet or media company. I hear all kinds of stories, from the absurd to the outrage-inspiring. I can only take a small fraction of these matters. Running a small law firm, resources are finite and I have to choose cases carefully. That said, I never would have guessed that one day I'd represent a Guatemalan church and its pastor in a lawsuit involving alleged drug trafficking, money laundering, a cocaine-smuggling pilot and one of the most irresponsible media companies ever. But sometimes a case is so unique, and a client so special, you have to say "yes."

Casa de Dios, or House of God, needed help. The church was founded in 1994 with a congregation of only three families, and in 25 years had grown to over 25,000 dedicated worshipers. The church and its pastor, Carlos "Cash" Luna, had been defamed by a Univision "investigation" that was replete with false charges obtained from the sketchiest of sources.[1] The fake news report was tarnishing the good name of the church, and deeply wounding the pastor who leads his followers with all of his heart and soul.

I was all too familiar with Univision. The Miami-based corporation had bought the slayed Gawker Media empire after Hulk Hogan had body slammed it—forcing it into bankruptcy. Univision had kept 99 percent of the Gawker staff employed after the purchase. I was learning more and more about worrisome practices by Univision's separate news division. I was representing the heir of the late Mexican icon and singer-songwriter Juan Gabriel in a lawsuit in state court in Miami against Univision for its false and defamatory reports that his own family members had caused the superstar's death. (In fact, Juan Gabriel died from natural causes after suffering a heart attack—his relatives were hundreds of miles away.)

My partner, Ryan Stonerock, and I met with two representatives of the Guatemalan church in the conference room of our office in Los Angeles. We covered the usual topics: the merits of the case, the expected defense by Univision, the cost of litigating a defamation case. They were all in. In the process, we learned how Univision chose to write about, and defame, Pastor Luna and his church.

In December 2018, Univision published a two-part project titled "Magnates of the Lord." Multiple online stories and TV segments stemming from the project claimed that Pastor Luna was funded, in part, by a drug trafficking and money laundering operation. We investigated and learned that these allegations were 100 percent false.

Univision's stories had the most unreliable source in the universe: a Colombian drug cartel pilot they had interviewed in prison. This guy wasn't just an incarcerated drug smuggler. He was known for habitually and recklessly filing frivolous lawsuits: He sued the judge presiding over his criminal case; he sued the prosecutors; he sued the DEA agents; he sued his own defense lawyers; and he even sued the president of the United States, as well as the first lady. All of these lawsuits were dismissed outright, and a federal judge identified the pilot as a "vexatious litigant" and prohibited him from filing any more suits. The judge presiding over the pilot's criminal case said on the record that he appeared "not mentally competent" and his *own lawyer* said, in open court, that the pilot was "delusional and paranoid." This was Univision's "source" for its story about Pastor Luna and his church.

* * *

Pastor Luna was dragged into the pilot's false story because he happened to live next door to the pilot's boss: a woman the pastor had met only in passing but did not know. Pastor Luna had no idea what she did, nor did anyone else, until she was arrested and the news broke. She was a drug smuggler, but not just any smuggler; she was Marllory Chacón, known as *"La Reina del Sur"* ("The Queen of the South"), described by the U.S. Treasury Department as "one of the most prolific narcotics traffickers in Central America."

Chacón had purchased a residential property next door to Pastor Luna's, years after the pastor had moved in. Over the years, they'd bumped into each other *only twice*: once when she moved into her house and he introduced himself as the next-door neighbor, and once when she saw him at a local restaurant and said hello. He didn't recognize her and thought she was one of the tens of thousands of congregants of his church, and said hello back. She reminded him she was his next-door neighbor, they talked for a minute or two, and that was it. He had no idea she was a drug trafficker, and certainly had no involvement with her or her operation.

Before the pilot's arrest, his job was knowingly transporting cocaine into Guatemala on behalf of a Colombian cartel. In his paranoid and delusional state, he claimed Pastor Luna was Chacón's adviser and right-hand man. (I spoke to the lead DEA agent who prosecuted Chacón and he confirmed that Pastor Luna had *no involvement whatsoever* in her operation. The pastor's name never even came up in his investigation. Chacón also emphatically denies the pilot's story.)

Univision interviewed the pilot when he was in prison for attempted murder and false imprisonment. The pilot made numerous completely delusional statements that would cause any rational reporter to disbelieve every word he said. But this was no rational news organization: It was Univision. So the reporter ignored all of the crazy stuff, and focused instead on the pilot's fantastical, and utterly false, allegations about Pastor Luna. There also was zero corroborating evidence, but Univision ignored that too.

We took on the case. Ryan and I were invited to fly down to Guatemala City to meet with the pastor and his staff. I cannot over-state how impressed I was with this man, his entire organization, every single person around him, and the spectacular building that he built for the church and its offices. The pastor, whose given name is Carlos Enrique Luna Lam, is one of the finest human beings I have ever met in my 51 years on this planet. Have you ever read or watched the original *Grinch Who Stole Christmas*, where his heart is two sizes too small, but then grows three times its normal size on Christmas morning? Pastor Luna's heart is at least 10 times the size of the average person's. He is so passionate about lifting up his poor country, combating corruption, helping people battle poverty, hunger and health issues. He is also a very relaxed and entertaining speaker. He is the very definition of the person you would like to hear speak for 40 minutes every Sunday morning. His message focuses on being a better person and helping your neighbor. That's exactly what he does every Sunday—two services each Sunday, with about 10,000 people at each service. I attended one myself. The pastor's sermon was all about being a good Samaritan, following the Golden Rule, and helping those in need, with a Bible lesson woven in.

Pastor Cash Luna and his wife, Sonia, with the church's logo and 11,000-seat sanctuary in the background.

THE CHURCH OPENED up its files to me—including its hundreds and hundreds of binders containing nearly every donation they've ever received. Whether someone gives the equivalent of $1 during a Sunday service, or tithes 10 percent of their income to the church, it's *all* accounted for. Every dime and every donation card, no matter how large or small. After Univision's story, the church was audited *five times* by five different organizations, several governmental and one a body that governs all churches in Guatemala. The church passed each one of those five audits with flying colors.

I attended the 7 a.m. Sunday service, and got to see what the church is all about. After at least 30 minutes of live music and short sermons by two co-pastors, and a prayer by his very articulate and equally passionate wife, Pastor Luna gave a 40-minute sermon. He is relaxed, naturally funny, self-deprecating, insightful and honest. He smiles a lot. He speaks from the heart, not just about being a good person, but about *truly* being a good Samaritan: having love for your neighbor, helping them as you would help yourself or your family. With tears in his eyes, the pastor tells his congregation how important it is to look out for others—and especially those most in need.

The church owns six large, state-of-the-art medical vehicles that traverse the country 24/7/365 providing free medical services to those who cannot afford them or do not have ready access to doctors or medical facilities. The church also runs a weekly food bank where it facilitates, through donations and hundreds of church volunteers, 2 million meals per year to needy families.

Univision's B.S. story could not be further from the reality of the man or the church. It portrayed him as a morally bankrupt person with an extraordinarily lavish lifestyle, who doesn't care about people and only cares about money. It said he flies around in a private jet, and lives in a giant mansion. The church *does* have a plane, which it purchased when it became too expensive and inconvenient to send the pastor and his staff around the region and Florida, where the church has a large presence, using commercial flights. Pastor Luna does *not* use the church plane when he goes on vacation with his family. He draws a standard salary from the church, and he also has a successful consulting business for other churches in Latin America that want to grow and thrive. All told, he does make a good living in a country with scarce resources. He also has a beautiful house: very tastefully designed with an interior that features pleasant Guatemalan furnishings and art—very little, if anything, is from outside the country. Labor is inexpensive—though he is still paying off the construction. So Univision's narrative about his house is far from the real story.

* * *

WE SENT Univision a letter demanding a retraction and apology in March 2019. Univision responded with the oldest reply in the book: They stood by their story. This even though their big investigative report had two sources: the cocaine-smuggling pilot whose own lawyer said he was "delusional and paranoid" and made "illogical and incoherent statements," and another admitted criminal who spoke anonymously. Plus, neither of these so-called sources corroborated *anything* that the other source said. For any responsible news organization, that would be a huge red flag.

The pastor wanted Univision to take back their lies and admit their mistakes. He just couldn't ignore this portrayal of him and the church, which was the diametric opposite of who and what they really are. Univision refused. We filed a defamation lawsuit in June 2019.

Why sue? Why not turn the other cheek? A large part of the motivation was Pastor Luna's deep concern that Univision would do the same thing to others. The lawsuit is as much about stopping Univision from defaming other people, as it is about having a jury determine that Univision's story was a total lie. The pastor feels it's not right to leave the lies out there, unaddressed.

Pastor Luna is an outspoken critic of corruption that plagues Guatemala and the region, and has for decades. Univision's lies harm his credibility in taking on corruption in the country and around Latin America. In fact, he suspects that someone corrupt, with connections to Univision, may have set up the story for the purpose of undermining his ability to fight corruption—to neutralize his effectiveness. The pastor and the church also want their charitable efforts—the six medical trucks, the massive food bank that feeds the poor, and other activities—to continue and grow. Univision's false story threatens those activities because it could sour members of the congregation and cause potential new members to stay away, thinking Univision's false charges are or might be true.

Univision recklessly put out false accusations, knowing it would cause a waterfall of harm to the church, the pastor and their important efforts. Univision ignored the clear signs that the pilot was a deranged and pathological liar. Pastor Luna is a great man, and his entire church and operation are comprised of great people. He, and they, are being tested by dark forces, and the church is determined to triumph in the end. This is my wish for them too, and my team is working hard to bring about that result. I always want to win for my clients—it's what they hire me to do. But with this case, I feel like I'm fighting on behalf of an even higher power.

SHOULD "CANCEL CULTURE" BE CANCELED?

O n July 7, 2020, a group of 153 artists, writers, and intellectuals made the public case that cancel culture should be ... canceled. *Harry Potter* author J.K. Rowling, one of the 153, tweeted out a link with the message, "I was very proud to sign this letter in defence of a foundational principle of a liberal society: open debate and freedom of thought and speech."

The piece, titled "A Letter on Justice and Open Debate," ran in *Harper's* and the magazine's website. "The free exchange of information and ideas, the lifeblood of a liberal society, is daily becoming more constricted," the letter says, citing "an intolerance of opposing views, a vogue for public shaming and ostracism and the tendency to dissolve complex policy issues in a blinding moral certainty. We uphold the value of robust and even caustic counter-speech from all quarters. But it is now all too common to hear calls for swift and severe retribution in response to perceived transgressions of speech and thought."

The signers include MIT linguist Noam Chomsky, feminist Gloria Steinem, musician Wynton Marsalis, former ACLU president Nadine Strossen, and Margaret Atwood, who wrote *The Handmaid's Tale*, a novel about a future America that has become a totalitarian state in which the Constitution has been canceled, and both dissent and discourse are strictly prohibited.

There was immediate backlash from people who had all kinds of opinions about the letter. Some said it was too vague. Others said it had an offensive or at least uncomfortable subtext coming just 43 days after George Floyd's death in Minneapolis galvanized protests and policy changes across the nation.

A few days after I read the open letter, I saw a 19-second video taken inside a Costco in Florida. In the video a white man—wearing shorts, flip-flops and a T-shirt that reads "Running the World Since 1776"—is going ballistic. He's screaming at the top of his lungs at the camera, which is a phone belonging to an elderly female customer who had asked him to please wear a mask in accordance with Costco's rules during the height of the Covid-19 pandemic. "I feel threatened!" he screams. "BACK OFF! Threaten me again! Back the f--- up and put your f---ing phone down!" As per usual in our digital age, the guy was quickly identified, down to his place of work as an insurance agent—and then immediately fired.

I can understand his employer's decision. This guy was (a) refusing to wear a mask during a global pandemic, (b) acting like a maniac, and (c) getting very close to people, yelling, with no mask on. Why? Because concerned folks around him asked him to follow the store policy and have some regard for public safety. Any reasonable employer would want him (and his lack of self-control, regard for safety, and common sense) as far as possible from the company and its clients. I would not want to be a client with him as the rep, nor would I want him in my employ.

When it comes to the "cancel culture" debate, I believe an important litmus test to apply, when thinking about whether something—or someone—should be canceled, is this: Does the punishment fit the crime? In this man's case, I believe it did. If he had acted this way at his workplace, to a co-worker or a client, he should be fired in an instant, no questions asked. He should not expect the employer to treat him differently if he goes on an unjustified rampage at a Costco, putting other people's health and safety at risk, plus verbally abusing and terrorizing them, including an elderly woman who could die from his lack of concern for her and others' safety.

* * *

THAT SAID, I also agree with the authors of the open letter and their opinion that vigorous debate, and even unpopular ideas, must be protected. Not only protected, but encouraged. When people become scared to speak freely or are punished for expressing an unpopular view, American society inches closer to being homogenous, and where freedoms and diverse thoughts are suppressed.

I hear from Republicans in liberal West L.A. and NYC all the time, that they are afraid to say *anything* for fear of being castigated by friends and neighbors who don't agree with their views. They're also afraid that if they were ever filmed speaking their mind, the footage could be used by someone to try to get them fired, or interfere with their clients or business partnerships. I imagine that Democrats in Southern and Mountain states (particularly rural areas) likewise feel they must keep their thoughts and opinions to themselves, rather than, for example, express their view that a woman has a right to choose, or that cities hit by gun violence should be allowed to ban assault rifles and other military-style weapons. A person should feel free to express, without fear of backlash, something as common or harmless as a thought or opinion.

The "I feel threatened" guy has the right to disagree with a store's mask policy. He can choose to not give that store his business, and shop online instead. He can even choose to picket outside the store, get on a soapbox and express his views about how much he hates this business and its mask policy. But once he steps inside a private business, breaks its rules, threatens and intimidates other customers, and puts their safety at risk, he has crossed the line. And if his employer —sickened by his conduct—decides to let him go, I can't disagree with that decision. I have employees myself, and if they were filmed acting that way in public, I would let them go too.

* * *

THEN THERE WAS the situation of Amy Cooper. The New York City woman was walking her dog in Central Park on May 25, 2020, and a Black man who was simply there to watch birds asked her to leash her dog (as the posted rules in that area required). She refused, it escalated, and she threatened to call 911. She told the man she was "going to tell [police] there's an African-American man threatening my life." His response: "Please call the cops." Cooper then called 911 while he recorded her on his cellphone. "There is a man, African-American. He is recording me and threatening me and my dog," she frantically told police. "Please send the cops immediately!"

The man was not threatening her. He simply asked her to leash her dog, per the posted rules. Cooper's use of the bird watcher's race struck a raw chord with many people, though I'm sure no one was more offended than the bird watcher himself. History's list of Black men (and women) dying at the hands of police officers is far too long. It so happened that George Floyd was killed on the *very same day*, 1,200 miles away, as a white officer kneeled on his neck for nearly eight minutes—while staring smugly at onlookers who implored him to get off of Floyd. Even while being filmed, the officer ignored their pleas, as well as Floyd's statement, 20 times, of "I can't breathe."

Cooper was quickly identified by online sleuths, vilified on social media, and fired from her job as a portfolio manager at investment firm Franklin Templeton. She also was pressured into giving her dog back to the rescue agency where she'd adopted it, because the video shows the dog thrashing and gasping for breath as Cooper holds its collar during the confrontation. (She later got the dog back.) The video of the encounter went viral on Twitter and has been viewed more than 40 million times.

Amy Cooper's life went down the tubes in less than a day. About six weeks after the confrontation, the Manhattan district attorney announced he was charging her with filing a false police report, a criminal misdemeanor that carries a maximum penalty of a year behind bars. Her behavior was terrible, without a doubt. It was offensive, bigoted, reckless and dangerous. The birder himself, a Harvard graduate and Audubon Society member named Christian Cooper (no relation), told *The New York Times* in an article published the next day, "It's a little bit of a frenzy, and I am uncomfortable with that. If our goal is to change the underlying factors, I am not sure that this young woman having her life completely torn apart serves that goal."

In addition to losing her job, Cooper was facing criminal prosecution, jail time, widespread shaming and ridicule, and the permanent stigma of being "the Central Park Karen." The "punishment" to Cooper is all of that. Not just the job loss, and not just the prosecution. The stigma is as bad as any of the rest. Did the punishment fit the crime? I'll leave that to the world to decide. It is an unfortunate situation all around, but also a learning experience for everyone. No one set a better example than the birder, Christian Cooper. He took the high road and announced that he would not cooperate with the criminal prosecution of Amy Cooper.

* * *

It's NOT a perfect measure by any means, but asking if the punishment fits the crime is one way to approach the "cancel culture" debate: weighing each case on its own merits. Apart from things like hate speech, if the "crime" is merely expressing an opinion—no matter how unpopular it is—then I don't see how harsh punishment is warranted at all.

Colin Kaepernick could be the poster boy for cancel culture. He played six seasons in the NFL as quarterback for the San Francisco 49ers and led his team to the 2012 Super Bowl. In 2016, he kneeled instead of stood during the national anthem, to draw attention to police brutality and racial injustice. Intense debate followed—about expressing one's views about systemic oppression, and respect for the American flag, national anthem, and soldiers who gave their lives to keep our country free. Kaepernick became a free agent after that season and was never again signed by a team. He was erased from the NFL because he engaged in peaceful protest, took a knee, and in the process was attacked by many who strenuously disagreed with him. If Kaepernick remained popular with NFL fans and viewers, notwithstanding his protest, he likely would have been signed and continued playing for years. But the demographics of NFL watchers, largely white, male, less interested in Kaepernick's message and more interested in respecting the flag and soldiers, meant team owners likely feared a backlash if they signed him. Thus, Kaepernick was canceled. Erased from the NFL rosters.

Not everyone felt the same way. *Time* magazine put him on its cover with the headline "The Perilous Fight" in September 2016, and then named him a runner-up for its 2017 Person of the Year. He graced the cover of *GQ,* which named Kaepernick "Citizen of the Year" in 2017. Nike made him the face of an ad campaign in 2018 despite major backlash. (The ad's copy reads: "Believe in something. Even if it means sacrificing everything.") He certainly had his supporters. They just weren't team owners.

Kaepernick's response to his detractors was, "To me, this is bigger than football and it would be selfish on my part to look the other way.... I am not looking for approval. I have to stand up for people that are oppressed.... If they take football away, my endorsements from me, I know that I stood up for what is right."

His former teammate Eric Reid, who took a knee with him, wrote in a Sept. 25, 2017, op-ed in *The New York Times,* "It baffles me that our protest is still being misconstrued as disrespectful to the country, flag and military personnel. We chose it because it's exactly the opposite.... [T]he brave men and women who fought and died for our country did so to ensure that we could live in a fair and free society, which includes the right to speak out in protest."

After George Floyd's death in May 2020, and as the Black Lives Matter movement and its important message surged in popularity, NFL Commissioner Roger Goodell released a video statement on Twitter apologizing for "not listening" to players about racism. "We, the National Football League ... admit we were wrong for not listening to NFL players earlier and encourage all to speak out and peacefully protest. We, the National Football League, believe Black lives matter. I personally protest with you and want to be part of the much-needed change in this country."

He never mentioned Kaepernick's name. Spike Lee criticized the apology as "weak ... piss poor and plain bogus."

When I was in high school, students and teachers would say the Pledge of Allegiance during weekly assembly. I always considered it a requirement for everyone. But my lovely young history teacher, Ms. Martin, didn't. She stood, like all of us, but she did not put her hand over her heart, and did not recite the pledge, as everyone did. Someone in class asked her why. "I don't believe in forced patriotism," was her reply. We all considered this for about six seconds, and then went on with our lives. Her boyfriend that year was another teacher at the school, Mr. DiMartini. He taught a class called "Current American Problems." I was in it, and we read the book *1984* by George Orwell. For those not familiar, it is about the most oppressive totalitarian government imaginable, which even limits the number of words that people are allowed to learn or speak, in order to limit their ability to think, including—God forbid—question the government. I put two and two together that year: Ms. Martin's nonparticipation in the pledge, and Mr. DiMartini's commitment to teaching *1984*. It made sense to me.

Kaepernick seems to be what the 153 signers of the Letter on Justice and Open Debate are addressing. He was canceled because he expressed his views on an important issue, in the face of strong disagreement. He didn't hurt anyone. Did not mean to offend anyone. He simply was doing what he felt was appropriate: not participating in the national anthem (like what Ms. Martin did with the Pledge of Allegiance when I was in high school), and drawing attention to a very important issue. The difference is that many people strongly disagreed with Kaepernick taking a knee during the national anthem, feeling it was extremely disrespectful to the flag and to soldiers who sacrificed everything for our country. If Kaepernick had taken a knee a minute before or after, and stood for the anthem, he would still be playing football today—but hardly anyone would have heard his message, and we would not still be talking about him or this issue.

So back to the test: Did the punishment fit the crime? My response: Where's the crime?

* * *

JOHN SCHNATTER STARTED a pizza business in 1984 out of a converted broom closet at his father's struggling tavern in Indiana. He sold his Camaro for $1,600 worth of used pizza making supplies. His pizza was a hit, and he had a knack for business. By 1994, he had opened 500 Papa John's Pizza stores; by 1997 there were 1,500, and by December 2019 there were nearly 5,400. It was a classic American success story. Then, in 2018, Schnatter was vaporized from the company he had founded and built.

Schnatter was in a meeting in June 2018 with a marketing team from an outside firm. He had stirred up controversy a few months earlier when he weighed in on the NFL's national anthem protests and partly blamed the league for hurting sales at Papa John's. Ironically, he was working with the marketing team on a PR strategy. At the very end of the meeting, he made an impromptu remark on how times had changed in the past 70 years, saying that "Colonel Sanders called Blacks n-----s" and yet never faced a backlash. (Schnatter used the actual word in the conversation.)

Someone leaked to the press that the Papa John's founder and CEO had used the awful slur. The punishment was swift. The board of his super-successful company threw him out and treated him like the enemy. He was forced to resign, which he did, with an apology. Within 12 hours of *Forbes* breaking the story, he was also out as a trustee at the University of Louisville. The mayor of Jeffersonville, Indiana—Schnatter's hometown—ordered the pizza mogul's name to be removed from the John H. Schnatter–Nachand Fieldhouse. It had gotten that name a year earlier after he donated $800,000 for the gym's renovation. Purdue University returned $8 million from Schnatter's charitable foundation and stripped his name from an economic research center on campus.

I have heard the audio. He certainly used the word, as he's

admitted and apologized for. Applying my cancel-culture test: Did the punishment fit the crime? And would you have the same answer if *you* were John Schnatter, canceled, kicked out and scrubbed from the company that you had founded and built, after quoting someone else who had used an offensive racial slur in the distant past?

* * *

APART FROM RACIST SPEECH, hateful speech, encouragement of violence or destruction, or other terribly unacceptable speech or acts, a person should be allowed to express a reasonable view, even if it is not the majority view, and not have to fear being attacked or scrubbed because of it. That is precisely what the Founding Fathers had in mind when they guaranteed the right to "freedom of speech" in the First Amendment. Anyone and everyone should be allowed to express their viewpoint, and to speak freely without fear of retaliation for simply exercising this fundamental right.

Problems arise when an expression of this First Amendment right is not respectful. The KKK should be canceled, even though hate speech has been held by the U.S. Supreme Court to be legally protected speech in such cases as *Matal v. Tam* (2017) and *Virginia v. Black* (2003). But beyond hate speech and other terribly unacceptable speech, while I don't condone disrespecting the flag or the national anthem, I strongly support people being allowed to speak their mind without fear of being canceled for it.

If someone wants to express how important they think it is for a woman to have the right to get an abortion, and someone else wants to express with equal passion how important it is for no one to be allowed to have an abortion, I encourage both sides to exercise their rights to free speech. That's what America is all about. But when someone crosses the line into interfering with the lives or safety of those who don't agree, that's where it needs to stop.

What about protesters who want to express how they feel about an issue or politician and go to that politician's house, with bullhorns, and shout and protest for hours, very loudly, and disrupt the life of that elected official and also his or her family members? That happened in Los Angeles and other cities during the BLM protests of 2020. It is completely unacceptable, in my view. I don't care if the speech is in full support of the issue that I care about most on earth —free expression needs to have reasonable limitations. Disrupting someone's family life crosses the line. Go to city hall, stand in the designated free speech area, hold up your sign, get on your soapbox and speak your mind, take to Twitter or Instagram and express yourself there. But leave an elected official's personal life and family alone.

Who in their right mind would want to become an elected official —with a modest salary, long hours, high stress level, general lack of appreciation by the public—if they can't even enjoy solitude in their own home because they have protesters screaming outside all day and night? People should be *encouraged* to run for office, without fear of being hunted down and treated like an enemy by whoever disagrees with them.

Stepping back, why is it not OK to kneel during the national anthem, but totally OK to vaporize someone from a successful company they founded for making a historical reference, quoting someone else who included a highly offensive word? Where do you draw the line between a stupid mistake, an ignorant blind spot, and a catastrophic career-ender? I don't have the answer for every situation. But I believe that less trigger-finger cancellation, and more thoughtful consideration of context—plus appreciation for viewpoints we disagree with, particularly when communicated in a respectful, law-abiding way—would benefit all of us. And when there is wrongful conduct: The punishment should fit the crime.

32

FLEETWOOD MAC & MY MOM

My mother was always a huge fan of Fleetwood Mac. Growing up, she would play the *Rumours* album over and over again, for years. It was the soundtrack of our home. She had lots of other albums, but rarely played them. She played *Rumours*. So I grew up listening to that album and, like my mother, never got tired of the songs. To this day, I love them all, and get excited whenever I hear one.

Fast forward a few decades to 2003: My mother was scheduled for a heart valve replacement surgery, which is an open-heart procedure, and very dangerous—risk of death and all of that. A few weeks before her surgery, I was driving on an L.A. freeway listening to the radio announce a giveaway of Fleetwood Mac tickets. I called in, and I was the lucky 11th caller—I won the tickets. They told me I would be put into a drawing for front-row seats. I got a call a few days later and lo and behold, I won those too. The ticket read: FLEETWOOD MAC, Section 1, Row 1, Seat 1. It was about the coolest thing I'd ever seen. And of course I had another ticket right next to it: Section 1, Row 1, Seat 2.

The concert was scheduled for six days before my mother's open-heart surgery, and I asked her if she would go with me. She was over the moon, but slightly reluctant because she was feeling a bit weak from her valve not working properly, and her surgery was coming a little late in the game. But she happily said yes.

We had a great time at the concert. I was standing up much of the time, while she was sitting next to me: watching, smiling, enjoying. My wife was a little jealous that I took my mom instead of her, but she understood the history and importance of this band to us, and the risks of my mom's major procedure six days later.

Her surgery was a success, by the way, and in 2020 she celebrated her 75th birthday.

33

ROAD TRIP TO 50

few months before I turned 50 in 2019, I was thinking about how to celebrate that milestone. Others around me were turning 50 and throwing parties. My wife and her twin sister had one that year, and it was lots of fun, attended by about 80 people. I started to plan one for myself, and made a reservation at a private salon with its own bar at a popular speakeasy in Hollywood that was a Victorian mansion converted into a private school in the 1920s where Charlie Chaplin sent his children.

But I've never been one for throwing a big party for myself; it always seems a little egotistical, and I don't prefer to be the center of attention. My wedding was the closest I ever got, but it was a traditional rite of passage and I shared the attention with my beautiful bride. I did not look forward to organizing, paying for, or frankly attending a big 50th bash. So I canceled the reservation at the venue.

I decided instead to take a road trip, on my own, through the South. I had wanted to visit the region in a meaningful way for the better part of 30 years. This was my opportunity.

Starting in Miami, where I had a scheduled court appearance for Pastor Luna (see Chapter 30), I would fly to New Orleans, drive to Natchez, Mississippi, and then follow part of the Natchez Trace

Parkway (a historic trail used by Native Americans before European settlers arrived, which became a 444-mile U.S. national park and two-lane road to Nashville, Tennessee). I planned a lunchtime stop in Jackson (the Mississippi state capital), and overnight stops in Clarksdale, Mississippi ("the birthplace of the blues"), Oxford, Mississippi (home to authors William Faulkner and John Grisham, and Ole Miss), and Memphis, Tennessee, eventually landing in Nashville for two nights, and then flying home the day before my birthday.

I really wanted to focus on these places: eat the food, hear the music, meet the people, visit the historical sites, and learn as much as I could about the struggles and successes that have defined this unique region of the U.S.

In New Orleans, I stayed in a historic B&B in my favorite part of town: Frenchmen Street, a recently renovated area with lots of terrific live music clubs playing jazz, blues and rock. I arrived in the afternoon on Halloween, which in New Orleans is a total spectacle. I bought a mask in the French Quarter, dressed in all black and people-watched, admiring the creative costumes and listening to one live band after another in the different clubs, all next to each other in a line. Many of the costumes were extravagant and spectacular—they really go all out in New Orleans on Halloween. I can't wait to go back.

The next day I gave a scheduled talk to a double classroom of students at Tulane Law School, at the invitation of Professor Amy Gajda, a First Amendment law expert who had supported our effort in the *Hulk Hogan v. Gawker* case. After the talk, she treated me to a late lunch at the historic Commander's Palace, where I experienced my first Sazerac (the unofficial cocktail of New Orleans—the town that invented cocktails), and enjoyed a lunch that included the best cup of gumbo of my life, a really good pan-fried fish, and their signature dessert: bread pudding soufflé that was light, not heavy, and *so* delicious.

* * *

THE NEXT DAY, I rented a car, and visited two plantation mansions on the way up to Natchez. Given my interest in civil rights (see Chapters 26 and 37), I wanted to see firsthand these places where our country's horrific legacy was the daily reality for slaves for hundreds of years. It is difficult but necessary to imagine the atrocities that occurred daily on these properties. The beautiful, historic buildings also were a sight to behold.

I first toured Houmas House, located on the Mississippi River. Under owner John Burnside in the 1850s, Houmas House had at least 550 slaves. It can be difficult to reconcile that fact with the beautiful architecture and historic artifacts in the home, like an original Gauguin painting and a clock once owned by Marie Antoinette. One of the owners of this house designed the Confederate Battle Flag. I felt physically ill when I learned this and saw the tiny display—tiny because it is so controversial. The man might as well have designed the Nazi swastika. But still, it is part of history, the house is now essentially a museum, and I am a perpetual student of history. So I took it all in, the same as if I were in Germany learning about the Third Reich.

One thing that blew me away in the house was the historic map on the wall depicting the many hundreds of plantations in Louisiana at the time of the Civil War. Few are left—nearly all of the mansions were burned to the ground by General Sherman in his march to the sea. Houmas House was spared because the owner, who was a native of Ireland, cleverly displayed a British flag in the front on the second-story balcony and told Sherman's troops that it was British soil and they needed permission from the queen of England herself in order to step foot on the land. Sherman's troops were confused and afraid to make an international mistake, so they skipped Houmas House and marched on, burning everything *else* in their path.

I also visited the Nottoway Plantation House, one of the largest antebellum plantation houses in the South. The 64-room home was built in 1858 by wealthy sugar farmer John Hampden Randolph. Most of the labor to construct the opulent mansion was done by Randolph's 155 slaves, who lived in 42 slave cabins on the property.

After walking through the 53,000-square-foot Greco-Italian main house I ambled up to the Mississippi River, where I watched a few barges float by. It is a beautiful mansion with a horrific past.

* * *

I STAYED the night in Natchez, in a historic mansion that is now a B&B. I had a terrific dinner at King's Tavern, one of the oldest buildings in all the South, dating back to 1769 (excellent food and drinks), and later went to Smoot's Grocery, a small blues club with an outstanding live blues band, which also played '70s hits like Fleetwood Mac in a unique blues style.

The next morning, I drove up to Jackson and visited the Mississippi Civil Rights Museum. The lady scanning my ticket advised, "Don't try to read everything; you'll never be able to do it. Just read what you can, and skip around." I thought: The heck with that, I'm going to read everything and learn it all! Boy, was she right. The place is so packed with detailed information, it's like a 20-volume encyclopedia on civil rights in the state of Mississippi.

There, the story of Emmett Till—which I had heard but never knew in all its excruciating detail—made an indelible mark on my psyche. Since that visit, I often think of him, and will never forget him.

Till was a 14-year-old boy in 1955. He lived in Chicago and was visiting family members during the summer, in rural Money, Mississippi, just a few miles north of Jackson. He was a fairly typical 14-year-old with a big sense of humor, who liked to laugh and play little practical jokes. At the time of my tour, I was the father of two 14-year-olds, and so I knew firsthand the rebellious but good-natured humor of boys that age.

Till was warned by his relatives not to upset any white people. But one evening, on a candy run to the little local grocery store up the road with a group of six other teens, Till thought it would be funny to do a wolf whistle to the lady behind the counter, who owned the shop with her husband, to see the reaction on his friends' faces. The woman, Carolyn Bryant, promptly told her husband, Roy, about the loud whistle.

Four days later, Emmett Till was dragged out of his bed by Roy Bryant and his half-brother, J.W. Milam, in the middle of the night. The men took Emmett to a farmhouse, where they severely beat and tortured him. They took him to the Tallahatchie River, shot him in the head, tied a large metal fan used for ginning cotton to his neck with barbed wire, and threw his lifeless body into the river.

Less than a month later, the men went on trial for the kidnapping and murder of Emmett Till. A jury of 12 white men took 67 minutes to acquit Bryant and Milam of all charges. Carolyn Bryant, when called to the stand, lied under oath. She testified that Till "grabbed her around the waist and uttered obscenities," but she confessed decades later that he never did—he just whistled. Even so, it would not have been justification to drag him out of bed, torture him and kill him. In the 2017 book *The Blood of Emmett Till*, she admitted: "Nothing that boy did could ever justify what happened to him."

The story of Emmett Till, the acquittal of his murderers, and the photos of his tortured body—which his mother insisted be released publicly so the world would know what they did to her 14-year-old boy—were front-page news throughout America. Till's story and image galvanized the fledgling civil rights movement in 1955. Rosa Parks said that she was thinking about Till when she refused to give up her seat at the front of the bus. According to the museum, people throughout America, of every race, creed and gender, suddenly felt the urgency of the civil rights movement.

The story of Emmett Till, during my road trip to 50, hit me like a ton of bricks. Still does. I could easily imagine one of my 14-year-old sons doing something like what Till did, just to see the reaction on their friends' faces. The thought of my own son being kidnapped, beaten, tortured and killed over an inconsiderate whistle at a stranger, strikes me to my core. I cannot fathom what Till's poor mother must have gone through—or worse yet, what the innocent teenager must have endured before he lost consciousness.

This story exemplifies to me the millions and millions of atrocities that Black people have suffered at the hands of white people since the first slave ship was packed up and put on the high seas toward America in 1524. Amazingly, the atrocities continue, as evidenced by the senseless murder of George Floyd on May 25, 2020, by four police officers in Minneapolis, and the mass protests that spontaneously erupted nationwide and around the world in response. Civil rights leader John Lewis wrote a final letter, published the day of his funeral in July 2020: "Emmett Till was my George Floyd ... he could easily have been me."

* * *

ALSO AT THE Mississippi Civil Rights Museum, I learned that when the U.S. Supreme Court ruled in *Brown v. Board of Education* (1952-1955) that separate is inherently unequal and unconstitutional, and ordered the integration of schools in America, the state of Mississippi announced defiantly that—notwithstanding the Supreme Court's directive—Mississippi would take *20 years* before starting the process of integrating its schools.

I was shocked that a state would or could so openly defy the United States Supreme Court order, and get away with it. As promised in 1955, the year of Emmett Till, Mississippi did not integrate its schools until 20 years after the *Brown* decision—yet another civil rights atrocity by whites against Blacks in America.

That education exhibit in the museum provides an enormous amount of detail on the tremendous imbalance in the 1950s education system in the South, including class size—which was many times larger for Black students than white students—the quality of educators, books and supplies, the number of schools per capita, the distance from schools to homes, and also the massive difference in the school year. Black children were expected to work the fields, picking cotton and other crops, for several months in the fall, while white children were in school. Black children had a school year of approximately four months, versus the eight-month school year of white children.

The concept of "separate but equal" in *Plessy v. Ferguson* (U.S. Supreme Court, 1896) was such a farce. It's amazing to me that it took nearly 60 years between *Plessy* and *Brown* to result in a favorable Supreme Court ruling, and then 20 *more* years for schools in Mississippi to finally *begin* the process of integration. The federal government should have required every school in the South to begin to fully integrate starting in 1955. Presidents Eisenhower, Kennedy, Johnson and Nixon completely dropped the ball on that. In '55, the full weight of the federal government should have put maximum pressure on the Southern school systems to fully integrate immediately.

* * *

AFTER THE SOBERING HISTORY LESSONS, I drove to Clarksdale, Mississippi, known for the famous Crossroads where Robert Johnson, an incompetent guitar player, disappeared for several months and returned as one of the greatest blues guitar players in history. One of his songs features the lyrics: "I went to the crossroad, fell down on my knees / Asked the Lord above, 'Have mercy, now, save poor Bob if you please.'" A legend quickly emerged that Johnson went down to the crossroads of Highways 61 and 49, at midnight, where he made a deal with the devil: his soul in exchange for blues guitar mastery.

It's a great town which (when not under Covid-19 restrictions) delivers live blues music to residents and visitors 365 days a year—which is a tall order, given that it's a town of only 14,300 people. I visited three blues clubs on a Sunday night, and was blown away by a blues lounge called Red's.

Spectacular music; no food except for the lady who sometimes pulls up her smoker outside and sells BBQ, basic beer, wine and soft drinks; a cash-only register; and true "juke joint" ambiance (the place is a total wreck)—it was wondrous. The lady with the smoker was there that night and I had, literally, the best baby back ribs of my entire life, bar none, and also the best homemade sausage of my life, bar none. They let you go out to get the food and bring it back into the lounge to eat.

I liked Red's so much, I wanted to replicate it in West Los Angeles, where I live. But the place would be lucky to break even, so I've committed to visiting Clarksdale and Red's as often as I can. (And I've kept my commitment—I visited a second time a few months later, and had dinner with iconic actor Morgan Freeman and his business partner Bill Luckett, a super nice guy and attorney who was mayor of Clarksdale a few years back. They co-own another amazing establishment in town: Ground Zero Blues Club.)

Red's at night, with the smoker outside for hungry patrons.

After Clarksdale, I spent a day and night in Oxford, Mississippi. I explored the town and the campus of Ole Miss (aka the University of Mississippi—but never call it that) on foot. It was here that James Meredith, the school's first Black student, showed up in 1962 to enroll following a federal lawsuit that ordered the state of Mississippi to enroll him and imposed a fine of $10,000 for each day it didn't.

Meredith was met with a riot of white racists who threatened his life, screamed racial slurs and other profanities at him, burned cars, damaged property and pelted the 500 National Guard troops—sent by President Kennedy—with rocks, bricks and gunfire. Two people died of gunshot wounds. Thankfully Meredith was not one of them.

While some students welcomed him, many did not, according to reports that cited first-person accounts: "Students living in Meredith's dorm bounced basketballs on the floor just above his room through all hours of the night. Other students ostracized him: When Meredith walked into the cafeteria for meals, the students eating would turn their backs. If Meredith sat at a table with other students, all of whom were white, the students would immediately get up and go to another table."

Even so, he persevered, and graduated Ole Miss in 1963 with a bachelor's degree in political science. A statue of Meredith walking into a monument that reads COURAGE stands in the middle of campus, in front of the admissions building, depicting the moment he bravely walked in, past a racist riot, to enroll.

The statue memorializing James Meredith's courage on the Ole Miss campus.

IN 1966, Meredith planned a solo 220-mile March Against Fear from Memphis to Jackson—and was shot by a white sniper on the second day. Others marched on his behalf, and after recovering from his injury, Meredith marched all the way to Jackson. He went on to become a civil rights icon, author and political adviser. At the time of this writing, the brave father of four is 87 and lives with his wife in Jackson.

* * *

THE NEXT DAY I drove to Memphis, where I visited the Lorraine Motel, the site where Dr. Martin Luther King Jr. was shot on April 4, 1968. The hotel is now a large civil rights museum, and I walked every inch of it, and read everything I could. The museum culminates in the very room that he stayed in, left exactly as it was at the moment he was shot, and the outdoor balcony where he was hit.

There's a view of the boarding house up a hill where his assassin lodged, stalked and fired the shot. An underground tunnel takes you to that boarding house with the room exactly how it looked the moment James Earl Ray fired the shot and fled, the window he used to rest his rifle, the actual rifle that he used, and the view down the hill to the hotel balcony.

The museum has lots of information about Ray and how he fled to London after assassinating Dr. King, and was picked up by authorities in England because he was carrying a gun, which is illegal in London. London authorities contacted U.S. authorities, who said that he was the main suspect in the assassination of Dr. King, whereupon Ray was arrested and extradited to Tennessee to stand trial. On his 41st birthday, Ray confessed to the crime and pled guilty. He was sentenced to 99 years, and died in prison at age 70.

I also learned at that museum that Rosa Parks was not the first person to be arrested in Montgomery, Alabama, for refusing to yield her seat on a bus to a white passenger. There were three others before her who did exactly the same thing, all of whom were arrested. (For more about them, see Chapter 26.)

In Memphis, I visited several blues clubs on Beale Street and ate tasty BBQ. The next day I drove to Nashville and took in a concert by an amazing band called Shovels & Rope, at the historic Ryman Auditorium, the original location of the Grand Ole Opry for 31 years, from 1943 to 1974. The venue is known for its acoustics, and they are spectacular.

The next morning, I explored Nashville and visited nearly every honky-tonk club on Broadway at night. The following morning, I traversed the city looking for the perfect Southern brunch before my flight home. I found it: biscuits, gravy, bacon, eggs and grits, in a beautifully restored historic building that used to be the railroad station, but is now a luxury hotel.

I returned home to L.A. late the night before my 50th birthday. On the day itself, I had a family get-together at my house. It was a perfect little celebration—better than any crowded late-night party at a Hollywood speakeasy. By the time I returned to L.A., I'd gotten my fill of crowds and clubs vibrating with amazing live music. I had a lot on my mind, reconciling the beauty, vibrancy, disturbing history and inspiring civil rights legacy of the South. On my birthday, I was overjoyed just having my family, and being home.

34

REFLECTIONS ON WORK

"Far and away the best prize that life has to offer is the chance to work hard at work worth doing." — President Theodore Roosevelt

I have spent more than two-thirds of my life working. From pushing shopping carts in a supermarket parking lot at age 15 to running my own successful law firm, every job I had taught me important lessons and shaped my outlook on work and life in general. I pass this outlook along to my sons more than they probably would care to hear. Here's what I tell them (or try to anyway):

- Working for someone else in a job where you are easily replaceable is not as fulfilling as one where you own the place and provide a product or service that is really important to others. With ownership and proper market strategy, you can become invaluable to customers or clients, and with that comes popularity and revenue.

- Whether you have a fulfilling job or are on your way to figuring out what fulfills you, always work hard, always show up on time (or early), and do the best job you possibly can that day (and every day); others will recognize your value and promote you.

- Don't settle for a job you don't like, and don't stay somewhere that does not make you happy. It's OK to walk away, politely, if you know you are in the wrong place.

- If you are selling something, whether a product, service, idea or yourself, always be available—don't ever close yourself off from an opportunity.

- If you ever have a business, never run out of product and always hire enough people to service the needs of your customers, promptly and with very high quality.

- Never underestimate the power of one-on-one relationships. You never know when a single person in your network of connections might bring an important opportunity—or change your life. Success usually comes from unexpected places. Be open to it coming from anywhere, at any time, and seize the moment when it does.

- The customer is always right. Customer satisfaction is all-important. If customers are not satisfied, they will go somewhere else—and with them, your revenues.

- Figure out what you love, and find a way to do it. Don't settle for something that does not inspire you, or satisfy you. Go find it—and do it.

- Believe in yourself. Believe you can achieve anything. Be optimistic. Think positive. Failure is usually self-inflicted. As automobile pioneer Henry Ford famously said,

"Whether you think you can, or you think you can't—
you're right."

- Always be kind. If everyone was kind, the world would be
  a far better place. If every person was nasty, the world
  would be unlivable. Do the opposite. Be kind, professional
  and courteous.

- Have fun. Fun should not be something that only happens
  after work or on weekends—life is too short. The more
  you enjoy your work, the better you will be at it. The more
  your employees, co-workers, and associates enjoy what
  they do, the more successful your business will be. If
  you're not having fun—what's the point?

All of this and much more I figured out on my own, mostly from
owning my own law firm for the past eight years, but also from
working at other law firms, working for a 150-person company as its
only attorney, clerking for a judge, working for a state senator, an
assemblyman and a county supervisor, working for my father, volunteering in the Rocky Mountains to maintain hiking trails, knocking
on doors with a clipboard in my hand and a smile on my face, and
bagging groceries and pushing shopping carts in a broiling, thankless
supermarket parking lot.

35

CORRECTING THE RECORD

T wo projects attempted to depict the *Hulk Hogan v. Gawker* lawsuit. One was the documentary film *Nobody Speak*, which was available on Netflix in 2017, the year after the trial. The second was the nonfiction book *Conspiracy* by Ryan Holiday, released in 2018. Both rehashed the case because it was juicy, packed with unexpected twists and, at times, stranger than fiction. The case also had far-reaching implications for the American media, particularly for journalists and outlets who act irresponsibly, cause harm to others, and then claim protection under the First Amendment. Gawker was ripe fodder for postmortem discussion and debate.

For *Conspiracy*, the author interviewed everyone involved: Terry Bollea (aka Hulk Hogan), Peter Thiel, Nick Denton, A.J. Daulerio and yours truly, among others. The book has a lot of detail that is generally accurate, and it is an interesting read. I do have two criticisms in particular. First, there are several passages that seem to imply that my main motivator was money. This is not true. While I do like money, it is not what drove me to work hard and win. I was driven by the fact that my client's privacy rights were savagely violated, that Gawker's actions were sadistic, and the implications of the outcome of the case on everyone in America: Would we prevail and uphold their right to privacy, or would the case fail and that right be severely weakened? Many of Gawker's top folks also seemed to get pleasure from Bollea's pain. I wanted to stop them, and I wanted that very badly. Gawker was my motivator. As were the people Gawker exploited and hurt, starting with Bollea, my client. At every turn in the case, until the end, Gawker's leaders thumbed their noses at us, and acted as though they could do anything, without consequence. All the while, the Gawker Media websites continued to trample on people's rights and engage in casual character assassination seemingly on a daily basis.

As discussed in Chapters 1 through 6, the Gawker case was a throwdown that pitted the right to privacy in America against the alleged "right" of a website to play a surreptitiously recorded video of a person naked and having sex in a private bedroom, against their objection, on the basis that the First Amendment supposedly allows it. I felt strongly, each and every day of the case, that we *had* to prevail so that privacy rights in America would survive, and thrive. If Bollea were to lose, Denton's twisted concept of "transparency"—that the "media" (which includes everything from individual bloggers to billion-dollar media conglomerates) are allowed into any location of a person's life, including their bedroom, to record what goes on there, and play it for all the world to watch—would become the new standard. I could not stand by and allow that to happen, at least not without a fight—all the fight I could muster. *That's* what motivated me in the case. Yes, it was nice to get paid for the many, many hours we put into the case, without which I could not afford to do the case in the first place. And as far as the money that came into the firm, the largest payees were my employees, my firm's vendors, our excellent co-counsel in Tampa, Uncle Sam (federal income tax), the state of California (state income tax), and then myself and my two partners. I still go to work every day trying to make a buck to pay my bills. So while the Gawker case was a great case to have, and I'm proud of our work and our victory, it certainly did not put me on easy street. I still drive the same 2004 SUV (which was only eight years old when I took the case), and I still live in the same starter house that Kathleen and I bought 20 years ago.

The second thing that *Conspiracy* got wrong—and it bothered me *greatly* when I read it—was its claim that my trial team selected jurors based on their demographics, specifically that we deliberately picked heavy women to be jurors. Nothing could be further from the truth. First, two of the six jurors and at least one of the alternates were men, and multiple women on the jury were not heavy at all. Second, we would have been happy with *any* of the 100 prospective jurors in the pool, with the exception of one juror way up around row seven or eight. (She was the one person out of 100 who answered questions, posed to the group, indicating she did not feel that privacy was very important.) But we never got near her in jury selection because all of the jurors were picked from the first two rows.

The jurors we ended up with (and did not challenge) we kept *solely* because of their thoughtful answers to questions posed to them during *voir dire*, the jury selection process. Their gender, race, weight and other personal attributes were *not a factor at all*—not one iota. We *did* challenge a few people, though we actually had no problem with those we challenged. We only did so because there was someone we liked *even more* a couple of chairs down—and if we didn't challenge someone, we'd never get to them. Gawker used up all or nearly all of their challenges because they seemingly were not happy with *any* of the jurors. All had answered questions in a manner that was not in Gawker's favor. When Gawker's lawyer asked who in the room agreed with the adage "I may not agree with what you say but I will defend with my life your right to say it," one prospective juror raised her hand and asked, "What about child pornography?" Gawker did not use one of its challenges on her. She became the foreperson. Good one, Gawker.

* * *

The Netflix documentary was a pure propaganda piece, and only rates a brief mention here. The filmmakers presented all of the evidence and arguments that Gawker presented at the trial, and virtually none of the evidence and arguments that we presented on behalf of Bollea. The objective of the documentary was to present that one-sided view, which was completely rejected by the jury in a huge way, and also was rejected by the trial judge in her post-trial rulings. The evidence we presented against Gawker at trial was massive—and conveniently omitted from the documentary. So if you want to see Gawker's side of the case, without anything else, go ahead and watch the film. But if you're interested in an account that is balanced and truthful, you won't find it in that film. There was one thing that made me chuckle: The film portrayed me as a total badass. I was OK with that.

* * *

ONE LAST THING TO say about the Gawker case: It was the wildest of rides on the most unpredictable of roller coasters. No book or film comes anywhere close to the real experience of living it every day from Oct. 15, 2012 (filing day), through Dec. 28, 2016 (payment day). It was an adventure I'll never forget.

36

POLITICS

This is not a political book. One might ask: Why is the author—who was a politics major in college, worked for two years for a California state senator, and is an attorney who represents the leader of the free world—*not* writing about politics in this book?

Reason: Political issues don't fit in this book, and would distract from the issues that are more important to me—like protecting people against irresponsible reporters, bloggers and mass media corporations.

Also, everyone has their own political views. I don't want to "turn off" readers by expressing strong political views substantially different from theirs. My clients and prospective clients might read this book and I would not want to lose some by expressing a "controversial" political view.

I *would* like to say this: The clients of my firm have a wide variety of political views, ranging from liberal Democrats to conservative Republicans. Many are in the entertainment industry in Hollywood, and others are in the Trump world on the other coast. I like all of my clients, and don't want anyone to think that my firm is not open to everyone, regardless of their personal views on the world. I certainly do not apply a political "litmus test" and only accept clients who agree with my own personal political views. If that were the case, I would have fewer clients.

All views are welcome at my firm, and I would hope that all people would feel comfortable being my clients, even if they might disagree with the political views of *other* clients of the firm. There are a few extreme exceptions, of course. Anyone who advocates or practices something that I consider loathsome, I would not represent, such as hate speech or criminal activity. But in terms of general politics: If President Obama, President Bush, President Clinton, or President Carter wanted to hire my firm, and as long as there were no conflicts with an existing client or matter, it would be my great pleasure to serve them, and I would do so to the fullest extent of my ability.

* * *

FOR THOSE WHO *really* want to know my political views, and can't accept the fact that I am not being forthcoming, I will say the following:

I consider myself to be politically "middle of the road." I vote for both Republicans and Democrats, depending on who the person is, their experience, their views on issues, the needs of the country, state, county or city at the time, and the other choices in the particular race. In California, and in the city of Los Angeles and LA County (where I live), Democrats dominate *all* of the elected offices: both U.S. Senate seats, all statewide offices like governor, lieutenant governor and attorney general, and all local offices like U.S. representative, state senator, state assemblymember, county supervisor (3rd District), mayor and city council (5th District)—my representatives. In the state of California, the two top vote-getters square off in the general election, even if they are of the same party. Thus, you often see two Democrats competing in the general election. For example, when Kamala Harris won her U.S. Senate seat, she beat U.S. Rep. Loretta Sanchez, also a Democrat, in the general election. Thus, voters in

California and Los Angeles often have the choice of which *Democrat* to vote for, of the two major candidates, not the choice between a Democrat and a Republican.

* * *

MY VIEWS on *economic* issues tend to be more conservative than most voters, including most Republicans. I think government taxes way too much, spends way too much, and is extremely inefficient, bloated, permits fraud, and constantly makes large-scale financial mistakes which cost taxpayers trillions of dollars. I feel (very strongly, actually) that government should be overhauled to be made extremely efficient —laser efficient—like the efficiency of buying something from Amazon, or ordering a ride from Uber: quick, cheap and the user experience is generally very good. Government functions the opposite of this, and always has. It doesn't have to be that way forever. If government were extremely efficient, responsive and automated, it would spend far less money, and there would be no need to tax people the amounts they are taxed today.

Many people pay more than 40 percent of their income, and sometimes more than 50 percent of their income, to combined federal and state income taxes. Those income taxes do *not* include the many other forms of taxes they also pay, including sales taxes, gasoline taxes, Social Security taxes, property taxes, capital gains taxes, employer taxes, estate taxes, and many more. I feel there should be a Taxpayers Bill of Rights, and it should include that anyone who earns under a certain amount, such as $500,000 for a household, should never pay more than a certain percent, such as 38 percent, of their income to combined federal and state income taxes and Social Security taxes. And those who make under $5 million should be capped at 45 percent. Capital gains should be factored in fairly as well, so that people with huge amounts of stocks, bonds or real estate, rather than traditional income, should be treated the same in terms of taxes.

I also believe that all government budgets (federal, state, county and city) should be balanced every year and there should be no borrowing by government except in case of emergency, such as the Covid-19 pandemic of 2020 or credit crisis of 2008. Even then, the government should not borrow more than 50 percent of its annual budget, and should pay off all borrowing within five years—so that the government quickly returns to a balanced budget. Also, in good years, government should save up a "rainy-day" fund, to avoid borrowing in the first place. Harvard University, through fundraising, has racked up a $37 billion "endowment," which is essentially a fund that it can use for anything it wants: to build new buildings, give its students free tuition forever, and so on. I don't see why the U.S., state and municipal governments can't keep costs low and save up a rainy-day fund for future needs, such as a major economic downturn or other emergency.

The U.S. government does the opposite. The last time the U.S. government had no debt was in 1835, when President Andrew Jackson (the seventh president of the United States) paid off the national debt. Since then, the country has been in debt. The U.S. national debt, as of the writing of this book, is about $28 trillion, and the debt per U.S. taxpayer is about $222,000 (*source: usdebtclock.org*). If someone were to knock on your door with a "U.S." armband and inform you that you and every taxpayer in your household *each* owe the U.S. government $222,000—and you all need to pay up now—you'd be pretty shocked. Well, that's the reality, except for the knock on the door and immediacy of the repayment requirement.

In 2019, pre-Covid 19, federal spending was $4.4 trillion and federal tax revenue was $3.5 trillion, leaving a total annual budget deficit of about $1 trillion (*source: Congressional Budget Office*). In other words, the government was adding $1 trillion each year to the national debt.

But in 2020, U.S. government spending skyrocketed, and tax revenue fell. Estimates are that spending will be $6.6 trillion in 2020. Tax revenue will be $3.3 trillion. That will leave an annual deficit of $3.3 trillion (*source: Congressional Budget Office*). The annual deficit is the same as the total annual tax revenue. That would be like a person earning $100,000 per year and spending $200,000 per year. All debt requires interest payments. The national deficit and national debt numbers are insane to me. I could go on and on about taxing and spending issues, but I would bore you even more than I have already. Bottom line, I consider my economic views to be far more conservative than most U.S. elected officials, both Republican and Democrat. We should tax and spend far less than we do, balance the budget and have a savings fund for the future—the way most American households operate.

* * *

ON ISSUES of *foreign policy and national defense*, I believe we should have a strong national defense, and strong foreign policy, but also we should not be spending trillions of dollars to fight wars in foreign countries, particularly when we *know* the war is unwinnable. How many countries need to wage a war in Afghanistan, and lose, before countries stop waging wars in Afghanistan? The U.S. should instead work with its foreign allies, provide leadership, create economic and diplomatic incentives and solutions, and avoid barbaric fighting and bloodshed. If we are attacked, we certainly should retaliate—with appropriate force, preferably as a collective force with our allies. But only an actual war waged against the U.S. should warrant an actual war waged *by* the U.S. against others. The terrorist attacks of 9/11 were truly horrific. That day, 2,977 Americans died. But it did not warrant full-scale wars in Iraq and Afghanistan, fought over the course of 10 to 20 years, costing U.S. taxpayers an estimated $2.4 trillion. Moreover, an estimated 111,000 people were killed in the war in Afghanistan from 2001 to 2020, including 31,000 innocent civilians. Many more casualties were in Iraq. The fact that Al-Qaeda killed nearly 3,000 innocent people on 9/11 does not justify the massive number of casualties, including some 10 to 20 *times* the number of innocent civilian casualties, and trillions of dollars, as a response. I certainly support the mission to capture or kill Osama bin Laden and all others who participated in planning and executing 9/11, but not the two all-out wars that were waged by the U.S. government from 2001 to 2020.

* * *

ON ENVIRONMENTAL ISSUES, I feel strongly that the environment is amazing and spectacular and should be protected and preserved. We are all just guests on the planet. The Earth is 4.5 billion years old, and modern life on Earth is only about 200 years old. There is no reason for a few selfish, irresponsible generations to wreak havoc on the planet by cranking up the temperature, melting the polar caps, flooding the coasts, causing polar bears to go extinct, and so on. Carbon emissions should be minimized. Water and air should be clean, not polluted. Products should be reused and recycled, and garbage buried in the ground should be minimized—or better yet, stopped altogether.

The two massive collections of floating debris in the ocean, known as the Great Pacific Garbage Patch, are absolutely insane. It never should have happened in the first place, and should be cleaned up, through a group effort of all countries who share the Pacific—with those countries making the largest contributions to the garbage patch providing the largest contributions toward its cleanup. When I read about marine animals like whales washing ashore dead with massive amounts of plastic in their digestive tracts, it makes me sick. Some might consider my environmental views to be not "conservative." I disagree. Conservation is conservative. Pollution, waste and destruction are radical.

* * *

ON CIVIL RIGHTS ISSUES, I believe that everyone deserves an equal chance at success, and those who succeed should be those who work hard, play by the rules, are creative in their approach, take thoughtful risks, and (as often happens in business) get lucky. Success should be colorblind. Success should be earned, not handed to anyone. Those who are raised with many things handed to them should have no better chance at success than those who start out in life with little or nothing.

Education including preschool, K-12, community college, four-year university, and higher education; grants and student loan forgiveness; and training and entrepreneurship programs (including small business loans) collectively should strive to become the "great equalizer." Institutions should value diversity, help those with great potential who start out in life with added challenges, and train them to be as successful as anyone else. But beyond education, it's up to each individual to work hard, persevere (never give up), be creative (find a way), and become as valuable as possible to the employer, the customer, and the economy. Those who do so should be rewarded. There should be no place at all for discrimination, other than on the basis of value and merit.

Another important part of civil rights is voting. The process of voting should be ridiculously easy, very quick, fully secure, strongly encouraged, and every legal vote should be counted—no exceptions. All politicians and all governments, federal, state and local, should strive to do this. Anything less is undemocratic. Voter roll purges, shrinking numbers of polling places, distance to polling places, long lines to vote, limited hours to vote, voter ID laws, not counting votes postmarked on Election Day, stopping vote counts and the many other ways that groups in power seek to suppress the vote of others, is akin to tyranny.

* * *

ON PERSONAL LIBERTIES, I feel that people should enjoy the greatest level of personal freedoms, provided (a) there is no danger to self or others, and (b) the personal freedoms do not interfere with other people's rights and freedoms—in which case there should be reasonable limitations and compromise. I agree strongly with the California Constitution, Article I, Section 1: "All people are by nature free and independent and have inalienable rights. Among these are enjoying and defending life and liberty, acquiring, possessing, and protecting property, and pursuing and obtaining safety, happiness, and privacy." If every government in America, from the U.S. down to each state, county, city and township, followed and valued each word in this sentence, we'd all be so much better off.

* * *

ON THE *GOLDEN RULE*, I think everyone should follow it, every day. "*In everything, do unto others as you would have them do unto you...*" Gospel of Matthew (7:12)

* * *

ON THE ISSUE of *ethics in journalism and media*, all journalists should follow the SPJ Code of Ethics. (See Chapter II.)

* * *

IF YOU ARE WONDERING, "Is Charles Harder running for office?" the answer is no. And that leads to one final thought here:

The institution of politics and government in America—from federal, to state, down to regional and local positions—is saturated with vicious personal attacks, mostly contrived or misrepresented so heavily so as not to in any way resemble the truth. As a result, lots of people who are excellent leaders, and might be outstanding at government, avoid politics altogether because of the reputational harm and emotional toll of the inevitable barrage of vicious false or misleading personal attacks in every election. The fact that million-aires and billionaires can spend unlimited funds to run ads and influ-ence outcomes is terrifying as well. The system is badly broken and needs to be fixed so that every well-qualified person feels comfort-able running for office, false attacks stop, and extremely wealthy people have no more influence on elections than anyone else.

37

THE INSPIRATION

Several things inspired me to invest the enormous amount of time and energy required to write this book:

First, my desire to share with the world my stories and viewpoints on the important issues in this book.

Second, my desire to leave a "legacy" of some sort. My children obviously are my legacy. But beyond them—if, for example, I were to be hit by a bus, and had no book—who would know the things I had done, or *why* I did them, or the importance of the issues I am committed to, or the problems that I see in our system and how they can be addressed? I cannot leave it to others to tell my story, because it either would not get told at all, or would be told unfairly—from the point of view of a reporter or small handful of them who might be influenced by the misleading and superficial critiques already written, with no ability to talk to me or otherwise understand what I am (or was) about.

I sometimes think of the father I once read about who had a terminal illness and spent his final days writing a long letter to his very young children, sharing his advice on various aspects of life because he would not be around to tell them himself. Fortunately, I'm around for my children and give them my advice daily, whether they welcome it or not. This book is a way of telling them, if they choose to read it, years into the future when they actually might care to learn, what I've done, why I did it, and how I feel about a variety of issues. If I'm not around to tell it in person, they will still receive it from me in this book—in my voice—rather than someone else's.

Third, I've always wanted to write a book like this one. Now I have.

Fourth, I was inspired by Leslie Gilbert-Lurie and her mother, Rita Lurie, who wrote a terrific book titled *Bending Toward the Sun*, about Rita and her relatives who survived the Holocaust by hiding in an attic for years, and how that horrific experience affected their family for the next two generations. I'm proud of Leslie and Rita for putting their time, energy, courage and emotions into that book, so that anyone and everyone on Earth, *forever*, will be able to hear that story —in their words. While this book addresses completely different subject matter, similar reasons inspired me to tell my story: to tell the truth, for the world to read, forever. And if my book inspires others to do the same, all the better. Everyone has an important story to tell, and should tell it.

NOTES

6. The Importance Of Bollea v. Gawker

1. "All people are by nature free and independent and have inalienable rights. Among these are enjoying and defending life and liberty, acquiring, possessing, and protecting property, and pursuing and obtaining safety, happiness, and privacy." —California Constitution Article I, Section 1

17. My Life as a Slug

1. Ansel Adams photo: *UC Santa Cruz*, November 1962, Gelatin silver film negative; Sweeney/Rubin Ansel Adams Fiat Lux Collection, University of California, Riverside, California Museum of Photography. For more imagery of UC Santa Cruz, google "UC Santa Cruz Minute" and check out the series of 1-minute videos showing the campus, 17 videos in all.

25. Amber Heard, Johnny Depp And a Media War

1. A detailed summary of the allegations and denials from both Heard and Depp, including numerous photos, can be found in a July 10, 2020, article in *The Canadian* bearing the headline: "Court is played recording of Johnny Depp begging Amber Heard to slice him with a knife."

30. Good Vs. Evil: The Incredible Case Of Pastor Cash Luna

1. His nickname "Cash" came from early childhood when he could not yet pronounce his name Carlos and it came out "Cash" instead. His parents thus started to call him by that nickname, and it stuck all his life. It has nothing to do with money, though Univision—with whom he was in litigation at the time of this writing—has made every effort to use his nickname to somehow falsely imply that he is corrupt.

ACKNOWLEDGMENTS

This book would not have been possible without the substantial assistance of Alexis Chiu, who was a thoughtful and helpful guide throughout the journey to publication.

I thank my clients over the 25-plus years of practicing law, without whom I would have no legal career or income.

I thank the terrific and talented attorneys and staff at my firm. They rendered the vast majority of the work on the cases discussed in this book, among many others. Each victory of the firm for our clients is *their* victory as much as mine. Some names of those who have been particularly instrumental are: my partner Ryan Stonerock, attorneys Dilan Esper, Lan Vu, Steven Frackman and Henry Self, our longtime office manager, Carla Drisdom, our longtime secretary Marcie Moreno, and my former partner Jeffrey Abrams. Each made invaluable contributions to our clients, cases and successes over the years. Thank you all so much.

I thank my bosses and co-workers at prior law firms, many of whom made it possible for me to succeed as an attorney. I also hope that my work with them helped them to succeed as well.

My amazing wife, Kathleen, has helped me (and the firm and its clients) in a multitude of ways, and I couldn't possibly thank her enough. I particularly appreciate her putting up with me, and also putting up with the publicity—including the occasional critique—that seems to come with the territory in high-profile cases.

My parents have been terrific to me, since birth, and I thank them from the bottom of my heart for their unconditional love, guidance and support throughout my life.

Many others, too many to mention, have helped me, my firm, my clients and cases along the way. To each of them, and hopefully you know who you are, a profound *Thank You* for your help, kindness and generosity.

Made in the USA
Coppell, TX
20 November 2023